D1443411

Day Trading on the Edge

Day Trading on the Edge

A Look-Before-You-Leap Guide to Extreme Investing

Leslie N. Masonson

AMACOM
American Management Association
New York • Atlanta • Boston • Chicago • Kansas City • San Francisco • Washington, D.C.
Brussels • Mexico City • Tokyo • Toronto

Special discounts on bulk quantities of AMACOM books are available to corporations, professional associations, and other organizations. For details, contact Special Sales Department, AMACOM, a division of American Management Association, 1601 Broadway, New York, NY 10019.
Tel.: 212-903-8316   Fax: 212-903-8083
Web site: www.amacombooks.org

This publication is designed to provide accurate and authoritative information in regard to the subject matter covered. It is sold with the understanding that the publisher is not engaged in rendering legal, accounting, or other professional service. If legal advice or other expert assistance is required, the services of a competent professional person should be sought.

Library of Congress Cataloging-in-Publication Data

Masonson, Leslie N.
   Day trading on the edge : a look-before-you-leap guide to extreme investing / Leslie N. Masonson.
      p.   cm.
   Includes bibliographical references and index.
   ISBN 0-8144-0573-8
   1. Day trading (Securities)   2. Electronic trading of securities.   I. Title.

   HG4515.95 .M376   2001
   332.64'0285'4678—dc21   00-063942

© 2001 Leslie N. Masonson
Contributing authors hold copyright on their respective chapters.
See chapter opener for details.
All rights reserved.
Printed in the United States of America.

This publication may not be reproduced,
stored in a retrieval system,
or transmitted in whole or in part,
in any form or by any means, electronic,
mechanical, photocopying, recording, or otherwise,
without the prior written permission of AMACOM,
a division of American Management Association,
1601 Broadway, New York, NY 10019.

Printing number

10   9   8   7   6   5   4   3   2   1

Dedication

To Marilyn, my beautiful, sweet, and loving wife of thirty years. I wish I could pay you back for all that you have given to me and our children.

To Dan and Amy, my delightful and terrific children. I wish them much health, happiness, and success in their endeavors.

To Dora Tuchman, my beloved grandmother, who, by giving me one share of PanAm Airways in 1957, spurred my interest in the stock market, which has only grown stronger over the past forty-three years.

CONTENTS

ACKNOWLEDGMENTS

Day Trading on the Edge would not have been such an information-packed book without the support and assistance of many talented and experienced individuals.

First, I want to thank Tim Bourquin, the former executive director of Day Traders of Orange County (now known as DayTraders USA, or DTUSA) and the co-founder of the Online Trading Expo. Tim was instrumental in placing the information and the link to my Day Trader Survey (see chapter 2, "Day-Trader Characteristics") on DTUSA's home page (www.worldwidetraders.com).

Richard Rueb, who took over Tim's position as executive director of DTUSA, also provided enthusiastic and continuous support. Richard contributed a perceptive chapter to this book, chapter 4, entitled "One Trader's Perspective on the Learning Process." I thank the many members of DTUSA and the over two hundred traders across the country who responded to the survey.

Teresa Lo not only provided a perspicacious interview (chapter 12, "Interviews with Traders") but also went many extra miles to help promote the survey not only in the chatroom on her Web site www. intelligentspeculator.com, but on other Web sites as well. She was always willing to keep pushing for more responses. I appreciate her review of the manuscript and perceptive comments.

I am truly indebted to the seven contributors who each provided a critical chapter in this book: John Piper, Gibbons Burke, Saul Nirenberg, Richard Rueb, Ryan Jones, Oscar Goldman, and Ted Tesser. Each contributor provided extremely useful insights that will serve the readers well.

I am profoundly grateful to eleven outstanding traders who provided their tremendous insights, knowledge, and experience to help others see the light: Teresa Lo, Alan Farley, Larry Pesavento, Ken Johnson, David Alexander, Michael P. McMahon, Tim Cho, Don and Robert Bright, Thomas L. Busby, and Chris Manning.

I thank the following CEOs for agreeing to be interviewed for this book and for their in-depth comments on the industry and on day trading: Robert A. Bright, CEO, Bright Trading, Inc.; Donald R. Bright, trader and director of education, Bright Trading, Inc.; Steven P. Goldman, CEO, Yamner & Co.; Gary Mednick, president and CEO, On-Site Trading, Inc.; David Nassar, CEO, Marketwise Securities, Inc.; Ronald Shear, CEO, Carlin Equities Corp.; Joe Wald, CEO and co-founder, EDGETRADE.com; and Kyle Zasky, president and co-founder, EDGE-TRADE.com.

I appreciate Omega Research's help in preparing figures for chapter 5, in particular Mitch Ackles and the graphics staff. I thank Herman Miller, Inc., for their furniture exhibit.

I thank the AMACOM staff, including Ray O'Connell and the editorial staff, especially Shelly Wert, for their superb job in getting this book published under a tight schedule.

I acknowledge Infopoll™ and especially Bob Lawrence and Jeff Wang for their assistance in developing a state-of-the-art fifty-seven question in-depth Survey for Day Traders. I signed up with the firm at www.infopoll.net, a fee-based service, and I was extremely impressed with the high level of survey sophistication and easy setup routine in preparing the survey questions.

INTRODUCTION

Is day trading stocks like playing Russian roulette? Individuals from all walks of life have embraced the self-directed trading revolution by taking advantage of the latest PC technology and fast Internet speed to trade stocks all day looking for the jackpot. Unfortunately, most of these individuals end up broke and not understanding what went wrong. On the surface, rapid-fire stock trading at low commissions seems fairly straightforward—buy low and sell high. However, as any experienced trader will tell you, it is anything but straightforward. Moreover, the regulatory authorities have found abuses at a number of trading firms—not fully disclosing the risks of day trading, as well as the claims made in these firms' advertising and marketing efforts.

It is hard to believe that intelligent people expect to find a pot of gold at the end of the day-trading rainbow. Most everyone is aware that over 50 percent of small businesses fail in the first year. Why should day trading stocks appear to offer a career with better odds of success? In actuality, the failure rate among traders has been estimated to be 80 percent to 90 percent.

If you have read most of the twenty-five day-trading books published in the past two years (as I have), you'd think it was not that difficult to succeed, since most of the books provide apparently viable day-trading strategies. How difficult could it be to follow a specific trading strategy, while having sufficient capital, the latest hardware and software, and getting real-time quotes, charts, and Nasdaq Level II data? Although all these things are important, you should not fall into the trap of believing that you can learn to day trade successfully by reading a book, buying the right hardware and software, and getting the most up-to-date data feeds. Actually, as you will see, the most critical aspect of trading that will determine whether you succeed or fail is your state of mind—the psychology of trading.

So, how does a perspective day trader decide whether or not to become a trader—either part- or full-time? Simple—by spending the time to thoroughly research the subject before putting dollars at risk. The goal of *Day Trading on the Edge* is to provide practical information on what day trading is all about—the good and the bad—and how to go about getting started if you are interested in pursuing it. This book is aimed specifically at the following audience:

1. The newcomer ("newbie") who does not know anything about day trading but is considering getting involved part-time or full-time. Newbies consist of individuals who are looking for a career change, retirees, college graduates, et al.
2. The novice day trader who is not doing well and has no clue what the problem is.
3. Online investors who have heard about day trading and want to learn more about it.

Day Trading on the Edge is not a "how-to" book on day trading. Instead, it focuses on the factors you should be aware of before you start to day trade, and whether you meet the minimum requirements. The book's goal is to present you with the facts about the day-trading profession without favoring one position over another. Make up your own mind, and do not be influenced by extraneous factors. Most books do not spend time on the risks of trading and the devastation that losses can inflict upon the trader and his or her family. In this book, seasoned professional traders who have witnessed these catastrophes discuss the negatives. Additionally, the advantages and possible returns attainable from day trading are explored. By having the whole picture presented, you will be in a better position to make the decision as to whether day trading is for you.

Day trading can be very lucrative. That is why so many people are getting involved. One of the larger day-trading firms claims that they know of a dozen day traders who use their firm who have profits of over $1 million a year. However, about 90 percent of those who venture into day trading leave with no profits. Therefore, it is important to get the facts, do your homework, decide if you have the psychological makeup, capital, and commitment, and get an education before you actually put money at risk.

Good luck—whether you decide to become a day trader or not! Believe it or not, making a decision *not* to day trade may be the best financial decision you've ever made to preserve your hard-earned capital! On the other hand, successful day trading can be very lucrative and enhance your lifestyle. Hopefully, after reading this book, you'll be in a better position to decide whether day trading is for you.

If you have any comments about the contents of this book, please contact me at: lesmason@frontiernet.net.

Leslie N. Masonson
Monroe, New York
August 2000

PART ONE

PRELIMINARIES— KNOW WHAT YOU NEED TO KNOW

1

WHAT IS DAY TRADING?

You are constantly being bombarded by newspaper and financial magazine ads, thirty to sixty second TV spots, and mail from online brokers with freebies or discount coupons trying to grab your stock trading business. You've seen the humorous ads from E*Trade and Ameritrade (e.g., Stuart, the red-headed computer nerd), and National Discount Brokers (passenger is placed in a jumbo jet's cockpit and expected to land it). Imagine an online broker paying $2.3 million for a one minute commercial during the Super Bowl (January 30, 2000)! Believe it or not, many of the ads during the 1999 World Series were for online brokers instead of the more traditional products we're used to seeing. Clearly, we are experiencing a burst in online trading volume and continual pitches for your business. The objective of these online brokers is pretty obvious—to bulk up their customer base and exponentially grow their commission income.

The profits of online brokerages are staggering. For example, the Senate's Permanent Subcommittee on Investigations Staff Memorandum on Day Trading (February 24, 2000) reported that fifteen online firms had gross revenues of $144 million in 1997, with an income of $22.2 million. In comparison to 1999, these firms grossed $541 million with a net income of $66.5 million. This revenue burst translates into a 275 percent increase and a 200 percent increase in income over three years. These financials are not shabby for a business still in its infancy.

Although the growth in online trading continues unabated, volume has dipped during the last two market corrections, Fall 1999 and Spring 2000. For the first quarter of 2000, online brokers added 3 million new online accounts, bringing the tally to 15 million accounts with over $1 trillion in assets. Moreover, trades via the Internet have risen to 38 percent of the combined volume of the New York Stock Exchange (NYSE) and Nasdaq.[1]

Day trading is very big business. Commissions drive the business. The more frequently individuals day trade, the more these firms make. While there are no published reports on the total earnings of the day-trading firms (which are all privately held), the larger firms are probably doing well with their bottom line.

A report by U.S. Bancorp Piper Jaffray[2] lists the firms with the largest number of trades per day (see table 1-1).

Online Trading and Day Trading Are on Two Different Planets

Don't be confused by the terms "online trading" and "day trading." They are not synonymous—they are light years apart in meaning. Online

TABLE 1-1. *Trades per Day Q1 2000*

Rank	Firm	Trades/Day	Market Share	Q/Q % Change
1	Schwab	293,318	21.4%	65.3%
2	E*Trade	214,573	15.7%	74.1%
3	Waterhouse	182,336	13.3%	69.9%
4	Fidelity	156,583	11.4%	69.5%
5	Ameritrade	129,709	9.5%	82.0%
6	Datek	121,261	8.8%	49.6%
7	DLJ Direct	44,100	3.2%	59.0%
8	Scottrade	34,494	2.5%	56.4%
9	Cybercorp	25,944	1.9%	82.5%
10	Suretrade	23,000	1.7%	74.2%
11	Tradescape	20,501	1.5%	NA
12	Dreyfus	14,292	1.0%	41.2%
13	NDB	12,963	0.9%	36.5%
14	Quick & Reilly	9,300	0.7%	181.8%
15	A. B. Watley	7,135	0.5%	50.1%
	Other	81,491		
	Total	1,371,000	100.00%	69.95%

Note: Q/Q change compares the first quarter of 2000 to the fourth quarter of 1999. Merrilly Lynch, American Express, and Morgan Stanley Dean Witter do not release their data. Tradescape recently acquired Cybercorp. Data from twenty-two online brokers are used in the preparation of this report.

trading refers to individual investors who execute their buy and sell orders for stocks and mutual funds over the Internet through an online broker for low commissions compared to phoning their order to a discount or full-service broker. The confusion lies with the word *trading* in the term online trading. The more appropriate term is "online investing." These investors are not trading but just making a few transactions a year using a less expensive and more automated method.

Actually, most individuals using online services transact only ten to fifteen buys and sells a year, hardly a blip on the radar screen compared to day traders, as we'll see in a minute. The term online trading should be thought of as online investing using the Internet instead of calling a broker to make a trade. As expected, a number of the full-service brokers (e.g., Merrill Lynch, DLJ) are now offering online-trading capability to fend off losing globs of their retail business to their online competitors.

Day trading is at the other end of the investing spectrum, on the extreme edge or fringes of investing. The term refers to individuals who execute numerous roundtrip trades (a buy and a sell) a day looking for fractions of a point to a few points per trade, but who close out all their positions by day's end. Day trading is speculating in a short time period. So, in summary, when you hear about or see ads about online trading be aware that the intent has little do with day trading unless that is the ad's specific focus. Be aware that some of the online brokerage firm ads on CNBC and CNNfn, for example, are for day traders or active traders and not for the typical online trading as we have defined it.

Online Trading Is Not Necessarily Direct-Access Trading

The advent of direct-access trading (DAT) has added even more confusion to the trading scene. DAT refers to the ability of a trader to deal directly with the market makers, bypassing any middlemen, thereby getting extremely fast and competitive executions. Direct-access trading is used by active traders such as day traders through specific firms offering the service to execute trades through an electronic communications network (ECN, such as RediPlus, ISLAND, and ARCA), as well as the New York Stock Exchange's SuperDOT system and Nasdaq's Selectnet, among others. An electronic communication network is a competing trading system that matches buy and sell orders internally and acts as an alternative to the traditional stock exchanges and market-makers on Nasdaq. Most full-service online brokers and many discount brokers do not provide DAT, so when selecting a broker, one of your first questions is: "Do you offer direct-access trading?" If the answer is no, then quickly move on to the next broker. DAT is required if you are involved in day trading, because it is a direct link to the market that offers rapid execution at a competitive price.

Day Trading—Easy Come, Easy Go

Day trading via the Internet has emerged as an easy way to make a quick buck while trading in the comfort of your home—or so it seems, based on the ads you've seen. And you don't even need a license. In today's Internet age, anyone who plunks down $1,000 for a PC and as little as $15,000 to $25,000 in "risk" capital (defined as money you can afford to lose to get started in this exciting field) at a brokerage firm can begin trading. And no prior investing or trading experience is needed, according to some of the ads of the day-trading firms. This flirting with the truth by some firms has led too many new day traders into financial straits, because they were not aware of the risks involved. Instead, they were mesmerized by the possibility of finding gold at the end of the rainbow.

Of course there are many successful full-time day traders who make between $50,000 to $250,000 a year and some over $1 million or more. But these millionaires are few and far between. However, the vast majority of neophyte traders lose all their starting capital and sometimes more within the first three to six months of trading. In reality, only 10 percent to 20 percent (and perhaps fewer) of day traders make consistent profits, according to various industry estimates. The rest drop out after taking a bath. But we're getting way ahead of the story.

Day Dreaming, Not Day Trading

Here's a possible day-trading scenario that you may believe represents reality in the day-trading kingdom:

You wake up at 8:30 A.M., have breakfast, scan *The Wall Street Journal* and *Investor's Business Daily*, flip on your TV to CNBC, and turn on your PC. Opening your online broker's Web site, you input your stocks for today's trading so they show up on customized tickers, you pull up real-time intraday tick charts on your watch list, and you get streaming news headlines. Now you're ready to do battle with the thousands of other day traders.

After making $500 to $2,000 profit on five or ten roundtrip trades by 2:00 P.M. you turn off your computer and take the rest of the day off. This sure beats getting up at 6:00 A.M., commuting for an hour or more, and working for someone else in a less than thrilling job environment.

Of course, this scenario is ridiculous and presents a completely false view of the day-trading world, but it is unfortunately what some potential day traders want to see in their reading of the landscape.

What Actually Is Meant by Day Trading Stocks

Day trading stocks consists of buying stocks (or selling stocks short) with the intention of making a profit and closing out all positions before the close of business that same day—whether profitable or not. A day trader may make a few trades (buys and sells) or hundreds of trades each day depending upon his or her strategy. The overriding factor is that all positions that are bought are sold by the close of business that day.

Using the New York Stock Exchange (NYSE) and Nasdaq, for example, the day trader ends all trading and closes all positions by 4:00 P.M. EST. Of course, a trader could trade in the after-hours market, but the volume of transactions is much lower, the spread between the bid-and-ask price of a stock is wider than it is during regular hours, and liquidity is poorer. Perhaps within a year or two there will be a twenty-four-hour global trading where these problems are not a concern.

In summary, the day trader's account is all in cash by the end of the trading day. All gains or losses are taken during the trading day. Normally, a day trader does not hold a position overnight because of the risk of a price decline on the next day's "open," assuming the trader is "long" the stock. A price decline can result from the release of a worse-than-expected earnings report, comments by Federal Reserve Chairman Alan Greenspan, market jitters, or other unforeseen factors.

A trader who normally holds stock positions overnight is typically referred to as a "swing" or "position" trader rather than a day trader. These traders may hold stocks for a few days (two to five) or a few weeks, respectively. The trader is looking to stay with the short-term trend and get out before it reverses severely. A "true" day trader does not hold any positions overnight no matter what the rationale may be. I would refer to an individual who both day trades and swing trades to be a "hybrid" trader. This two-way approach may cause difficulty for the trader, since he or she is not following one clear-cut methodology. But some traders successfully use this hybrid approach by keeping two separate accounts—one for each type of trading.

A Brief History of Day Trading

Day trading did not just appear on the scene in the 1990s out of no-where. "Professional" day traders (traders who trade at a firm using the firm's capital, not their own) have been around for hundreds of years. Don Bright, of Bright Trading, a firm of professional day traders, pro-vides his insights into the origins of day trading and the trading on exchanges:

> It is quite interesting that the American public, in general, and the investing public, in particular, know so little about the inner workings and methods of the securities industry. Having spent over a decade as a "floor trader" and "market maker" and many more years as an "upstairs trader" (trading in an office environment off the trading floor), I have come across thousands of people who have what seems to be a genuine interest in the field of day trading stocks for a living. Unfortunately, these Wall Street neophytes and "trader wan-nabes" for the most part have no clue as to what really tran-spires on the floor of any of the major stock exchanges.
>
> I have advised most of these people to move to a city that has a major stock exchange, get a job on the trading floor, and keep their eyes and ears open. This is surest way to really see how things work. And, in my opinion, if a potential trader doesn't know how the system works, then he or she should not be playing the game. Based on my experience, most people will not take this route to become a trader be-cause it is too difficult, too time consuming, and doesn't pro-vide instant gratification. As expected, 99 percent of these individuals will fail in pursuing their day-trading dream.

And they are shocked when they fail and don't understand why. They are totally blind-sided by the huge risks for the uninitiated.

Based on all the media attention to the stock market swings, many individuals think that day trading is the latest rage. Actually, day trading has been around for over two hundred years. Let's review a bit of the history [of day trading] so that you understand the basic structure of the securities markets.

A stock exchange is an organized market for the trading of stocks and bonds. Stock exchanges exist in major financial centers of the world. Members of an exchange buy and sell for themselves or for others, charging commissions. The largest and best-known exchange is the New York Stock Exchange (NYSE), which was founded in 1792 under the Buttonwood Tree. It handles more than 70 percent (in market value) of all transactions.

Only companies that have met certain stringent listing requirements may be traded on an exchange. These securities are called "listed" securities as opposed to "over-the-counter" (OTC) securities. The American Stock Exchange (AMEX), also based in New York City, and regional exchanges account for the remainder of the listed securities. Those exchanges have varying listing requirements. Unlisted shares, often of smaller companies, are traded in the growing Nasdaq market.

The over-the-counter (OTC) market is composed of thousands of far-flung stock and bond dealers and brokers who negotiate most transactions by computer or telephone. For the most part, dealers purchase securities for their own accounts and sell them at markup prices. Many U.S. OTC issues are quoted on Nasdaq (National Association of Securities Dealers Automated Quotations), a computerized system.

A company can usually list its stock on only one major stock exchange (with some recent changes, dual listings can occur), although options (e.g., put and call options) on a stock may be traded on other exchanges, such as the Philadelphia Stock Exchange or the Chicago Board Options Exchange. The different exchanges attract different kinds of companies. For example, the AMEX, for years, attracted many companies in the energy field.

Newer electronic exchanges typically trade the stock of small, emerging businesses, such as high-tech companies. The AMEX lists small- to medium-size businesses, including many oil and gas companies. The NYSE primarily lists large, established companies.

The NYSE uses a "specialist" system. At a stock exchange, certain brokers specialize in handling specific stocks. These specialists operate on the floor of the exchange, the area where all trading takes place. The floor of the NYSE, for example, is an enormous room that measures about 100 feet wide by 183 feet long, with a ceiling 79 feet high. Brokers pack the floor during trading. They often use bargaining and negotiating to execute larger trades, and they take bids for the highest prices. The process is noisy and frantic, and brokers use hand signals to communicate above the chaos. In U.S. exchanges, only trades over a certain number of shares are negotiated on the floor. For smaller trades, orders commonly go to specialist brokers directly via computer.

Specialists sometimes act as dealers instead of as intermediaries or brokers, trading directly in the stocks of their firms' accounts. (For this reason, they are also known as "broker-dealers.") They do this when market trends favor the trading of certain stocks, and investors have not ordered enough trades to clear the market or balance supply and demand. Floor traders trade only in stocks owned by their brokerage firms and never act as intermediaries.

The specialist system is probably the best example of a day-trading environment. The specialists on the NYSE and regional exchanges have, in many cases, inherited the job from someone in their family. Up until the 1987 "crash," family firms owned many, if not most, of the NYSE memberships, or "seats." The specialist does not want to take home any open positions in the group of stocks he or she is responsible for. He or she is charged with the job of making "fair and orderly" markets and has many rules he must follow. For example, a specialist cannot initiate an "uptick" [increase in price over the last trade] nor can he take the bulk of any public order. The specialist can participate in, but not initiate, any movement of the stock. He or she is responsible for determining "opening" and "closing" prices, based on the orders present, and participating on the "other side" of any imbalances. Day trading provides the liquidity needed in an open marketplace.

With the tremendous growth in online trading on the Internet a new genre of traders has come about. They are interested in new technology companies listed on the Nasdaq, whose rules are known by the "market makers" (who are the professionals of their marketplace). They call themselves "day traders," but, for the most part, they are simply "retail" customers of a brokerage firm who have little if any knowledge of this very competitive and risky business.

For the most part, buying and selling shares via the Internet on either the NYSE or the Nasdaq is fine for investors but should not be confused with a method for actual trading. In the early 1990s the "DOT," or "Designated Order Turnaround" system of electronic trading was developed. This allowed the "upstairs trader" to trade directly with the NYSE specialist or OTC market makers. This electronic system has developed to such a degree that a high percentage of all NYSE trades are done via DOT or "SuperDOT." Now, armed with quick execution ability, professional traders are able to compete effectively off the trading floor. This system has evolved and improved to the state-of-the-art system known as RediPlus. RediPlus and other ECN systems allow trading to actually take place in cyberspace. The trading of listed securities is every bit as fair as trading on the trading floor. This is due, in part, to the tight scrutiny of the NYSE specialists.

On the retail level, customers of brokerage firms are enabled to enter orders (not execute, just enter) electronically via the Internet. This has been a boon to the volume of trades, while taking away the need for "registered representatives" (stock brokers).

In the mid 1990s, with the advent of what is called the "Small Order Execution System," or SOES, many small trading firms opened to take advantage of the disparity in OTC market-maker markets. This system was used effectively for only a few short years. It allowed traders to trade between the professional market-makers' markets. It wasn't long before a system commonly known as "SOES-Busters" was put in place to take away any advantage that the SOES traders had.

"Professional" stock trading is done by about 7,500 men and women who are licensed, registered traders. A few firms have hundreds of these dedicated professionals in offices nationwide. Stock trading should be left to the professionals. Over the years, only a small fraction of these experts have been able to make any money when trading at home. (In the industry we call this "hermit trading," referring to the fact that one is out of the much needed environment of other professionals.) If our professional traders have a difficult time trading away from the office, it must be very tough for the non-professional retail customer.

And that was Don Bright's take on the day-trading scene. Don's extensive trading experience and an interview with him are provided in chapter 13, "Interviews with Firm CEOs," as well as in chapter 12, "Interviews with Traders."

Professional Day Traders vs. Retail Day Traders

You should be aware of the major distinction between a "professional" day trader and a "retail" day trader. Don Bright and others define a professional trader as an individual who is licensed, has investment experience, and has a full-time position at a trading firm trading the firm's money. A "retail" day trader trades his own money at a day-trading firm or from home (known as "remote" trading).

"Professional" traders work for investment/brokerage/trading organizations as employees or possibly as independent contractors obtaining a percentage of the profits from their trades. These traders typically trade in 1,000-share lots or multiples thereof, are provided with a trading line (trading capital plus margin—sometimes ten times the normal margin requirements), and have wide latitude in their trading throughout the working day. Most of these companies electronically monitor their traders' performance throughout the day to ensure compliance with their trading policies as well as to protect the firm from a trader going astray and carrying a big losing position.

This monitoring must be ongoing or else the firm can be hit with a huge disaster. Remember the stories in the past few years about traders who put their employers in bankruptcy by covering up or running up huge losses before the employers became aware of the situation (e.g., trader Nick Leeson at the Barings Bank in 1994–1995).[3] These traders were not day trading stocks but, rather, options, futures, or other derivatives.

There is another definition of professional espoused by many day-trading firm officials. They define a person who trades full-time for his or her own account as a professional day trader, trading either at an office or at home. These traders use their own capital and are often referred to as "retail" day traders, since they are customers of day-trading or other brokerage firms. Therefore, you should be aware of the different meanings of the term "professional" and who is using the term. Where you see the term "professional," it will most likely refer to "retail" day traders unless otherwise specified.

Day Trading by Individuals

Since 1994, and perhaps earlier, a handful of companies (e.g., Spear, Leeds & Kellogg; Schonfeld Securities, and Bright Trading, among others) offered individuals a complete trading workstation for day trading their own accounts in their offices. These firms, mostly based in the New York City area, provided individuals with a margin account (sometimes with ten times the normal margin) and a terminal containing streaming real-time quotes, charts, news, and rapid order execution. The orders were routed to various sources, including SOES (Small Order Execution System), Instinet or Selectnet for competitive price execution (between the bid-ask) on Nasdaq stocks.

These firms charged traders commissions averaging one to two cents a share as well as charging for the use of their terminal and information feeds. Typically, these firms did not provide the individual with any training or account monitoring. Therefore, most individuals that decided to day trade for a living at that time had some previous experience in the markets—they were ex-brokers, investment bankers, and floor traders.

This is in sharp contrast to today's typical newbie (beginner) day trader, who may have limited stock market experience, minimal knowledge of trading basics, and no idea what the risks are. For today's neophyte day trader the odds of success are slim to none. According to Don Bright, "99 percent of today's traders will not make it." These are pretty daunting odds. Even so, hordes of potential day traders are still contacting online and direct-access brokers, buying trading software, and attending trading conferences and day-trading seminars in record numbers.

Day Trading Setup

In 1994, when real-time quotes became available via FM, cable TV, and satellite dish, the opportunity for day trading from home became viable for the individual. Also, there were a number of discount brokerage firms that offered reasonable commissions—much less than the big firms—which made day-trading profit potential viable. For example, with a roundtrip commission of $90, making $0.50 per share on a trade of 1,000 shares resulted in a profit of about $410.

I started day trading NYSE and Nasdaq stocks in 1994 using the following setup:

- Gateway 486DX2 computer with Windows 3.1 ($2,700).
- Omega Research TradeStation software (for real-time tick-by-tick charts and technical analysis tools) ($700).
- BMI (as the real-time quote service via satellite costing about $240 per month plus $500 for the 3-foot satellite dish), now mergered into eSignal.
- Waterhouse Securities (for handling trades at $45 each). Buying power at Waterhouse was recalculated only at night. For example, if you had $100,000 in your account, you could do two 1,000-share trades of $100 using your $100,000 of margin. The buying power was not readjusted upwards after each roundtrip was completed! So you could not trade for the rest of the day.

From 1994 to 1996, my day-trading equipment and services setup was typical for the "remote" (at-home) day trader. At that time there were only three or four providers of real-time continuous quotes (e.g., Signal, Data Broadcasting, BMI, and Telemet), a few real-time charting programs, and a handful of discount brokers. Deep discount brokers were nonexistent in those years.

I upgraded my trading setup in March 1999:

- Gateway Pentium II GP6-450 with Windows 98 ($2,400).
- myTrack "gold" trading software package including AIQ software, broker execution, real-time feed, and real-time intraday technical charting for $69.95 per month over the Internet at 50Kbps speed. Frontier Internet service costs $19.95 for unlimited usage. Buying power is now calculated in real time, so after each sale my buying power rises accordingly.
- Commissions run $12.95, except for NYSE limit orders, which cost $15.95.

Thus, in a few short years, technology has greatly increased, software has more features at lower cost, and commissions have dropped over 70 percent. All these advancements have fueled the growth of online trading and day trading.

Today, there are over twenty-five deep discount brokerage firms that offer trades for $4.95 to $15.95 each and many larger ones that charge $14.95 to $19.95 for active traders. Over the past five years commissions have dropped dramatically, now averaging about $15 to $16 a trade, which greatly increases the profit potential even for a very active trader. Today, online transactions cost about as much to make as long distance phone calls did only a few years ago. This shows how technology has transformed the landscape.

Currently, commissions have leveled off and will most likely remain at existing levels unless there are structural changes in the way that trading is handled in the future. A few organizations are offering "no" commissions—but be careful about the spreads and the execution prices (which can kill you). Just remember the old adage, "There is no such thing as a free lunch." This applies to all dealings in the day-trading arena.

Since 1997, many day-trading firms (now called direct-access firms) have sprung up to offer their services to "wannabe" day traders who either trade at the firm's office or in some cases from their homes using proprietary software. Refer to chapter 7, "Ten Steps to Selecting a Trading Firm" to get a handle on the process.

A Day Trader's Dream Setup

Today, anyone can become a day trader at home using the Internet in two weeks or less with minimal expense and training. A top-of-the-line desktop computer, with one or two large 21-inch flat screens, trading software, and an Internet connection all can be had for less than $5,000.

Of course, you'll need a brokerage account and start-up capital. The suggested minimum starting capital is $25,000 to $100,000, so that you can trade multiple positions simultaneously. And your initial capital is doubled if you use a margin account (similar to a two-edged sword, as we'll see later). It may take a week or two to get the necessary forms from a brokerage firm and have them processed to begin trading. Some firms have online registration, so that all you have to do is fill out the forms online, print and sign them, and send them with a check to get the account active. Electronic signatures are now acceptable, so the entire account registration process may take minutes instead of days.

One of the potential problems of day trading from home is that no one is monitoring your account's status except yourself. And you can be your own worst enemy by making a few big mistakes, resulting in losing all your capital and more (if on margin). Also, your Internet connection may be slow and may get knocked off a few times a day—most often when you are just about to make a trade. So you must get a consistent internet service provider (ISP), or better yet, get a cable modem, digital subscriber line (DSL), or integrated service digital network (ISDN) in your area by contacting your phone company and cable provider. More about this in chapter 6, "It's All about Connections."

Information on Day Trading

Obtaining reliable data on all the aspects of day trading is difficult. There have been a number of reports issued by regulators and govenment agencies, but they have not provided much in the way of comparative data. Chapter 2, "Day Trader Characteristics," contains a survey that provides a much needed look at how day traders go about their business and how profitable they are. Refer to that chapter for never-before published statistics.

A few reports have been issued on online trading or day trading practices by different organizations. The key findings of these reports are summarized in chapter 14, "Regulatory Findings on the Day-Trading Industry."

The number of day traders plying their trade at day-trading firms for their own accounts has been estimated at about 7,500 countrywide. Perhaps another 20,000 (my guess) individuals are day trading from home either part or full time. Estimates on the number of day traders who are unsuccessful and leave the profession range between 70 percent to 90 percent, depending upon the source. These individuals have lost a portion of their initial capital, all their starting capital, or more than their starting capital (if they have to cover margined funds that turned into losses).

Because of the constant turnover of day traders, the day-trading firms, which number fifty to sixty nationally, need to advertise to bring in new clients and, of course, to keep those traders who generate numerous trades and high commission traffic. According to J. William Lauderback, a spokesperson for the Electronic Traders Association, the top nine trading firms control approximately 93 percent of onsite trading business and about 15 percent of Nasdaq daily dollar volume—over 350,000 transactions and over 120 million shares. These firms are as follows:

- Tradescape.com Securities LLC (doing business as Momentum Securities LLC)
- Mt. Pleasant Brokerage Services
- Heartland Securities (Datek)
- Broadway Trading
- Cornerstone Securities Corporation (name changed to Pro-Trader Group in February 2000)
- On-Line Investment Services, Inc. (parent company is GS Hold.com)
- Andover Brokerage
- On-Site Trading, Inc.
- All-Tech Direct, Inc.

Day-Trading Expo

When you see ads for an expo on a subject for the first time, you know that it's "hot." The first ever International Day Trading Expo was held in Ontario, California, in November 1999. A few thousand individuals attended to hear expert speakers and see exhibitors show their wares. I attended the second expo, dubbed the International Online Trading Expo, held at the Marriott Marquis on February 18–20, 2000, in New York City. The expo name was changed to "online" instead of "day" trading to include the expanding universe of online investors.

By the large crowd—over 5,000—you could not tell that the weather outside was horrendous. Snow had just begun to fall, and the winds were kicking up. Attendees were not in the least bit deterred by the weather.

I got to the Expo about thirty minutes after it opened, and I expected to see a minimal crowd so early in the morning, especially with the bad weather. Was I wrong! The exhibit hall was already open, and thousands of mostly young males were prowling the booths looking to grab any information packet they could about the day-trading phenomenon. The exhibit hall contained the booths of day-trading firms, organizations that provide trading courses and training, software, books, and newsletters, and many live "demos" of software and trading systems.

I would estimate the ratio of males to females was ten to one. A host of prominent speakers and sessions on all aspects of day trading took place on Saturday and Sunday. Most speakers were industry veterans, and from the comments I heard from those attending the sessions the quality was very good to excellent. By attending for three days I obtained a unique perspective on the insatiable demand for information on day trading and DAT.

Here are some of my observations on that expo:

- There were over a hundred vendors in the exhibit hall promoting online and direct-access trading companies, training courses, technical analysis software, new computer hardware, and software.
- A few vendors had large flat screens with crystal-clear resolution to display the trading screens and real-time quotes.
- The exhibit hall aisles were packed all the time, even during educational sessions.
- The bookstore booth was fully stocked with hundreds of trading titles, and a huge number of books were sold on all aspects of trading.

■ Vendor demos were given every fifteen to forty-five minutes with fancy screens and software, and giveaways were common.
■ There was a big scramble to obtain a handout after a certain speaker finished his well-attended (crowd of seven hundred) session. When he announced at the end of the session that he had brought only a hundred handouts, a stampede to the podium occurred!

Focus of This Book

This book is different from most other day-trading books, which focus on how to make money day trading using a specific technique or methodology. *Day Trading on the Edge* instead focuses on what the potential day trader should know before putting even one dollar on the table. The risks of day trading are clearly delineated, since day trading by inexperienced individuals is a deadly game—financially and psychologically.

In *Day Trading on the Edge,* you will learn:

■ How day trading got to where it is today.
■ What you need to know in order to trade from home, including the importance of selecting the best communications link to the markets.
■ Money management principles to reduce risk of loss.
■ How to go about getting the best trading education to reduce your learning curve.
■ A ten-step process for selecting a trading firm.
■ Specific findings from a fifty-seven-question survey of over two hundred day traders.
■ Viewpoints of two experts on the importance of psychology in the day-trading equation.
■ Experiences and insights of seasoned traders, as well as the attributes that separate the successful traders from the many unsuccessful ones.
■ Viewpoints of CEOs of trading firms on the day-trading phenomenon.
■ Tax-planning tips for traders.
■ Abuses by day-trading companies uncovered by regulators.

■ A viewpoint on why you should not be a day trader.

■ Where day trading is headed in the future.

After reading and absorbing the wealth of down-to-earth information in this book, my hope is that, if you plan to day trade as a career or just part-time, you do your homework, determine if you are really cut out for the tremendous market volatility—the fits and starts—and then carefully assess whether or not you believe that becoming a licensed "professional" trader is a realistic goal, one that you should pursue.

Notes

1. "Battle of the Brokers," *The Industry Standard,* May 22, 2000, p. 188.
2. *Online Financial Services Report—First Quarter 2000,* U.S. Bancorp Piper Jaffray.
3. "The Informer," ed. William P. Barrett, *Forbes,* May 29, 2000, p. 34.

2

DAY-TRADER CHARACTERISTICS

Uncovering detailed information about day traders, their performance and trading characteristics, is difficult. I know, since I tried. To determine if day trading is for you, it is important to know the "real" picture on how existing day traders perform. That is the purpose of this chapter—to provide insight into day traders' scorecards and what the average day trader's profile looks like.

Not surprisingly, the large day-trading firms that I contacted did not want to release any information about their "retail" traders' performance. The Securities and Exchange Commission (SEC) obtained some demographic information in its February 25, 2000, *Report of Examinations of Day-Trading Broker-Dealers,* which will be referenced in a later section. The SEC obtained data from 294 day traders who traded at eleven firms, so none of the data reviewed was from "remote" traders (at-home traders, if you recall the first chapter).

The SEC information was extracted from customer account forms, U-4 filings, and/or firm questionnaires. The SEC did not have answers to questions that they may have wanted to ask. For example, the SEC would have liked information on the trading and investing experiences of the individuals on whom they received information. But this information was not shown in the documents they reviewed.

Before you decide to put even one dollar into a day-trading account, you should be aware of as much information as possible about the *actual performance* and characteristics of day traders. This information includes:

■ How successful existing day traders are
■ How much capital they started with

- Their overall profitability
- Their average profit and loss
- Their 1999 trading profits or losses
- Their use of margin
- The technical tools and indicators they use
- Their brokers
- Their trading software
- Their strengths and weaknesses

Because of the limited amount of public information on day traders, I had no choice but to develop my own Day Trader Survey. I posted the survey on a Web site for access by interested day traders. I was fortunate enough to get assistance from the DayTradersUSA (www. DayTradersUSA.com), who highlighted the link to my survey on their home page, as well as mentioned it at their meetings, and included it in their e-mailed newsletter. Also, Teresa Lo, who runs the Web site (IntelligentSpeculator.com), was extremely active in promoting the survey on her chatroom and those of other sites frequented by day traders. Lastly, On-Site Trading, Inc. provided assistance in soliciting their traders, as well—twenty-five traders responded. Without the generous help of these three parties this survey would have been dead in its tracks.

Infopoll™ Used for the Survey

The survey was set up on Infopoll™ (www.infopoll.net)—a top-notch polling site that hosts surveys and provides real-time analysis and cross-referencing of questions. The most amazing aspect of Infopoll™ was the ability to view real-time survey analysis in colorful graphics and tables (with percentages) at any point in time. Moreover, the software provided speedy cross-tabulations and reports, as well as an effortless spreadsheet download for further analysis. I highly recommend Infopoll™ to anyone considering surveying or polling.

The survey period spanned February 25, 2000, through May 25, 2000. At the top of the survey I put the phrases "Day Trader Survey (Stocks Only)" and "Only for traders who transact more than 4 round-trips on an average day," since I wanted only active stock traders to participate. Over 215 day traders from all over the country responded to the survey which contained fifty-seven questions. Most questions allowed only one answer, but there were a few fill-in questions and a few questions that allowed multiple answers.

Respondents had to go to the Web site and either click their mouse on one of the question choices or type a few keystrokes to answer open-ended questions. Unfortunately, the survey results were not drawn from a random sample, since I had no control over who responded. Thus, it is not a scientific survey. Also, the respondents were self-directed by their own motives—hopefully good ones—to participate.

I would have preferred performing a statistically valid survey, but I found it very difficult to get traders to respond, in general. Therefore, I did the best that I could in requesting assistance to spread the word about the survey. Nevertheless, I believe that the information from the survey represents the existing day-trader environment. I removed a handful of responses that would have skewed the data.

Survey Coverage

The survey covered the following seven major areas:

1. *Demographic Factors*—Age, gender, zip code, marital status, education

2. *Financial Background*—Annual income, net worth

3. *Investment Experience*—Investment portfolio value, years of experience, investment vehicles

4. *Day-Trading Practices*—Reasons started day trading, Nasdaq versus NYSE stock trades, margin usage, trading at home or at firm, name of firm, full-time or part-time trading, communications setup, name of trading software, and previous profession.

5. *Day-Trading Statistics*—Length of time day-trading, 1999 day-trading profit or loss, trading tools used, beginning and ending capital in day-trading account, profit or loss for first three months of trading, length of time before consistent profit was made, number of trades a day, number of stocks traded in a day, average share price of stock traded, point goal for each trade, percent of short sales, percent of profitable trades, average amount of winning trades, average amount of losing trades, percent of time limit orders are used, percent of time stop loss orders are used, percent who averaged up a position and what percent of the time, and percent who averaged down a position and what percent of the time.

6. *Day-Trading Courses*—Percent of traders taking a course, cost of course, length of course, course name, course rating.

7. *Day Trader Strengths and Weaknesses*—Percent of traders having specific strengths and weaknesses.

Demograhic Factors

Age, Gender, and Marital Status

Surprisingly, only 18 percent of traders surveyed were below age thirty. Another 27 percent were between ages thirty-one and forty, 31 percent were between ages forty-one and fifty, and 24 percent were over fifty-one. Based on the premise that day trading is a young man's game, I expected many more day traders to be in the twenty to thirty age bracket than the survey indicated. The finding that 55 percent of the traders were above age forty-one was unexpected. See table 2-1 for the comparison.

The SEC results were very close to my survey results, except for the thirty-one to forty and forty-one to fifty age brackets. There were more younger traders in the SEC sample. Perhaps the fact that the SEC surveyed only traders at day-trading firms (compared to my survey sample, which had over 90 percent of the traders trading at home) was the reason for the age difference.

Not unexpected was the finding that 93 percent of the traders were male, and only 7 percent were female. Just over two-thirds of the respondents were married, 26 percent were single, and 8 percent were divorced.

To determine whether marital status had any bearing on performance, I cross-tabulated single and married persons with their trading results. The results are shown in table 2-2.

Observations

Many more singles (67 percent) than marrieds (50 percent) were full-time traders. Twice as many marrieds (28 percent) as singles (14 per-

TABLE 2-1. *Age Comparison of Traders*

Age	Day Trader Survey	SEC Survey
Below 30	18%	20%
31 to 40	27%	37% (age 30–39)
41 to 50	31%	20% (age 40–49)
51 and over	24%	23% (50+)

TABLE 2-2. *Marital Status and Trading Results*

	Single	Married
Full-time trader	67%	50%
Starting trading capital		
Less than $50,000	61	62
$51,000 to $99,999	26	13
$100,000 or more	14	28
Current trading capital		
Less than $50,000	31	37
$51,000 to $99,999	19	18
$100,000 or more	50	45
Length of time to make a consistent profit:		
Never	19	14
1 to 3 months	17	24
4 to 9 months	40	36
10 to 12 months	4	8
Over 1 year	19	18
Percentage of profitable trades		
Less than 50%	55	47
More than 51%	45	53
Average amount of winning trades		
$100 to $249	21	26
$250 to $500	33	29
$501 to $999	7	19
$1,000 to $1,999	21	15
$2,000 to $2,999	12	6
$3,000 or more	7	7
Average amount of losing trades		
$100 to $249	45	35
$250 to $500	17	25
$501 to $999	19	20
$1,000 to $1,999	12	13
$2,000 to $2,999	2	2
$3,000 or more	5	5
1999 average net profit or loss—day trading	$50,553	$70,082
Percent of traders making a profit	66.7%	76.4%
Average net loss in first three months	($3,632)	($1,959)
Percent of traders making a profit	32.0%	42.6%

cent) began with over $100,000 of starting capital, but about an equal number (67 percent) began with starting capital of only $25,000. Typically, larger starting capital provides a cushion for losses (depending upon the person's risk-control parameters) and will allow the person to have a longer day-trading experience.

Fifty percent of the singles had a current trading capital of over $100,000 compared to 45 percent of married persons. However, we don't know how much capital, if any, was removed or added since either group began trading, or how much was solely due to trading profits.

More singles (19 percent) than married persons (14 percent) never made a consistent profit day trading. Married persons had a larger number of profitable trades (53 percent) compared to singles (45 percent). On the other hand, singles had larger profits per trade and less losses per trade than married persons. Although the number of trades for married traders was a higher percentage, they had worse performance on the profit and loss of each trade, which is the more important criteria. For example, 33 percent of the singles earned a profit of between $1,000 to $3,000 on each trade, compared to only 21 percent of the married traders. On the losing side of the ledger, 45 percent of the singles lost less than $250 per trade compared to only 35 percent of the marrieds.

Regarding overall profitability, marrieds earned about $20,000 more than singles in 1999 trading profits ($70,082 compared to $50,553) and had lower losses in their first three months of trading (−$1,959 versus −$3,632). Moreover, 76 percent of marrieds had a profitable 1999 compared to only 67 percent of singles. For the first three months of trading, 44 percent percent of marrieds made a profit compared to only 31 percent of singles.

About 27 percent and 28 percent, respectively, of singles and marrieds took a day-trading course.

Married day traders, as a group, appear to outperform single day traders in most of the areas measured. More marrieds were full-time traders, had more trading capital, had more profitable trades, had higher 1999 profits, and had fewer losses. Thus, marrieds appear to have the overall edge. Again, remember that these results cannot be stated with any degree of statistical certainty because the sample was neither statistically valid nor randomly drawn.

Education and Domicile

Forty-seven percent of the day traders had a college degree, while 21 percent had a master's degree or higher. Twenty-four percent had some college, while only 9 percent had a high school degree. To determine whether education had any bearing on performance, I cross-tabulated each education category with trading results for 1999. The results are shown in table 2-3.

Based on the data from this survey, it appears that the more formal the education, the better the annual performance, in general. This makes intuitive sense as well. On an individual basis, there were traders in each category who made much larger returns than the averages.

Almost 70 percent of the survey respondents owned their own home, 19 percent rented an apartment, 8 percent rented a house, and 4 percent had other arrangements.

Financial Background

1999 Annual Income

In 1999, two-thirds of the respondents had an annual income of between $51,000 and $200,000; about half of this group earned less than $100,000. Seventeen percent earned $50,000 or less in income, while 15 percent earned over $200,000 per year. (See table 2-4.)

My survey and the SEC survey had a similar percentage of respondents earning a salary ranging between $100,000 and $200,000. The SEC sample had more traders on the fringes—about 25 percent at $50,000 or less and 25 percent at more than $200,000. Again, it is hard

TABLE 2-3. *Education and Trading Performance*

Education	1999 Average Annual Profit Earnings
High School	$27,333
Some college	$41,106
College	$46,943
Master's degree or higher	$51,591

TABLE 2-4. *Trader Annual Income*

Annual Income	Day Trader Survey	SEC Survey
0 to $50,000	17%	23%
$51,000 to $99,999	38	24
$100,000 to $200,000	30	28
$201,000 or more	15	25

to explain the different results of the surveys, except to say that they were both drawn from nonrandom samples.

Net Worth

Respondents were asked about their total net worth—no exclusions were mentioned in the question, such as not to include the value of their home. Twenty-two percent of the traders had a net worth of less than $100,000, 12 percent had a net worth of $100,000 to $199,999, and another 12 percent had a net worth of between $200,000 and $299,999. Fourteen percent had a net worth of between $300,000 and $500,000. Another 15 percent had a net worth of between $500,000 and $1 million. Fourteen percent had a net worth of over $1 million and less than $2 million. And 9 percent had a net worth beyond $2 million.

Interestingly, 54 percent had a net worth of over $300,000. This is probably due to the 55 percent of the respondents who were over age forty-one and who had accumulated more assets. Quite unsettling was the response that 22 percent of the traders had a net worth of less than $100,000. If they had to put down a minimum of $25,000 to begin day trading, then this represented 25 percent or more of their net worth. This is certainly money they could not afford to lose, especially if they were young and newly married. (See table 2-5.)

TABLE 2-5. *Trader Net Worth*

Net Worth	Day Trader Survey	SEC Survey
0 to $50,000	10%	6%
$51,000 to $99,999	12	7
$100,000 to $199,999	12	10
$200,000 or more	66	78

Clearly, the SEC survey respondents had a higher net worth than those from my survey. I don't have an explanation for this since the SEC respondents were younger than my sample group and would be expected to have a lower net worth.

Investment Experience

Length of Time Investing

The respondents were asked about their investing (not their trading) experience in a separate question. The responses were quite disturbing, since only 18 percent had less than one year of investing experience and another 16 percent had between two to three years of experience. This means that just over one-third of the traders had less than three years of investing experience but were already involved in day trading—some for over a year, as we'll see later. The problem is that these individuals are day trading the markets with minimal investing background and experience. Lack of knowledge and perspective on how the markets behave over the long run can have a devastating impact on the trader who is not prepared to deal with both Bull and Bear Market scenarios.

Continuing with the investment experience statistics, we found that 18 percent had between four and five years of investing experience. Twenty-nine percent had between five and fifteen years of experience. Another 13 percent had between sixteen and thirty years of experience. And lastly, almost 6 percent had more than thirty-one years experience.

Investment Vehicles

As expected 96 percent invested in stocks, 51 percent invested in mutual funds, 36 percent invested in options, 16 percent invested in futures, and 15 percent invested in bonds. Respondents were allowed to choose more than one category in answering this question.

Investment Portfolio Value

Astonishingly, 23 percent of the respondents had between zero dollars and $50,000 of investment portfolio value—including their retirement accounts. And another 16 percent of the traders had a portfolio value of $51,000 to $100,000. Should any of these individuals with limited investment portfolios be day trading at all? I wouldn't think so.

Hopefully, you realize that the initial funds that are placed in a day-trading account should not be needed for other critical purposes (e.g., college education, down payment for a house, retirement, and so on). Your mindset should be that if you lose your entire initial starting capital you can afford to do so without impacting your lifestyle or causing any financial hardship. If this is not the case, then you probably should postpone your foray into day trading.

Completing the breakdown of portfolio value, 17 percent had a portfolio value of between $100,000 and $200,000, and 10 percent had a value between $200,000 and $300,000. Twelve percent had a portfolio valued at $300,000 to $500,000. Nine percent had a portfolio value between $500,000 to $1 million. Lastly, 14 percent had a portfolio value beyond $1 million.

Day-Trading Practices

Reasons for Pursuing Day Trading

In an open-ended question, respondents were asked to give their reasons for pursuing day trading. Their answers were enlightening. Here are representative responses (each bullet point represents one individual's response):

- Freedom, flexibility, fun.
- Less risk versus buy and hold.
- Interesting and profitable.
- Low-cost business start-up.
- Thirty-year love of trading, now made possible by direct-access trading.
- Excitement and control that I have to make money anywhere in the world.
- Possible to earn a great living (I realized from the very beginning that it would take a lot of time and extreme discipline).
- Lifestyle improvement, financial reward directly related to performance.
- Work at home when I want to, no boss, no coworkers to argue

with. I make much more money than I've made at any job I've had. I sleep late and trade every day.

- Large potential income, independent contractor status, ability to live wherever I want.
- It is a passion, a calling. That is the "super" reason.
- I am very grateful that there's a way to build capital that doesn't involve catering to the whims of a bizarre culture.
- The main reason I day trade is that I enjoy it. Day trading is a turn on, it is like making love all day long.
- Trading is a competitive and intellectual challenge, and I make money.
- I appear to be good at making money this way. I enjoy taking profits on the short side. Nice steady, average daily gains around $400 to $600 for the past ten months. I read everything. I understand what is hype and what is real news. I do not mind reading SEC filings and usually interpret them well.
- I have never had a boss that I could get along with. Day trading is more lucrative than consulting in my field.
- It is a small business of my own in which I can make $500 to $1,000 per day, and I don't have to commute or interact with people. I can do this on my own terms in my own house. I like computers. I like being at home, and I like being able to spend time with my family. I studied for three solid months before starting, and I read twenty books and every Web site I could find.
- This is the best and most rewarding business in the world.
- Bad advice from a Wall Street broker. I realized I could make my own mistakes and then found my track record working conservative trades was more lucrative than my high-tech day job.
- Work for myself and excel at what I like to do.
- Fun, money, challenge.
- Excellent financial upside, work at home for myself, guarantee of more secure retirement.
- Freedom from daily work, affinity for trading.
- Huge opportunity and great lifestyle.
- I always wanted to own a seat on the New York Stock Exchange and be a floor broker. The computer and ECNs allow me to partially fulfill this dream.

In summary, the following reasons appear over and over again as to why someone becames a day trader:

1. Complete freedom to do what I want, where I want.
2. Challenging pursuit.
3. Low-cost business entry with great profit potential.
4. Monetary rewards are high.
5. No need to deal with bosses, employees, and office internal politics.
6. More leisure time and more time to spend with my family.

Instruments Traded Most Often

Almost 95 percent of all respondents traded stocks most often, 15 percent also traded stock options, while only 6 percent traded both indexes and index options. Lastly, 9 percent traded futures. Respondents were allowed to choose more than one category in answering this question. Remember that the survey was geared to getting active stock traders to participate, so these results were expected.

Stock Exchanges Used

About 53 percent of the respondents traded only Nasdaq stocks, while 42 percent traded both the Nasdaq and NYSE stocks. Only 5 percent traded NYSE stocks only.

Use of Margin

Eighty percent of the respondents used margin, and 26 percent used margin 100 percent of the time. About 21 percent of traders used margin between 50 percent to 99 percent of the time. Thirty-four percent used margin less than 50 percent of the time. Of the margin users, 72 percent indicated that they were not able to obtain more than 50 percent margin from their broker-dealer. This is the standard margin agreement of firms dealing with "retail" traders.

Trading at Home vs. Trading at a Day-Trading Firm's Office

By an overwhelming majority of nine to one, the day traders surveyed were trading from home rather than at a day-trading firm. This preference probably has to do with a number of convenience factors, such as:

- Obtaining the necessary computer hardware, trading software, communications link, and online broker easily;
- Not having the hassle of a two-way commute to a day-trading office;
- Being able to be at home for young children while still earning money;
- Not being surrounded by other traders who could negatively influence their trading plan; and
- Being able to concentrate on trading without interruptions.

Another factor that may enter the decision process to trade at home is that the trader can make his or her own mistakes without anyone watching and criticizing. This actually could be a positive or negative reason to trade at home, since a mentor or supervisor at a firm may be able to stop a trader from making common costly mistakes.

The number of full-time day traders (including "professional" and "retail") has been estimated to be between 5,000 to 7,500 at trading firms and perhaps another 5,000 at home. If my survey is accurate regarding the ratio of at-home traders to at-office traders (9:1), then perhaps there are as many as 37,800 at-home full-time traders (56 percent are full time traders according to our survey so 9 × 7,500 × .56 = 37,800). If my survey is inaccurate by 50 percent, then the number of full-time at-home traders could be almost four times more than the current day-trading industry estimate. Actually, no one really knows how many traders play the market from home. But one thing is for sure—the number keeps growing all the time.

Trading Firm Used

Respondents who traded at home were asked the name of their trading firm or broker. The three most often named were: MB Trading, Datek, and Cybercorp.

Other brokerages mentioned less frequently were (in alphabetical order): Ameritrade, E*Trade, Fidelity Investments, Interactive Brokers, MyTrack, Schwab, Scottrade, and TD Waterhouse.

Communications Connections

Day traders were asked what their main communications link was to obtain their real-time data. As expected, the Internet was the main link used by two-fifths of all respondents. But, surprisingly, 60 percent of respondents had faster connections—cable modem (28 percent) and digital subscriber line, or DSL (20 percent). And 7 percent used integrated services digital network (ISDN). Another 3 percent used a completely different method. So, in total, six out of ten day traders were very aggressive in obtaining speeds beyond the 56Kbps modems, which is the standard on the Internet. Faster connections result in obtaining real-time data more rapidly and executing orders and receiving confirmations more quickly. Saving seconds can have a positive impact on trading results, especially in fast-moving high fliers.

Software and Real-Time Charting

Among the most popular software packages that traders used for displaying their real-time data including intra-day charting, according to the survey, were Real Tick III, CyberTrader, eSignal, quote.com, myTrack, and QCharts.

Overall, almost 25 percent of all traders used Real Tick III, Cyber-Trader came in second place with 8 percent usage, and eSignal took third place at 5.3 percent. Other packages mentioned less frequently include Datek Streamer, TradeStation, Quicken Quotes, PC Quote, Windows on Wall Street, and A.T. Financial.

If you are looking for top-notch trading software that is used by many day traders, check these out. And remember to check references, refund policies, and cancellation policies very carefully.

Full-Time vs. Part-Time Trading

Fifty-six percent of all traders were full-time, while the remainder were part-time. Of the latter group, 48 percent traded part-time five days a week (most likely a portion of the day due to other commitments), 23 percent traded three days a week, 15 percent traded four days a week, and 13 percent traded two days or less a week.

To determine if part-time traders did as well as full-time traders, their performance was analyzed separately. (Refer to table 2-6.)

Based on the data, it appears that full-time traders had an edge in both the three-month and one-year time frames. However, there were traders in each category who did significantly better or worse than these averages.

TABLE 2-6. *Comparison of Full-Time and Part-Time Traders*

	Average 1999 Profit	Average First Three Month's Loss
Full-Time	$58,840	($1,083)
Part-Time	$39,370	($2,391)

Previous Profession Prior to Becoming a Day Trader

Traders were asked to reveal their previous profession prior to day trading. As expected, traders came from all different backgrounds. However, about 20 percent of the respondents had banking, brokerage, finance, or financial analyst experience. This finding makes sense, since these individuals were looking to benefit from their experience in a new career. These financially oriented individuals, as a group, should have a leg up on the average person who has no prior financial or investing experience.

Other professions mentioned included self-employed business owners, military, postal worker, physician, sanitation worker, software and computer engineer, contractor, salesperson, assembly line worker, lawyer, and real estate salesperson and investor.

In summary, the day traders surveyed came from different backgrounds and hoped to make day trading a successful career.

Day-Trading Statistics

Day-Trading Experience in Years

The vast majority of traders surveyed (68 percent) had been trading for less than two years. Of that group, 20 percent had been trading for only one to six months, 21 percent for seven to twelve months, and 27 percent for between one and two years. Thus, 41 percent of the traders surveyed were "newbies"—trading for one year or less as of the time they filled out the survey (March to May 2000)!

Only 10 percent of the traders had been trading for two years, 9 percent for three years, 4 percent for four years, 4 percent for five to six years, and less than 2 percent for seven to ten years. Just over 2 percent had been trading for more than eleven years.

Day Trading during 1999

Forty-four percent of all traders surveyed had traded for the entire year in 1999. On the other hand, 23 percent had traded between six and eleven months. Sixteen percent had traded between three to ten months, and 17 percent had traded from one to three months. For 1999, in summary, 56 percent had traded for less than one year.

Total 1999 Profits and Losses from Day Trading

The average day trader surveyed had a 1999 profit of $65,644. The winning traders (74 percent) had an average 1999 profit of $92,296, and the losing traders (26 percent) lost an average of $11,176. So on the whole, day traders did very well in 1999. Remember that 1999 was a very good year for the stock markets—the Nasdaq soared 86 percent, far outpacing the S&P 500 and Dow Jones Industrials.

Tools Used to Trade Stocks

Respondents were allowed to choose more than one category in answering a question on the tools they used to trade. Just over 70 percent of respondents used technical analysis (charts and indicators) when trading stocks. Additionally, almost two-thirds also used Nasdaq Level II (market maker bid and ask prices). About 60 percent of the traders used intra-day tick charts (charts that are created by using each trade and then combing the ticks into a one or three minute bar chart, for example), and 58 percent traded on news. Fifty percent also used price screens. Although 52 percent used candlestick charts (a special chart type that won't be discussed), only 13 percent used point and figure charts (a special chart type that won't be discussed). Lastly, 35 percent used information on the futures prices, indexes, TICKS (net number of stocks advancing minus the number of stocks declining), TRIN [(advancing stocks/declining stocks)/(advancing volume/declining volume)], and new highs and lows to guide them in making their trades.

The use of these tools or indicators is an individual preference of traders. Although traders use different tools to trade, their results speak for themselves. There is no one set of tools that is used by all traders, and there is a wide range of opinion as to which tools are the most useful. A beginning trader should be aware of the tools available and select the ones that have the most relevance and provide the most financial benefit. Therefore, the newbie should read books on technical analysis.

Starting and Ending Capital in a Day-Trading Account

Almost 64 percent of all traders began trading with between $25,000 to $49,000. (Most likely the true number is closer to $25,000, since most firms want that as a minimum to open the account, and that is what most traders put up.) About 11 percent started their accounts with between $50,000 to $74,999. (Most likely the true number is closer to $50,000, since some firms want that as a minimum to open the account.) And only 4 percent started with capital ranging between $75,000 and $100,000. Interestingly, 21 percent of traders began with more than $100,000 in their account. As noted earlier, this tended to be the married traders.

As far as the current capital in their accounts, 36 percent had between $25,000 to $49,000. Twelve percent had $50,000 to $74,999, and 7 percent had between $75,000 to $99,999. Nineteen percent had between $100,000 and $199,999. And another 19 percent had between $200,000 and $750,000. Lastly, 7 percent of all traders had more than $1 million in their accounts.

These data are difficult to interpret because some traders had been trading for years and had built up a large account compared with fairly new traders who had only been trading for a few years.

Unfortunately, we have no way of knowing what traders actually did, since a question about whether they took money out of their account was not asked. My guess is that the traders did not take money from their accounts, since the more principal in their account, the more stock they can buy, and that is leverage higher by using margin.

By reviewing the spreadsheet of all the surveyed data, I was able to determine that most traders had more capital than they started with, which probably means that they had been profitably trading their account. Another possibility is that they put more capital in their account, but the survey did not ask that question.

Profits and Losses in the First Three Months of Trading

Traders provided information about how much they made or lost in their first three months of day trading. *Only 40 percent of all traders* surveyed *made any money in their first three months.* In the winner's group, the average gain was $14,486, and for the losing group the average loss was $10,814. If we combine both groups, then the average trader lost $615 in the first three months.

Length of Time Required to Become Profitable

Seventeen percent of all traders required more than one year before they first made a profit in their accounts. About a quarter of the traders required one to three months before making a profit. Another 25 percent of traders required six months to make a profit. Fifty percent of traders required seven to nine months to make a profit. And 12 percent indicated that they never made money.

As you can see by these findings, you should not expect to make a profit as a day trader for about four to nine months on average. And about 30 percent of all traders surveyed took twelve months or longer, or they never made a profit at all. That is the reason you have to understand what you are getting involved in.

Number of Stocks Traded per Day

Half of the respondents indicated that they traded between one and three individual stocks per day. Another third indicated that they traded four or five stocks a day. Six percent of the respondents traded six or seven stocks a day, while another 6 percent traded eight to ten stocks a day. Lastly, only 6 percent traded more than eleven stocks in one day. So, in summary, 82 percent of all traders traded only one to five stocks in one day, a much smaller number than you might have guessed.

Round-Trip Trades Made in a Typical Day

Forty-two percent of all respondents indicated that they made between one to five trades (round trips) in a typical day. Another 30 percent made six to ten round trips in a day. Fifteen percent of the respondents made 21 to 30 trades a day. About 7 percent of the respondents made 31 to 50 trades a day. Only 2 percent of the respondents made between 100 and 199 trades per day. And only two traders made between 200 and 300 trades in a typical day.

So the traders in our survey were not the rapid-fire, mouse-clicking maniacs conducting hundreds of trades a day for a small incremental profit, which is often how the media portrays the typical day trader's modus operandi.

Shares Traded per Transaction

Almost 22 percent of all traders traded 100 to 200 shares per transaction. About a quarter of all traders traded between 201 and 499 shares per transaction. Approximately 18 percent of all traders traded exactly 500 shares. About 23 percent traded exactly 1,000 shares per transaction. Only 9 percent traded between 600 and 999 shares per transaction. Only 2.6 percent traded an average of 2,000 shares per transaction, less than 1 percent traded 3,000 shares, and only 2.6 percent traded between 5,000 and 10,000 shares per transaction.

Average Price per Share

One-third of all traders purchased stocks ranging in price from $51 to $100 per share. Twenty-two percent of all traders purchased stocks ranging in price from $21 to $50 per share. Seventeen percent purchased stocks ranging in price from $101 to $200 per share. Only 12 percent of all traders purchased stocks at less than $10 per share. Another 12 percent of all traders purchased stock at $11 to $20 per share. And only 2 percent of the traders purchased stock above $200 per share. Traders were not interested in very low priced or very high priced stocks—but bought stocks between $21 to $100 per share.

Point Goal for Each Trade

One-quarter of all traders were looking for a one-dollar-per-share profit on each trade. About 21 percent of all traders were looking for $2 to $3 per share profit. Interestingly, another 21 percent of all traders had no point goal in mind when they traded. Only 5 percent of all traders were looking for $4 to $5 per share profit. Almost 6 percent of traders were looking for more than 5 points per trade. Only 3.2 percent of all traders were looking for $\frac{1}{8}$ of a point, 5.2 percent were looking for $\frac{1}{4}$ of a point, 9 percent were looking for $\frac{1}{2}$ of a point, and 5 percent were looking for $\frac{3}{4}$ of a point.

Short Sales

Thirty percent of all traders never put on short sales. Another 30 percent put them on only 10 percent of the time. About 12 percent of all traders used shorts 20 percent of the time, and another 12 percent used shorts 30 percent of the time. Lastly, about 60 percent of traders put shorts on between 40 to 60 percent of the time. Clearly, shorting stocks is performed only by a small number of traders. Being on the wrong side of the market can have devastating financial consequences. Even though shorting is the way to make money in a down market, traders are reluctant to play that side of market.

Percentage of Profitable Trades

Forty-five percent of all traders indicated that 60 percent to 70 percent of all their trades were profitable. Ten percent of all traders indicated that 80 percent or more of their trades were profitable. Only 6 percent indicated that 20 percent or less of their trades were profitable, 13 percent indicated that their trades were profitable in 30 percent of the cases, 13 percent had profitable trades in 40 percent of the cases, and another 13 percent had profitable trades in 50 percent of the cases. That means that about 39 percent of the traders were profitable 30 percent to 50 percent of the time. As you will see after reading the interviews with traders in chapter 12, it is not necessarily your winning percentage that determines your success as a trader but the average amount of your winning and losing trades.

Average Amount of Winning Trades

Thirty-one percent of all traders indicated that they made a profit of $250 to $500 per trade. About 25 percent of all traders made only $100 to $249 per trade. About 16 percent of all traders made between $501 and $999 per trade. Another 16 percent of the traders made between $1,000 and $1,999 per trade. Another 6 percent indicated a per trade profit of between $2,000 and $2,999. Two percent of the traders made between $3,000 and $4,000 per trade. About 1 percent of the traders made $4,000 to $5,000 per trade. And about 2 percent of traders made between $5,000 and $10,000 per trade. Lastly, another 2 percent of the traders made an average of $10,000 or more per trade.

Thus, over 55 percent of the traders made between $100 to $500 a trade and 74 percent traded 100 to 500 shares. This means that they were taking profits after a move of about a point ($1.00).

Average Amount of Losing Trades

Traders kept their losses small as evidenced by the fact that 40 percent of all traders lost an average of $100 to $249 per trade. Another 20 percent lost between $250 and $500 per trade. Another 21 percent of all traders lost between $501 and $999 per trade. Only 3.5 percent of all traders lost between $2,000 and $4,000 per trade, and 3.4 percent lost $5,000 to $10,000 per trade. Only one trader lost more than $10,000 per trade.

Getting Out of a Losing Position

Traders were queried as to when they get out of a losing trade. Over 60 percent of the traders got out before they lost a point. Actually, 20 percent of the traders got out when they were down between ⅛ to ¼ of a point. And another 20 percent got out when they were down between ½ of a point to ⅞ of a point. Lastly, 21 percent got out after losing 1 point. Approximately 8 percent of the traders got out after a 2 point loss, and another 8 percent got out after losing 3 points. And a whopping 22 percent got out of a trade after losing 4 or more points. Since we don't know the price of the stocks that were being traded, we cannot criticize these traders for taking too much risk.

Limit and Stop Loss Orders

Almost 60 percent of all traders placed limit orders (an order to buy a stock at a specific price and not any higher) on their trades all the time. Another 25 percent used limit orders 75 percent of the time, and 14 percent used them half of the time. Another 7 percent used them only a quarter of the time, and another 7 percent never used limit orders.

As far as stop loss orders (an order to sell a stock once it trades below a specific price that you select) are concerned, a whopping 62 percent of all traders did not use them. Only 7 percent of all traders used stop loss orders all the time. About 5 percent of the traders used these orders 75 percent of the time, 10 percent of the traders used these orders 50 percent of the time, and 16 percent used them 25 percent of the time.

Savvy traders use limit orders to buy stocks and stop loss orders to limit losses. Traders who do not use stop loss orders can see their losses mount and their capital get depleted. One of the keys to successful day trading is to use stop orders to limit your potential losses.

Averaging Up and Averaging Down Positions

Traders were queried on whether they were averaging up and averaging down their stock positions. Averaging up means buying additional shares as the price of the stock is rising, and averaging down is buying shares as the price is dropping. Most seasoned traders would agree that averaging down a losing position is usually a big mistake and shows a lack of discipline. Nevertheless, according to our survey, about half of all the traders surveyed averaged down! This is the path to the poor house, not to becoming a millionaire!

Almost 57 percent of the traders averaged up a position, and 75 percent of them indicated that they did this 25 percent of the time. About 20 percent of the traders who averaged up did it half the time. Only about 6 percent of the traders who averaged up did it 75 percent of the time.

About 46 percent of the traders also said that they averaged down a position, but only 76 percent of those traders averaged down 25 percent of the time, 17 percent averaged down 50 percent of the time, 5 percent averaged down 5 percent of the time, and about 1 percent averaged down all the time. So, they did not average down very often—typically 25 percent or less.

Day-Trading Courses

Only about 28 percent of all the traders surveyed had taken a day-trading course or seminar. Of those, one-quarter indicated that they took the course for free. About 17 percent indicated that the cost ranged between $200 and $500, 10 percent indicated that the cost ranged between $500 and $1,000, and another 17 percent indicated that the cost ranged from $1,000 to $1,500. Seventeen percent indicated that they paid between $1,500 and $3,500 for the course. Lastly, 12 percent paid $4,000 or more for a course.

As far as the course length was concerned, about 40 percent of the respondents indicated that the course was only one or two days long. Twenty percent indicated that the course lasted one week. Another

13 percent took courses lasting three to four days. About 4 percent indicated that their course lasted two weeks, another 4 percent indicated that their course lasted three weeks, and another 12 percent took courses that lasted four weeks. Only 2 percent took courses that lasted five to six weeks, and another 2 percent took courses that lasted seven weeks or longer.

Five traders indicated they took the Online Trading Academy course, two indicated that they took Tony Oz's course, two traders indicated that they took the Pristine course, three took a course with Bright Trading, five took a course at the Online Trading Expo, and the remainder of the traders took other courses.

The course ratings varied widely, and only 18 percent of the courses were rated excellent. Another 16 percent were rated very good. Thirty-one percent were rated good, but 22 percent were rated fair, and 11 percent were rated poor. In selecting a training course you have to be very careful. Once you have read chapter 3, "Basic Training," you'll know exactly what steps to take to ensure that you take the right course.

Day Trader Strengths and Weaknesses

Greatest Strengths as a Trader

Traders were queried on their greatest strengths. They were allowed to give multiple answers to the question. Fifty percent of the traders indicated that they had patience, that they were disciplined, and that they "swung for singles instead of home runs." Forty-five percent of the traders cut their losses quickly, and 35 percent indicated that they achieved consistent results. Only one-quarter of all traders limited the number of trades that they made each day, as well as let their profits run. Only 13 percent of all traders took a few days off after a losing streak.

Greatest Weaknesses as a Trader

Traders were queried on their greatest weaknesses. They were able to indicate multiple answers to the question. Fifty-five percent of the traders indicated that they took profits too quickly, another 33 percent indicated that they could not cut losses quickly enough. One-fifth indicated that they got "whipsawed" (knocked out of positions) too often.

Another 22 percent got too emotionally involved with the trade. Twelve percent were influenced by CNBC, other traders' chatrooms, and other individuals. Nine percent felt that they made too many trades in a day, and 9 percent felt they made too few trades each day. Only 5 percent of all traders surveyed indicated that they had overcome all their weaknesses—that means that 95 percent still have work to do. Remember that the more weaknesses you possess as a trader, the higher the probability of failure. And the reverse holds true as well—the more strengths that you possess as a trader, the higher the probability of success.

CHAPTER

3

BASIC TRAINING

Knowledge is critical to trading success. Every field of endeavor requires training; otherwise, the end results can be disastrous. Without a comprehensive education in the basic and advanced concepts of day trading you will not get very far, and you'll pay a high price in having lost most of your starting capital. Whether you believe it or not, day trading is a tough business. Becoming a successful trader can take an individual months or years of hard work. And if the trader does not have sufficient capital, he or she may quit too early, before turning a profit.

If day trading were easy, everyone would be doing it and making a ton of money. It's astonishing that so many wannabe traders believe that they can excel at day trading with minimal experience, training, and capital. They do not equate day trading with a "real" job. They perceive day trading as a "magical" domain where there are no rules of engagement. Unfortunately, reality comes quickly to those who jump in without doing their homework. If there were a test or license required to day trade, I'm sure the number of potential traders would greatly diminish.

Just as you wouldn't consider flying a plane without the proper training and licensing—including simulated flying and flying next to a co-pilot, as well as studying for and obtaining a pilot's license—you shouldn't rush into day trading without the proper preparation. Most likely you don't want to spend a year or more taking basic and advanced training programs, reading books (e.g., investing, technical analysis, and trading), studying the markets, paper or simulated trading, and mastering various day-trading techniques. But that is what the average person should probably do if he or she wants to greatly increase his or her chances of being a successful trader. Probably only one person in ten thousand will approach day trading in this methodical manner.

Most individuals interested in day trading want instant gratification—they want to begin clicking their mouse to enter trades as soon as possible. And they are raring to go after taking a one week course. They are chomping at the bit and can't wait to trade. The thirst for instant wealth by day-trading stocks has been caused by the media blitz, as well as the constant barrage of online broker ads focusing on the excitement and fun of trading.

Any field of endeavor requires knowledge, skill, and practice *before* you actually begin the job. These factors apply in spades to day trading. The reason is very simple. The original stake in your day trading account can be wiped out in a few months (or less in a wild market environment) if you don't know what you are doing. Instead of losing your $25,000 to $50,000 of principal by trading poorly, invest a portion of this money upfront in education and training. You'll be glad you did. Don't forget that, in the day-trading arena, knowledge is the edge that can turn the odds in your favor. The more in-depth your knowledge the better. But knowledge alone won't make you a successful trader. You must also possess certain personal attributes, including a passion for trading, discipline, patience, decisiveness, and being unemotional about your trades.

You may feel that because you were successful in another career, because you have a higher level of intelligence than the average person, because you have a college degree and perhaps a master's degree, or because you've been fairly successful with your stock and mutual fund selection, day trading stocks should not be difficult to master. You couldn't be more wrong in your thinking. Comparing investing to day trading is like saying that the skill level required to play in Little League is similar to that of playing in the major leagues. Nonsense!

Successful day traders come from all walks of life and have different backgrounds and varying levels of intelligence. A high IQ is no *guarantee* of success in day trading and actually can be a hindrance. Of primary importance is whether or not you have a burning desire to be a successful trader. If your primary goal is to make a lot of money quickly, then you are doomed to failure. Second, successful traders educate themselves before they risk a cent in their trading account. Many new traders first lose their shirt and then bemoan the fact that they neglected to get educated. What a backward and expensive way of handling their money. Either way, an education is a must. So, why not educate yourself before starting to trade? Taking the education route up-front should improve the odds in your favor, as well as greatly reduce the very expensive learning curve.

What Educational Resources Are Available

Luckily for the new trader there are myriad resources to choose from. There is no lack of educational Internet sites, courses, seminars, books, video and audio tapes, conferences, psychologists (focusing on traders), and mentors to enable a potential trader to obtain a solid education. Your problem will be to determine which method of training to select, which supplementary training tools are needed, and which of the resources best suit your needs. Remember, most of the resources that are available, as in any field, are probably mediocre with high price tags. Caveat emptor!

You can benefit from using numerous resources, but your time and budget are probably limited. Therefore, you have to know where to go and what to look for. That is the purpose of this chapter—to lead you in the right direction.

The minimum age to open and trade an account at a brokerage firm is eighteen–twenty-one depending on the state. If you are currently entering college or are in college, you should consider majoring in finance and investments, economics, or business. Take as many investment courses as you can, and master the subject matter presented. You will not learn anything about trading in your college courses, but the core information will be helpful in putting the whole picture together. Similarly, on a master's level, focus on investments, finance, economic theory, and other related courses.

Investing and Trading Education

For those of you who are searching for supplementary education beyond college, there are entities that offer courses in areas such as economics, corporate finance, derivatives, futures, investment analysis, portfolio management, technical analysis, options, fundamental analysis, trading, and test preparation courses—Chartered Financial Analyst; series 3 (Commodity Futures Representative); series 6 (Investment

Company and Variable Contracts Products Representative); series 7 (Account Executive Training Program for the General Securities Registered Representative Examination); and series 55 (Limited Representative–Equity Trader). One well-known institution offering courses in most of these subject areas is the New York Institute of Finance (www.nyif.com), (800) 227-6943 or (212) 390-5020. Their office is located at Two World Trade Center, New York, NY 10048. They also offer distance learning courses, books, and seminars.

Also, look for noncredit investment-related courses given by universities, colleges, community colleges, and other institutions of higher learning. For example, Golden Gate University in San Francisco offers a technical analysis course. Use the Internet to search for these courses. Understand that these courses provide basic information related to investments and economics, but they do not provide any education regarding day trading. In the near future don't be surprised if you see some courses related to online trading and perhaps day trading or direct-access trading eventually pop up at college and university continuing education programs.

Quick View of the Landscape—Attend an Online Trading Expo

One great way for a beginner to get a quick fix on what day trading and direct-access trading is all about is to attend an online trading expo. These events have sprung up recently—since November 1999—and now there are expos offered by three competing organizations. These expos provide not only educational forums but also a gathering place to speak with experienced traders and experts in the field. They also offer an exhibit hall chock full of vendors offering to sell you their direct-access trading, training, trading software, technical analysis packages, books, and other related services. You won't have a problem getting information at these events. Make sure you bring an empty suitcase with wheels to lug home all the brochures, T-shirts, and other stuff you will collect. Once you get home you can review all the material and make follow-up phone calls to get more information on subjects of interest.

The first day-trading expo, dubbed the International Day Trading Expo, took place in California in November 1999 and snared over two thousand eager attendees. The success of that event, and the mushrooming demand for more information about online trading and day trading has resulted in two more organizations sponsoring similar conferences. Every potential trader, as well as experienced traders, should consider attending an expo to see what's happening in the day-trading arena and the latest developments in direct-access trading, hardware, software and trading systems. Everything you need to get started is presented at these expos, but your have to use your best judgment in looking for products and services with substance rather than hype.

Here is a run down of the online expo scene:

International Online Trading Expo—This three-day information-packed first-ever expo billed for direct-access and Internet traders had its groundbreaking exhibition in Ontario, California, in November 1999. More recent expos changed this title, using "online" trading to replace "day" trading to capture a larger audience of active traders and potential traders. The second expo had a blow-out in New York City in February 2000 with an estimated 5,000 attendees crushed into the exhibit hall. Other expos were a regional two-day session at Ft. Lauderdale in July 2000 and a three-day expo in Ontario, California, in August 2000.

At the three-day event, there was a large exhibit hall housing 125 exhibitors. The conference rooms had multiple concurrent sessions (six scheduled time slots in two days with a choice of five topics) by top-notch industry experts. The keynote address coupled with all the other activities provided an outstanding educational experience. The three-day conference registration fee was $299 ($99 admission for the two-day event), and an exhibit-hall-only pass is free, if you preregister. Audio tapes of most sessions and keynote speeches were available at the expo, as well as at a higher price after the conference. For more information, contact the organization at (800) 390-3085, or *www. OnlineTradingExpo.com.*

Online Traders World Expo—This expo had its first three-day exhibition in March 2000 in Oakland, California (about 1,800 attendees) and another one in Dallas in October 2000. This expo was similar in content and focus to the International Online Trading Expo. The March expo cost $225 to attend, had forty-seven high-quality speakers (many of whom spoke at the other expo) in its two-day session track, and had almost ninety exhibitors. For more information contact the promoters at (800) 610-2629 or www.onlinetradersworldexpo.com. Audio tapes of most sessions and keynote speeches were available on site as well as at a higher price after the conference.

Money Show—This three or four day investing extravaganza provides well-known investment gurus and an exhibit hall full of vendors hawking their wares—online brokers, mutual funds, investment managers, newsletters, books, software—to the crowd of thousands (attendance is 6,000 to 12,000, depending on the city). Multiple concurrent educational sessions provide an opportunity to attend numerous sessions of interest. Certain sessions are repeated. The show is given three times a year, in Las Vegas, Orlando, and San Francisco. The four-day San Francisco event in August 2000 had 230 workshops with fifty-four speakers, 145 exhibitors, and five special event panels. Audio tapes are available.

The show is usually free if you are a subscriber to a newsletter sponsor, own one of many mutual funds, or do business with one of the exhibitors, or if you respond to an ad in a financial publication. Day trading and direct-access educational sessions are not currently part of the Money Show curriculum. The Money Show has been operating for over twenty years and has grown in size and subject coverage. And it has been very successful for the promoters, exhibitors, and participants.

Online Investor's Expo—To keep pace with the surge of interest in active online trading, including direct-access trading, InterShow, the sponsor of the Money Show, has scheduled its first Online Investor's Expo in Las Vegas on November 17–19, 2000, as well as two additional expos planned for 2001 in Fort Lauderdale (April) and Las Vegas (November). The price of admission is $99 for the three-day event. This show is a direct competitor to the other two online trading expos. To obtain more information about any of these shows and audio tapes, contact InterShow at (941) 955-0323, (800) 970-4355, or Web sites at www.moneyshow.com or www.onlineinvestorexpo.com.

Omega Research's OmegaWorld—This once-a-year three-day conference focuses on trading strategies (back-testing and forward-testing, including custom-designed indicators) using Omega Research's Trade-Station and OptionStation software for day traders, position traders, and swing traders who trade futures, commodities, stocks, and other derivatives. Hundreds attend—most of whom use Omega's software. The 2000 conference was held in New York City in June, and the 2001 conference is tentatively scheduled for San Francisco. There was a choice of three preconference full-day workshops for a fee of $295. The regular conference was $895. During the conference there were multiple concurrent sessions with eight highly regarded speakers per time slot. Some sessions were repeated on subsequent days. Keynote addresses were presented by Ralph Acampora, Tushar Chande, Bill Cruz, Sue Herera, David Nassar, John Piper, and Charlie Wright. Over forty exhibitors were in the exhibit hall for the three days. Audio tapes of most sessions and keynote speeches were available on site as well as after the conference. The educational tracks presented by forty speakers included:

- Day Trading
- Technical Analysis
- Trading Psychology
- Trading Strategy Development
- Money Management
- Options
- Cycle Analysis/Pattern Recognition

For more information, contact Omega Research at (800) 556-2022 or visit www.omegaresearch.com.

Selecting a Day-Trading Course

Even if you have a bachelor's or master's degree in finance, investments, economics, or business, you still need a comprehensive day-trading education. Fortunately, there are many seminars and courses available to choose from that can provide you with basic as well as advanced concepts. These educational resources include day-trading firm training courses, online trading expo educational sessions, private training companies, and individuals (successful traders).

In order to be prepared to trade, you must be knowledgeable in the following subject areas:

- Money management.
- Risk management.
- Order execution, direct-access trading intricacies, and routing systems.
- Technical analysis.

■ Nasdaq Level II (if you decide that this tool is pertinent to your trading style).
■ Trading psychology.
■ Trading strategy and techniques.
■ Trading software proficiency.
■ Fundamental analysis (e.g., to select best stocks to trade).

Before spending one dollar on your training program, you must do your homework, otherwise you may be throwing away good money. As in any field, a few training courses are exceptional and have an outstanding reputation, while others are fair or poor. And you'll find that price does not give you a clue as to which is which. In general, courses lasting for a few days may charge $250 to $750 a day, those lasting for a week may charge $3,000 to $5,000, while those courses running a few weeks to a month may charge over $5,000.

Day trading firms that offer training programs may allow you to work off the training fee against commission dollars, if you decide to trade with them either on site or remotely. This, of course, is not the case with most third-party vendors, unless they have a direct tie-in to the day-trading company.

You many feel that training courses are too expensive for your budget and that you can learn just as much by reading books, hearing audio tapes, viewing video courses, studying on your own, and working side-by-side with mentors (real day traders) for their insights and methodology. All these avenues are different approaches you can take, but they may not cover all that you have to know to start trading successfully.

If you don't obtain a thorough education up front, then expect to take big losses when you actually begin trading—well beyond the most expensive training course you could have taken. There is no substitute for knowledge. You wouldn't consider flying a Piper Cub without studying the basics, practicing flying with a trained pilot, and passing a test to get a license. Why would you think that there is a shortcut to learning how to day trade? Don't be foolish at the outset. Spend your money on training—you'll be glad you did.

Obtain Critical Information—Don't Be Bashful, Be Bold

Above all, your goal is to select the best training for your individual needs and to get the biggest bang for your buck. Therefore, you should compile a list of potential firms you want to contact regarding their training capabilities. This list should include day-trading firms and third-party vendors. You can obtain basic information on their Web sites and by phoning them. Be sure to check references very carefully. Check into their refund policy and whether you can retake the course if you "don't get it" the first time through.

Question, Questions, Questions

The information you should request from each training company (and day-trading firm offering training) includes:

- Length of time that the organization has been offering the training program (or course).
- Number of different training programs offered.
- Training program objectives.
- Detailed description of each program.
- Cost of each program.
- Length of each program (number of hours a day, excluding all breaks).
- Number of instructors used in each course.
- Biographies of the instructors (they should all be *active*, successful traders).
- Training methods used, such as simulated trading, real-time trading, paper trading, group exercises, case studies, and videos.
- Use of exams, tests, and trading situations.
- Action taken if a student cannot master specific segments of the course.
- Whether final exams or trading tests are given after course completion.
- Whether the firm encourages a potential trader to do additional work to master the subject of day trading outside of the classroom.
- Whether the firm permits a student to take the course over again at no cost if he or she does not feel comfortable about mastery of the material.
- Maximum number of students permitted in each course.
- Whether each student has an individual workstation (or shares it) during the course.

- Number of individuals that have completed the training program since its inception.
- Number of individuals that have completed the training program in each of the last two years.
- Number of individuals that have failed to complete the training program on the first attempt in each of the last two years.
- Percent of the individuals who took the course and rated it poor, fair, or unsatisfactory.
- Whether the organization would provide the e-mail addresses or names and phone numbers of at least twenty students (with their permission) who have successfully completed the course.
- Whether the organization would provide the e-mail addresses or names and phone numbers of at least twenty students (with their permission) who have failed the course or dropped out before completing it.
- Emphasis (high, medium, or low) placed on the following trading tools: Nasdaq Level II; Time/Sales Screen; Technical analysis tools (standard and advanced tools, bar charts, candlesticks, and point and figure charts); real-time tick charting; reading the tape; reading a customized ticker; and indicators—TRIN, TICK, up volume, down volume, T-bond yield, S&P futures, put/call ratio (put options divided by call option on the CBOE), and VIX (volatility index).
- Amount of time spent on explaining the risks of day trading.
- Whether the firm provides full disclosure about all the risks of day trading, including the high probability that the trader may lose his or her entire starting capital and possibly more capital if using margin.
- Whether the firm requires that the individual sign a formal contract before taking the course (if not, indicate what paperwork is required to be completed, if any).
- Whether a copy of the contract can be seen beforehand to review.
- Whether individuals taking the course can obtain a 100 percent refund if they feel that the course did not meet their own objectives.
- Whether the firm prescreens individuals before scheduling them to take the training program.

- Whether the firm is currently developing any additional training programs.
- Whether the firm is planning any enhancements to existing training programs.
- What the attendee will be able to accomplish after completing the course.
- Whether the firm offers "live" mini-training sessions, a training segment sample on videotapes, audio-tape sessions, or a Web site demo so that a potential attendee can get a feel for what the training is like before taking the course.

If you have difficulty in obtaining answers to these questions from any firm, then perhaps that is a sign that the firm is not for you. If the firm is not willing to disclose the critical information about its course content and other factors, then it may be trying to hide a mediocre operation. On the other hand, if you ask a firm for twenty references and it offers to give a hundred references, that would be impressive, assuming that you carefully check them out.

Reference Checking the Right Way—Twenty Questions

Checking references is a critical part of your training course selection process. To get the most information from the references, you should ask specific questions. You may want to tape record their answers with their permission so you can listen carefully later on and not miss anything. If permission to record is not given, then be ready to jot down their answers on a preprinted sheet containing all the questions with a space for the answers.

Consider asking the references the following questions:

1. What process did you use to select your training program?
2. Which firms or trainers did you look at?
3. Specifically why did you select the organization that you did?
4. What was the length of the course and its cost?
5. Did the course brochure or marketing materials accurately describe the training that you actually received?
6. How much experience did you have in day trading before you took the course?
7. Did the course meet your needs? If not, why not?
8. What were the best parts of the course?

9. What were the worst parts of the course?
10. How would you rate the quality of the instructors?
11. How many individuals took the course with you?
12. Did you have your own workstation, or did you have to share it?
13. Was the material covered at a good pace, or was it too slow?
14. How would you rate the course on a scale of 1 to 10, with 10 being the highest rating?
15. How do you think the others attending the course would rate it?
16. How many individuals left before the course was completed?
17. Do you know why they didn't complete the course?
18. Was the course worth the money? Explain your answer.
19. What can you do now that you couldn't do before you took the course?
20. Would you ever take a course from this firm again? Why?

Day Trader Survey Results

In our Day Trader Survey (see chapter 2), we asked respondents about their experience with day-trading courses. The sample size was small (sixty-two individuals actually took courses), so these findings should not be considered as definitive.

Here are the highlights of the survey. Only 29 percent of all day traders surveyed took a day-trading training course. As far as the price paid for the course was concerned:

- 25 percent paid nothing (probably taken at an expo at the educational workshops—but there was an admission for the expo)
- 21 percent paid $200 to $499.
- 12 percent paid $500 to $999.
- 15 percent paid $1,000 to $1,499.
- 11 percent paid $1,500 to $2,999.
- 6 percent paid $3,000 to $4,000.
- 11 percent paid over $4,000.

As far as the length of the training was concerned:

- 42 percent took a one or two day course.
- 11 percent took a three or four day course.

- 24 percent took a one week course.
- 5 percent took a two week course.
- 3 percent took a three week course.
- 10 percent took a four week course.
- 2 percent took a five to six week course.
- 3 percent took a seven week or longer course.

Thus, only 47 percent had a training course longer than a week, and 42 percent took a course lasting only a day or two—certainly not in-depth training.

The course ratings were as follows:

- Excellent, 20 percent
- Very Good, 16 percent
- Good, 30 percent
- Fair, 21 percent
- Poor, 13 percent

Not unexpectedly, 43 percent of the courses were rated fair or poor, and only 20 percent were rated excellent. This indicates that you must carefully assess a course you want to take or you may make a bad choice—losing time and money!

Because this was a small sample size coupled with the wide universe of companies that provided training, the survey results did not provide a consensus on the worst or best courses. It would not be fair to any training company and/or instructor to give it a rating based on only one or two comments. That is why reference checking is critical. Moreover, if you can get a preview of the course via a CD-ROM or a live presentation, or a presentation at an expo, that would be ideal.

Day-Trading Courses Offered by Vendors

Most day-trading firms offer training courses either directly, through an affiliate company, or through a specific third-party vendor. You can obtain training program information directly from their Web sites. Following is an alphabetical listing of representative firms to check out with your due diligence approach:

Day Trading Institute (www.daytradingschool.com) (334) 344-7787; (800) 970-9791

- Offers day trading S&P 500 and Dow Jones futures with applicability to stocks, bonds, futures, options, and commodities.

■ Offers live commentary of trading over the Internet in Trade Room offering.

Legend Trading Seminars (www.tradingSeminars.com) (212) 509-2322

■ Offers Two-Day Introductory Day Trading and Swing Trading.
■ Offers Two-Day Advanced Trading and Swing Trading seminars.

Manning Advanced Trading Seminars (415) 885-3408; (800) 684-7100

■ Offers three-day intensive seminar for day and position traders of stocks and options; heavy focus on charting and using selected indicators.
■ Offers free three-hour introductory seminars in selected cities.

Pristine.com (914) 682-7613; (800) 999-0979

■ Offers one- and three-day, and two-week seminars on swing trading (one- to three-day trades).
■ Offers six-month mentorship program.

TCI Corp. (www.tcibalt.com) (646) 756-2803; (800) 540-1160

■ Offers day trading, swing trading, and long-term trading.
■ S&P 500, E-mini, stocks, currency.
■ Offers live demos at eleven regional offices.

Teachmetotrade.com (801) 531-7696; (877) 998-3224

■ Offers interactive training CD (six hours).
■ Offers seminars.

The Electra Group, LLC (www.electratraining.com) (914) 332-0030; (800) 925-9893

■ Offers two-week workshops, three-day intensive seminars, and a two-day national seminar covering trading Nasdaq and NYSE stocks.
■ Offers simulated trading.

The Traders Club (www.tradersclub.net) (212) 332-2626

■ Offers online distance learning and on-premises seminars for stock trading.

■ Offers advanced one-on-one training.

Trader Tech University (www.tradertechuniversity.com) (310) 281-1676; (800) 978-6379

■ Offers a three-day S&P day-trading course held monthly in Atlanta.
■ Offers Seminars With Masters.
■ Offers private consulting to develop a trading plan.

TradingAcademy.com (949) 930-2088; (888) 841-8418

■ Offers seminars and boot camps; virtual mentoring.
■ Offers free two-hour introductory seminars in selected cities.
■ Offers twelve interactive CDs, Nasdaq Level II, and Direct-access Trading.

Tradingschool.com (626) 963-2057

■ Offers ten multiday workshops on different subjects for day traders, including a mentor program.
■ Offers online education.

TradingTutor.com (520) 529-0469; (800) 716-0099

■ Specializes in S&P 500 trading, both swing and day trading.
■ One-on-one interface with Larry Pesavento via phone, fax, or e-mail. He has thirty-five years of experience and a unique trading methodology.
■ Offers a day of real trading; also available if the student visits Tucson, Arizona.

Velocity Trading, Inc. (www.velocitytrading.com) (617) 641-0309

■ Offers a two-day day-trading boot camp.
■ Gives a course monthly in Newton, Massachusetts.

Description of Manning Advanced Trading Seminars (MATS)

To gain insight into the content of a trading seminar, I attended a free seminar in New Jersey on May 31, 2000, called Mastering Trading, given by Chris Manning, a thirty-two-year-old full-time trader, and founder of a major seminar provider. I found out about the seminar from an ad in *Investor's Business Daily*. This was a three-hour preview session to his three-day Manning Advanced Trading Seminars (MATS) given on June 17–19, 2000. I attended both the preview and the three-day course.

At the three-hour preview session I expected to get a lot of hype about the three-day course and very little useful information. I was mistaken. Manning provided many useful insights on how to read charts, how to use technical analysis patterns, managing risk, and when to buy and when to sell. Only at the end of the preview did he briefly mention the content of the three-day seminar.

Chris Manning has been presenting seminars for a few years in the United States, United Kingdom, and Australia, drawing solid attendance. On a recent U.K. seminar, he had 250 attendees. The one I attended had 90. Each seminar day is independent of the previous day, but for true neophytes the three days are highly recommended, since each day builds upon the knowledge of the previous day.

Manning has spent years testing many technical indicators (using back and forward testing of different time periods and different parameter settings on indicators) using Omega Research's TradeStation to select the few that work. He has used many software packages and knows their strengths and weaknesses. He has strong opinions on which technical indicators and settings are the best, as well as which software packages do the best job in particular areas.

Here is an outline of the major subjects covered in the three-day seminar:

Day 1: Successful Investing—How to Get Started

A. Steps and tools to get started
How to get started in the business of trading, using step-by-step checklists.
A list of Manning's all-time best investing Web sites.
Learn how to diversify your portfolio via an asset allocation exercise.
Criteria checklist to select a broker with a proven track record.
Discussion of how to use all the different types of buy and sell orders.

Detailed charting software comparison.

How to test your strategy via paper trading before using real money.

B. Stock selection strategies using fundamentals to select winning stocks

Checklist of fundamentals and the levels that are tested to give the best result.

How to determine the proper valuation of a company (to determine undervalued opportunities).

Strategies that beat the market using the *Investors Business Daily*.

Day 2: Mastering Trading

Mastering charts—indepth review of key principles and buy and sell points.

Tested indicators to recognize when to be in the market and when to be out.

How to utilize Telechart 2000 charting software with Manning's Telechart Quick Reference guides.

Exercises to learn how to draw the trendlines that matter most.

Indicators that reduce false breakouts.

When to buy and when to sell with razor sharp precision.

Summations and proprietary groupings of all major chart patterns including reversals, breakouts, triangles/pennants/wedges, gaps, candlesticks, and Fibonacci retracements.

Professional traders' option secrets.

Distinctions to make trading stock splits profitable.

Trading profitably with news.

Nontraditional methods of trading using upgrades and downgrades.

Day 3: Live Workshop and Advanced Trading Strategies

Nine of the most consistent trading strategies Manning has uncovered in years of modeling and testing.

How to identify stocks massively undervalued and undiscovered (The famous $1.6 million strategy).

Exiting positions using the six different targets.

Advanced indicators to determine market turning points.

Summary of all main proven exit strategies.
Professional's trading plan.
Live trading with a master trader.

The three day seminar—Saturday, Sunday, and Monday—lasted from about 9:15 A.M. to about 6:00 P.M. each day. Manning was the only speaker, and he answered all attendee questions using his wealth of knowledge and experience in a direct manner. Based on discussions with attendees during the seminar, I found that they felt they had received excellent training and a solid approach to trading the markets. Since I have an extensive investing and trading knowledge base, I felt that at times the seminar was moving too slowly, but it's hard to please a diverse crowd every minute of the day.

Other than that criticism, I felt that this seminar provided solid material for the new and experienced trader. This multiday seminar provided a specific methodology for trading, coupled with an understanding of how to use charts along with fundamental analysis. It also provided guidance into the proper way to execute tight money management stops. In summary, I believe that a trader could greatly improve his or her results by implementing the numerous time-tested strategies taught at this seminar. For further information on this seminar, call Manning Advanced Trading Seminars at (800) 684-7100.

Video and CD-ROM Training Courses

There are a growing number of videos and CD-ROMs on technical analysis and trading, and more are being added each day. The downside of these kinds of courses may be the return policy. In most cases, once you open the package you cannot return the item. Therefore, see if there is a guarantee or a fair return policy prior to buying one of the packages. You may find the same information in a book published by the same author for a much lower price.

Here are some videos and CD-ROMs, listed in alphabetical order:

A Stock Traders Guide to Trading: The S&P 500 Futures, with Hal Massover
Cutting Your Trading Taxes in Half, with Ted Tesser
Day Trading 101—Myth vs. Reality, with David Nassar
Day Trading Today, with Oliver Velez

Disciplined Trading: How to Trade Your Way to Financial Freedom, with Van Tharp

Full SPECTRUM Trader, Inc. (Fullspectrumtrader.com) (712) 684 5239 (fourteen-hour course and CD-ROMs)

Fundamentals of Direct Access Trading—Online Day Trading Course by Online Trading Academy (CD-ROM only)

High Probability Chart Reading, with John Murphy

How to Get Started in Electronic Day Trading (home study course), with David Nassar

Martin Pring's Introduction to Candlestick Charting, with Martin Pring

Martin Pring's Introduction to Technical Analysis, with Martin J. Pring (CD-ROM, not video)

Maximizing Trading Systems and Money Management, with David Stendahl

Pinpointing Entry and Exit Points, by John Clayburg

Power Day Trading: Successful Strategies to Increase Profits, with Marc Friedfertig

Swing Trading, with Oliver Velez

Technical Analysis for Short-Term Traders, by Martin Pring

The Intelligent Online Trader: Disciplines, Tools, Technique and Technology, with Robert Deel

Trade Simulator Pro (CD-ROM, not video)

Trading with NASDAQ Level II Quotes, with Mike McMahon

Books

Books are always an excellent source of detailed information. Unfortunately, there are hundreds of books on investing and trading. You may be overwhelmed. Consider going to the following Web sites for investment and trading books, videos, and audio tapes. Check for the best deals.

www.traderspress.com

www.traderslibrary.com

www.amazon.com (go to book section—select category of book desired)

www.pristine.com

www.primapublishing.com

The following sections list books that I recommend a beginning day trader consider reading:

Technical Analysis (in order of preference)

The Technical Analysis Course: A Winning Program for Stocks & Futures, Traders & Investors, by Thomas A. Meyers (Probus Publishing Company 1989). *Note:* A revised edition is also available.

Technical Analysis of the Futures Markets, by John J. Murphy (New York Institute of Finance, 1986).

Technical Analysis of Stock Trends, by Robert D. Edwards and John Magee (AMACOM, 1997).

Martin Pring on Market Momentum, by Martin J. Pring (International Institute for Economic Research, 1993).

Technical Analysis Explained: The Successful Investor's Guide to Spotting Investment Trends and Turning Points, by Martin J. Pring (McGraw-Hill, 1991).

Point & Figure Charts

The Three Point Reversal Method of Point & Figure Construction and Formations, by Michael L. Burke (Chartcraft Inc., New Rochelle, NY, 1993).

Point & Figure Charting: Essential Applications for Forecasting and Tracking Market Prices, by Thomas J. Dorsey (Wiley, 1995).

Trading (alphabetical listing)

A Beginner's Guide to Day Trading Online, by Toni Turner (Adams Media Corp., 2000).

Amazing Life of Jesse Livermore, by Richard Smitten (Traders Publishing, 1999).

Candlestick Charting Explained: Timeless Techniques for Trading Stocks and Futures, by Gregory L. Morris (Probus, 1995).

Day Trading into the Millenium, by Michael P. Turner (Traders Resource, 1998).

Market Masters: How Successful Traders Think, Trade and Invest* And You Can Too, by Jake Bernstein (Dearborn Financial, 1994). (out of print)

Market Wizards: Interviews with Top Traders, by Jack D. Schwager (Harper and Row, 1989).

Pitbull: Lessons from Wall Street's Champion Trader, by Martin "Buzzy" Schwartz (HarperBusiness, 1998).

Reminiscences of a Stock Operator, by Edwin Lefevre (Wiley, 1993).

Short-Term Futures Trading: Systems, Strategies and Techniques for the Trader, by Jake Bernstein (Probus, 1993).

Stock Trading Wizard: Advanced Short Term Trading for Swing and Day Trading, by Tony Oz (Tony Oz Publications, 1999).

The Day Traders: The Untold Story of the Extreme Investors and How They Changed Wall Street Forever, by Gregory J. Millman (Times Business Books, 1999).

The Education of a Speculator, by Victor Niederhoffer (Wiley, 1997).

The Long-Term Day Trader: Short-Term Strategies to Boost Your Long-Term Profits, by Michael Sincere and Deron Wagner (Career Press, 2000).

The New Market Wizards: Conversations with America's Top Traders, by Jack D. Schwager (HarperBusiness, 1992).

The Way to Trade: Discover Your Successful Trading Personality, by John Piper (Financial Times Prentice-Hall, 1999).

Tools and Tactics for the Master Day Trader, by Oliver Velez and Greg Capra (McGraw-Hill, 2000).

Trade Your Way to Financial Freedom, by Van K. Tharp (McGraw-Hill, 1998).

Trading as a Business, by Charlie F. Wright. (Published by the author; may be still available from Omega Research.)

Trading for a Living: Psychology, Trading Tactics, Money Management, by Alexander Elder (Wiley, 1993).

The Trading Game: Playing By the Numbers to Make Millions, by Ryan Jones (Wiley, 1999).

Investing (alphabetical listing)

A Random Walk Down Wall Street: The Best Investment Advice Money Can Buy, by Burton G. Malkiel (Norton, 1996).

Extraordinary Popular Delusions and the Madness of Crowds, by Charles Mackay, LL.D. (Harmony Books, 1980).

How I Made $2,000,000 in the Stock Market, by Nicholas Darvas (Carol Publishing Group, 1993).

How to Make Money in Stocks, by William J. O'Neil (McGraw-Hill, 1991).

*101 Investment Lessons from the Wizards of Wall Street: The Pros'
Secrets for Running with the Bulls without Losing Your Shirt,* by
Michael Sincere (Career Press, 1999).

Riding the Bear: How to Prosper in the Coming Bear Market, by Sy
Harding (Adams Media Corp., 1999).

Secrets of the Investment All-Stars, by Kenneth A. Stern (AMACOM,
1999).

*Stocks for the Long Run: A Guide to Selecting Markets for Long-Term
Growth,* by Jeremy J. Siegel (Irwin, 1994).

24 Essential Lessons for Investment Success, by William J. O'Neil
(McGraw-Hill, 2000).

*Winning the Loser's Game: Timeless Strategies for Successful Invest-
ing,* by Charles D. Ellis (McGraw-Hill, 1998).

Taxes

*The Traders Tax Solution: Money-Saving Strategies for the Serious
Investor,* by Ted Tesser (Wiley, 2000).

The Trader's Tax Survival Guide, by Ted Tesser (Wiley, 1997).

Monthly Magazines

AAII Journal (www.aaii.com) (312) 280-0170 (Investing, not a day
trading focus)

Active Trader (www.activetradermag.com) (800) 341-9384

Online Investor Magazine (www.onlineinvestor.com) (800) 778-
8568

Futures (www.futuresmag.com) (888) 898-5514

Technical Analysis of Stocks and Commodities (www.traders.com)
(800) 832-4642

Newspaper

Investor's Business Daily (www.investor.com) (800) 831-2525

Internet Resources

There are myriad sites that provide excellent information about investing and trading, some without charge and some for a fee. A few of the
best sites to look at are as follows (all sites begin with www.):

bigcharts.com
bloomberg.com
cbs.marketwatch
clearstation.com
dorseywright.com
greentradertax.com
http://fifunu.yahoo.com
HardRightEdge.com
IntelligentSpeculator.com
jagnotes.com
murphymorris.com
pring.com
pristine.com
http://quote.yahoo.com
schaeffersresearch.com
siliconinvestor.com
stockselector.com
syharding.com
taxtrader.com
tradersedge.com
tradertechuniversity.com
tradingmarkets.com
wallstreetcity.com
worldwidetraders.com
yahoo.finance

ONE TRADER'S PERSPECTIVE ON THE LEARNING PROCESS

Richard V. Rueb

Have you ever wondered why college takes four years and graduate school takes two more? Why couldn't the academics just get on with it quicker? They could surely teach the elementary stuff in a month or two. Why take four years? I'm sure you've wondered about this but been afraid to ask. Well, throughout this past three years, I've figured it out. *Pace!* Pace is the special element that facilitates learning.

Traders new to the business want to learn all about trading *"yesterday"* so they can start active trading *today*! You can't learn it all in a day! Grasping all the complexities of the financial markets will take you some time. This chapter may be used as a roadmap for learning what you need to know. Taking the time to properly learn will possibly save you more capital than you can imagine.

The mind can take in a lot of data, but time—seat time—is required for assimilation of data into memorable and usable information. Ultimately, knowledge gained can be converted to wisdom and, hopefully, used as quick-witted instinct!

Traders are generally impatient people in a hurry to make more money. But impatience breeds failure, and it is extremely hazardous to your wealth. What a novice trader needs to realize is that, regardless of

Copyright © 2001 Richard V. Rueb. All rights reserved.

how smart he or she is, the financial markets are complex, and there is much to learn.

Forget about knowing everything. It's impossible! Just focus on what's pertinent to your chosen style of trading. However, remember that you don't yet know your trading style. You need time, education, and drill training to learn your own style. People spend six years getting a Ph.D. in finance, and they are still not qualified to trade directly with the market; however, academia certifies they're qualified to teach college courses.

Direct-access traders have many advantages over those who don't know what they know; however, even though they have the added advantage of direct-access to the markets, they still need the clear knowledge from structured, well-paced education to succeed. I call it TIQ—Trader Intelligence Quotient.

Pace is required to facilitate education. Information should gradually and repeatedly be pushed into our minds over time, in order for our minds to comprehensively grasp new concepts, ultimately converting the information into knowledge. This is never truer than when we are dealing with wealth, except when we are dealing with our health and/or the health of others.

Structure and schedule are essential to control the flow of information into the brain to create the building block effect.

Curriculum—what is going to be taught—is sorted out in advance and provided by competent instruction at the proper pace and within the correctly sized pipeline, so that all ingredients necessary for successful trading are indelibly etched into your brain before your capital is put at risk.

I believe the minimum elapsed time for learning short-term trading is six months, and beginning traders should remain in a state of supervised, governed training for that period. To get traders "paying commissions" many brokers are hesitant to protract the training they control over that long a period—so they provide just what *they think you need* in a week or two! A week or even a month is not enough time!

I know a broker who will not allow you to trade on his brokerage's floor until you have taken their basic and advanced course. That's better than many; however, their combined two courses take less than three weeks elapsed time, and it's all emersion training, so there is no time for knowledge absorption (seasoning). It is very profitable. For the person with a typical IQ, developing TIQ takes months—not weeks.

I'm concerned that the Securities and Exchange Commission and National Association of Securities Dealers allow brokers to teach such intricate information to new traders in a week (or two)! I don't care how many disclosures brokers require new traders to sign.

Traders will sign anything. They want to trade. Simply put, nobody is smart enough to learn all that there is to know about trading the short-term financial markets in a week or two.

One more important requirement for adequately learning this business is attitude. The new trader needs to completely shift away from his or her investment paradigm (beliefs). Many short-term traders migrate into the business from an investing experience base—perhaps ten to thirty years of investing in mutual funds and/or 401k contributions, so they come to the trading pit with preconceived attitudes (e.g., dollar cost averaging, double down, buy and hold). These attitudes lead traders astray. New traders need to shift completely away from this investment paradigm.

Investing values and trading values are at opposite ends of the financial knowledge/instinct spectrum. What we must do is shift our paradigm from investing to trading, even though it is very difficult to do. We don't dollar cost average. We never double down. We set stops and then execute them. Traders that don't keep their stops become investors awaiting recovery of their "long term investment" made as a short-term trade, gone south.

So, forget all you ever learned about investing. You are entering a new world, not just a subset of the investing world. Traders make the world go round. Investors watch the world go round. You need seat time to learn how to accomplish this. It won't happen in a week or a month. It will take months of seat time focused directly on the important topics I will outline and define in the following pages. You'll make mistakes. Count on it! Mistakes are OK as long as they are little ones. Mistakes made while trading 100-share lots minimize the financial impact of mistakes while demonstrating the impact to the money pile. As you make the 100-share mistakes, just imagine the impact it would have been on 1,000 shares or 10,000 shares. Trading is not a part-time profession. It takes 110 percent of your focus and energy to succeed.

The American university system has long used the structure of freshman, sophomore, junior, senior, graduate, and postgraduate to schedule and pace the appropriate basic information into the brains of young minds. U.S. military forces have mastered the element of repetition in their training curriculum to get the point across—avoid getting killed or maimed while fighting the enemy. Being an old product of both those learning systems, I can attest to the functionality and effectiveness of their combined processes. So many "would be" traders (who never make it) come to this new "trading" business thinking they are already seasoned business men and women. They think that they need to be told what should be done only once and they'll be on their way to riches. Many are greedy and impatient and will probably blow their life savings before the "war" even starts or before they even know what the "war" is all about.

Traders need the same learning process as a military recruit who arrives at boot camp. They need haircuts and discipline before they sit down and eat their first good meal! Now that you know what I suspect about you, let's see if you can get past this major learning barrier and allow some very important information into your thinking to subsequently convert into wisdom, which could mature into instinct.

Remember this: I am not the best trader, the most profitable trader, or the smartest trader, but I am here trading after three years, so I possess one important element many others don't—staying power. What I do know is that there are no comprehensive trader education centers offering what is proposed here.

Structure

Every moving element in the system of the universe oscillates within a structure. My suggested structure for learning trading is packed into just six elements: basic trading, execution, momentum, chart analysis, leverage, and trade planning.

You're probably thinking: Those elements sound simple and generic. There can't be that much to learn about only six elementary focus points!

Pace

How much time should a trader invest in studying these basics? Probably ten years is not too much; however, let's be realistic. A month is not long enough, and two years may be too great a time investment for seasoned business people. You might as well go to law or medical school or become an electronics engineer. After thinking about it, teaching these basics, and studying the elements, I've arrived at the optimum structured learning pace: six months minimum to one year maximum. That's much more time than brokers want you to invest before paying trade commissions. We're not brokers, but we need brokers, and brokers need us. Once you are a graduate of such a course, you'd be one lucky broker's client for life.

Instruction

Military training is compacted into a twelve to fifteen week immersion training segment, while college academia is protracted out to four to six years. Humans can't stand constant immersion instruction without time to reassess their focus. One must respect the learning curve of any new science or art one is thrust into.

My personal experience over three years of trading is one of intermittent learning and trading. People need breaks. My problem at the outset was that I did not have a visually clear picture of the knowledge I needed before risking capital. Remember, this industry is new—made possible only by the access technology of the Internet. The content of my first course was information packed, but since I was informed of so much, I forgot far too much.

Caveats

It's extremely dangerous for "traders-in-training" to experience immediate success when first trading. Immediate gains promote false euphoria and are a cancer that will kill you (your capital)! A false sense of accomplishment fuels the human ego and produces a feeling of euphoria. Euphoria is bad for traders. All emotion is bad for traders. Traders need to think while in their learning stage and then become reactionary in their application state. Traders need to experience several plateaus of the learning process before putting much of their capital at risk.

Remember this: There are two processes occurring simultaneously when learning to trade: education *and* training. Yes, they are distinctly different.

Successful traders use technical analysis to choose stock plays, apply instinct to enter and exit trades, follow momentum to pace entry and exit, and leverage capital to explode profitability, all the while executing a well-planned trading strategy.

You should understand what's needed. I've identified the six major areas where "learning" traders need to focus their education. Once you know what you need to know about each of these elements, you will know how to get it and you will know whether the business is for you. It usually takes about a month to know whether the business is right for you. The business takes tremendous concentration.

Curriculum

My recommendation is to have six compacted weeks of training spread over six months, with trainees practicing in structured drills what they learned in each successive prior class during the three intervening weeks between the six distinct classes. A description of each program segment is provided in figure 4-1.

Content

The trading college I envision would consists of 180 hours of direct instruction accompanied by 720 hours of structured trading seat time plus 600 hours of structured postmarket study and research for a *total 1,500 hour investment*. That's a very serious six months. Most people probably won't want to work that hard. The college would probably go broke awaiting willing students.

Minimum elapsed time is six months—maximum time is twelve months. It would not matter whether students complete it in six or twelve months. It's entirely up to the individual to determine his or her appropriate pace with the proviso that the college be completed within

FIGURE 4-1. *Overview of the Optimum Trader Training Curriculum*

■ Trading 101	Month One	Basic Trading
■ Trading 201	Month Two	Execution
■ Trading 301	Month Three	Chart Analysis
■ Trading 401	Month Four	Momentum
■ Trading 501	Month Five	Leverage
■ Trading 601	Month Six	Trade Planning

a year. I believe any more than a year would be counterproductive because the synergy of focus would be diluted.

Instruction should be provided by competent traders teaching what they know how to do. Not every trainee will get it, and there will be washouts. This college would not graduate traders not possessing the basic aptitude needed to trade—just as you can't graduate from flight school unless you "cut it" in the cockpit.

Optimum Schedule Overview

This overview details the general structure of the 180-hour classes delivered in one-week (thirty hour) segments each month for six months. (The actual curriculum is proprietary to the author.)

In the first week of in-depth training, the trading student will be:

- Exposed to all elements of direct-access trading.
- Warned about all the caveats.
- Introduced to various execution methods available for Nasdaq and NYSE.
- Instructed on interpretation of Level II momentum.
- Provided a roadmap of various alternative chatroom and advisory services.
- Told about the over three hundred Web sites available supporting the financial markets.
- Introduced to primary technical analysis.
- Provided an overview of the use of leverage (options).
- Pretested on knowledge of the financial markets.
- Informed of the distinction between Internet brokers and direct-access brokerages.
- Schooled on the mechanics of available multiple brands of direct-access software.
- Posttested on what they learned during the week.

Following each week of in-house training, students will be provided a detailed roadmap of drills and exercises to practice all the elements of what they were exposed to in the week of training. They have three weeks to practice everything they learned in the week of in-house training.

The postcourse precision exercises developed by each week's instructors are an integral element of each of the six education levels. While the detail is proprietary, students may be assured that, when followed, these exercises will enable them to cement the information presented in the week of in-depth training. For the student to assure grasp of the information, these exercises need to be practiced over and over during the three intervening weeks between classes, according to the plans provided by the instructor. Students will learn and relearn, so retention will be elevated from the average of 10 percent to 70 percent (gross estimates). The object of the precision drills is to establish a structured environment to facilitate the instrumental conditioning so crucial for students to continue learning the material covered once they leave the classroom.

An important factor in trading from home is to be connected with bandwidth equivalent to that available to professional traders at the trading floors around the country. The college will assure, as part of the tuition, that students are properly equipped, connected, and trained on the use of all of their intellectual trading tools as well as physical equipment. "Computers are computers" is not entirely true. In the vision of the college, a trader's workstation is the total professional collection of many components, not just the computer, from saved favorites of all important Web sites, lists of stocks available for shorting, and the names of market makers to all the networking ingredients of the trader's "system," including a glossary of financial terms, right down to conversion charts from decimals to fractions.

Trading 101: Month One—Basic Trading

- ■ Week 1 Rigorous basic trading training (breadth).
- ■ Week 2 Simulated instructor's precision drills.
- ■ Week 3 Get connected to high-speed bandwidth.
- ■ Week 4 Establish multimonitor home trading station.

Following three weeks of home exercises, the student returns to class for the second week of instruction on one of the most important elements of direct-access trading—execution. This week begins the second month of training. Without trying to "teach" it here, just remember there are myriad methods for executing trades in the financial markets. Traders need to learn how to do it with instinct. This week-long block of instruction followed by another three weeks of practice drills will enable that learning to occur.

Trading 201: Month Two—Trade Execution

■ Week 5 Second week—In-depth trade executions.
■ Week 6 Employ instructor defined trading regimen.
■ Week 7 Practice various execution skills.
■ Week 8 Simulated instructor's precision drills.

It's clearly my opinion that you can't trade intelligently without the use of technical analysis. That's why you have not been encouraged to trade with large share size yet. Until you have mastered the elements of execution and have learned to recognize momentum, there is not much point in confusing you with technical analysis. Now, at this point in your learning cycle, it is time to grapple with the complexities of technical analysis. You will now be taught how to identify support, and resistance, use relative strength index (RSI), Stochastics, MACD, Fibbonacci Ratios, bull flags, triangles, up trends, down trends, and so on.

Trading 301: Month Three—Using Technical Analysis

■ Week 9 Third week—Analyze technical indicators.
■ Week 10 Employ instructor defined analysis techniques.
■ Week 11 Follow instructor provided technical analysis drills.
■ Week 12 Continue trading 100-share lots.

After another three weeks of home exercises, students return to class for the fourth week of intense instruction on what I label "momentum." Momentum entails all the elements of Level II screens and market maker behavior. By the time you reach this point in your curriculum, Level II and market makers will be well known to you, but you will probably not yet fully understand and appreciate all of the nuances of one of the most important elements of direct-access trading. During this week, you will be taught all the elements of trading that involve use of Level II. You will learn how to identify "momentum" and the lack of it. Following another three weeks of practicing the identification of momentum and executing small 100-share lot trades, you will return to the college for your fourth block of training on technical analysis.

Trading 401: Month Four—Momentum Interpretation

■ Week 13 Fourth week—Interpretation of momentum action.
■ Week 14 Employ instructor defined daily research regimen.

- Week 15 Master interpretation of market maker behavior and momentum.
- Week 16 Begin live trading of 100-share lots.

The fifth week is when you will be exposed to the leverage options provide, but you will not go away without knowing how to control the tremendous risk in using them. I am not advocating the use of borrowed funds to buy stock; however, leverage is an extremely important factor in capital growth. Leverage within the financial markets is achieved through the use of options. With options you can control much larger blocks of stock than with holding the underlying stocks. There are at least twenty-five different strategies for the use of options; however, that's too many to learn quickly. You need five sound primary strategies and five secondary strategies to employ when it's not practical to use your primes.

Trading 501: Month Five—Trading Leverage

- Week 17 Fifth week—Understanding leverage.
- Week 18 Employ instructor defined leverage techniques.
- Week 19 Limit to learning only ten options strategies well.
- Week 20 Begin trading 200-share lots.

In the final week you will learn how planning trades and then trading your plan reduces your risk substantially. Remember that during each of the six separate weeks of in-house training you will not only review prior material but you will also be exposed to previews of material to be covered in future weeks. As you can see from perusing this schedule, I've limited trade share size to 100-share lots until this last week, when you *may* be ready to try larger lots. Try 200 only if you are trading profitably with 100-share lots. Remember to ignore the cost of commissions for small share size lots while you are in the learning mode. Commissions are just another element of your tuition.

Trading 601: Month Six—Trading Style Plan

- Week 21 Sixth week—Develop trade strategy plan.
- Week 22 Convert knowledge to wisdom.
- Week 23 Trader IQ—Test your knowledge.

■ Week 24 Trade 300-share lots indefinitely.
■ Week 25 Graduate from college.

This curriculum is designed to be cumulative. Just remember that not only is there much to learn, but also there is much you have to keep constant track of. At the risk of repeating myself, trading is a full-time profession in which you must remain constantly focused. If you are not constantly focused on it, you will lose. If you don't "feel" like trading, play golf.

Summary

There you have it—my vision of the optimum learning environment. In the best of all worlds, renowned instructors from across the trading community would strive to become members of the faculty. I am personally acquainted with several eligible professors; however, I'm looking forward to being introduced to more, because such a college would need about twenty. The main campus of such a college would be located centrally for easy air travel, reasonably priced lodging and food, and some leisure time attractions.

I don't know how much the tuition would be for a college like this; however, I wouldn't expect it to be cheap. Graduate schools charge about $50,000 for an MBA. Proficiency in trading could be worth far more. What would make such an educational opportunity unique are competent instructors with superior trading/training proficiency. I would want the instructors to teach only that particular subject matter in which they excelled by demonstrated expertise as proven by documented trading records or previous highly rated student evaluation ratings via structured critiques.

In the financial markets, successful traders can average more than $5,000 an hour using optimum capital and well-balanced leverage. Few individual earners can lay claim to such a financial achievement.

New traders keep asking me how much capital is needed to trade. My recommended trading account size is only $30,000 to $50,000—never any more than $100,000. And half of the $100,000 would be trading built capital. The reason a trader's account remains modest is that wise traders pay themselves weekly (and sometimes, daily) once consistent profitability is achieved.

Recently, a master trader showed me how to convert $10,000 into

$300,000 in just five short months all the while reducing his account size by taking substantial weekly withdrawals. What this trader demonstrated is that it's possible, even during volatile market conditions (March to June 2000) to convert $10,000 to $50,000 in very short order and keep on growing it while protecting the initial investment as well as the gains by removing large chunks from constant risk.

Another special benefit of a college like this would be the camaraderie interaction with fellow trading students would build. It is proven that bonding is the "glue" that sticks people together and helps people stick to their chosen paths.

I recommend that all new traders join DayTradersUSA.com in order to network with experienced traders. Experienced traders should offer their expertise as DTUSA mentors.

The final thought: Have you ever pondered the rigorously constant vigil that FAA agents apply to the skies to maintain airline traffic safety? Think of trading the financial market as equivalent to that vigil, because that's what you're in for!

Don't trade unless you want to!

PART TWO

PLACES—
WHERE TO TRADE?

5

DAY TRADING AT HOME

Now that you've completed Part One, you should have a good handle on what day trading is all about in general, as well as how to go about obtaining a solid day-trading education. Do not shortchange yourself and skip the education process; otherwise, your chances of survival—let alone success—are slim.

Once you've spent the time and money educating yourself about the basics of day trading, your next decision is where to trade. Luckily, you have only two choices—trade at home (known as "remote" trading) or at day-trading brokerage's office.

This chapter focuses on what you need to have to trade from home. The following chapter (chapter 6, "It's All About Connections") provides guidance in selecting the right communications link (e.g., Internet, DSL, Cable) to your broker from your home. And chapter 7 will give you a detailed process to go through for selecting a day-trading firm, if you decide that is the path you want to take instead of trading from home.

Goals of Top Day Traders

Before getting into the specifics of home trading, let's review what top traders perceive their goals to be:

■ 100 percent concentration on day trading without any interruptions during trading hours.

- Making a net profit each day.
- Closing out all positions by the end of the day.
- Minimizing risk and preserving capital by cutting losses *very* quickly.
- Using margin, as needed, to leverage trades and increase profits.
- Using a specific methodology or trading system (back-tested and forward-tested) to determine buy and sell points.
- Leaving emotions outside the trading environment.
- Learning from mistakes and not repeating them.
- Keeping a log book (diary) of all transactions, with notes on which trades went well and which didn't and the reasons why.
- Taking a few weekdays off, especially after a losing streak.
- Paying no margin interest, since overnight positions are not taken.

As you read through these goals, you probably said to yourself that you agree with all of them, that they make sense, and that to achieve them should not be a problem. You would be right until your last observation. It is very hard to achieve them—ask any trader in the business about his or her experiences. Unfortunately, many new traders, as well as experienced traders, fail to achieve most of these goals and lose their entire stake. By far, the major obstacle to achieving trading success is your mind not your bank account. More about the importance of mastering the psychology of trading in chapters 8 and 9, written by two experts.

Day Trading Is a Business

If you expect to be a successful day trader, then you must treat day trading as a business—not as a hobby or pastime. Unless you truly believe it is a business, you probably will not give it the attention it needs. Since you are using hard-earned money to day trade, you don't want to throw it away by having a nonprofessional or lackadaisical attitude. Some individuals day trade part-time and do very well. That is possible, but even part-time trading must be treated as a business. Trying to day trade while working another job is suicide—neither you nor your employer is getting the full benefit of your talents.

Day trading is very hard work, according to those who have been down the road. On the surface it may appear fairly simple: pick a stock

→ select a buy point → put in your buy order → receive the confirmation → decide to sell it → put in your sell order → receive the confirmation → record your profit or loss.

True, the mechanics of executing trades are simple once you learn how to do them. However, determining what stock to buy and when to buy and sell take a lot of experience, as you will find out in your first week of trading.

Characteristics of a Home Trader

Some individuals like to work by themselves, and others like to have people around. You have to decide for yourself whether working at home or at a trading firm is best for you. Once you have read this chapter and the next two chapters, you will be able to make up your mind as to which road you want to take.

Typically, home trading is a good choice for individuals with the following characteristics:

- Independent thinker who doesn't want or need input from others
- Self-motivated
- Does not need much social interaction
- Can concentrate better without distractions
- Hates commuting and wasting time
- Disciplined to focus on trading
- Self-confident
- Patient
- Decisive

What Should Your Setup Include

You should have a separate office that is large and bright enough for your needs. It should be properly ventilated and air-conditioned. Then you need the following items to day trade:

1. Computer system.
2. Communications link.
3. Online brokerage account.

4. Trading and quote software.
5. Desk and chair.

Let's cover each of these items.

Computer System

You may already own a PC with a Pentium II, a 15-inch or 17-inch monitor, a 10 GB hard drive, a 96 MB RAM, a 56Kbps modem, and a printer. This system may be sufficient to run your trading software and connect to your broker without difficulty. However, if your system has fewer features than these, then you should spend the money for a new PC system. Remember, in day trading speed is the name of the game—a slow computer can impact your ability to get fast quotes and trade executions.

Moreover, if you are sharing a PC with others in your family, you should consider upgrading solely for your trading business. The current PC prices are very reasonable, and you can buy an excellent desktop computer for $1,500 to $2,000. A budget system will run about $1,000.

In a new system, go for the following *minimum* components:

Pentium III processor 500/100 MHz (or equivalent processor)
128 MB 100 MHz SDRAM
Microsoft Windows 98 or NT (preferred by many for its stability)
10 megabyte hard drive
17-inch flat screen monitor (but 19-inch flat screen or larger is
    highly recommended)
v.90 modem
Iomega ZIP100 drive

Of course, as part of the package, your PC will be equipped with a CD-ROM drive, a 3.5-inch 1.44 MB diskette drive, sound card, graphics card, software, and so on. Try to get Office 2000 or Small Business since they provide word processing, a spreadsheet, and other useful integrated software.

For $2,500 you can get a top-of-the-line PC with a Pentium III—733 (or 800EB) or Athlon 600-850, 19-inch flat screen monitor (get the highest resolution you can afford), 20GB hard drive, v.90/DSL modem. Considering the focus of your business, I would recommend the best system you can afford. Also, strongly consider a second monitor that will provide you with added capability to see critical information without having to keep hitting the mouse to change screens. Some of the "professional" traders have four screens!

One excellent source for information on PCs is *PC World* magazine (www.pcworld.com), which ranks the best PC systems. For example, the July 2000 issue cover story was the "Best of 2000," which ranked the best desktops, notebooks, hardware, software, and Web sites. Many Web sites also contain information on PCs.

Communications Link

As a trader you want a fast and reliable connection to your broker to receive real-time data and to make trades. If you can afford digital subscriber line (DSL), cable, or other methods of communication, then you should strongly consider them. I use the Internet with a 56Kbps modem, and I'm satisfied with the service. However, I have no choice because of where I live. I will definitely consider higher speed modes of communications once they are offered to me. Because of the importance of your communications link, the next chapter is devoted to this subject, including the need for back-up arrangements in case of problems.

Online Brokerage Account

To execute trades you need to sign-up with an online brokerage firm. You have a wide choice of firms—full-service, discount, deep discount, and direct-access. In the day-trading arena not all firms are created equal with regard to cost per transaction, execution speed, access to ECNs, and customer service. There are many online brokers, and the largest ones were listed in table 1-1.

If you think that all you have to do is select the online firm with the lowest commissions, then you have a misconception about what day trading is all about. What you are looking to achieve is getting the best executions you possibly can in the quickest time. Seconds in this business can cost you thousands of dollars of profits or losses, especially with high-flying stocks.

Day traders need a direct-access broker—pure and simple. Direct-access means that your order is routed to a market maker without involving an intermediary. This means that your order is quickly executed at the best available price, based upon the type of order you are using (e.g., market order, limit order, buy stop, sell stop, market-on-close). Many of the popular online brokers do not offer direct access; therefore, you should bypass them.

You should be concerned about the spread between the bid-and-ask price of a stock and what you can buy or sell it for. If you pay just ⅛ of a point more for a stock when trading 1,000 shares because of a delayed or poor execution, then you've paid $125 too much, even though your online broker charged you only $8 for the trade. You lost $117 on this transaction right out of the gate. Direct-access provides the mechanism to avoid this situation.

Of course, if you are not day trading but position trading (over a few days) instead, then a regular online firm may be suitable as long as you use orders other than market orders. However, your best bet is a direct-access broker.

According to the Senate's report, entitled *Day Trading: Everyone Gambles But the House*, the average day trader pays about $16 in commission for each of twenty-nine average trades per day at day-trading firms (see a review of their report in chapter 14). Therefore, just to break even these traders must generate *daily* profits in excess of $464 to cover commissions. Annualizing this data, the average trader has to generate a profit in excess of $111,360 to cover costs, assuming twenty trades a month. Yes, commissions at direct-access firms are about $16, but you get the best executions you possibly can. How else are you going to overcome these fees—each brokerage firm's commissions are the same for remote traders, as well.

You may be familiar with some of direct-access firms, such as Tradescape, On-Site Trading, Inc., EDGETRADE.com, Marketwise Securities, Inc., Broadway Trading, and Carlin Equities Corp. There are many others. One Web site that contains a review of sixty firms and delineates their services is www.sonic.net/donaldj. Check it out. Also, look for ads in *Investor's Business Daily* and contact the firms for information as well as their Web sites.

There is a specific process you should go through in selecting one of these brokerages. Many of the questions you should ask and the information you should request is contained in chapter 7, "Ten Steps to Selecting a Trading Firm." Just adapt the questions to "remote" trading instead of onsite trading.

Trading and Quote Software

Before making a final selection of your direct-access broker, you should realize that the brokerage offers trading software and real-time charting and quotes. The software they offer should be part of your selection process. Some firms have only one software package—but with multiple levels of sophistication and pricing. Demo the software. Again, chapter 7 covers the bases on this as well.

If you decide to use an online broker, then you'll have to obtain charting and real-time quote software. Among the most popular packages used by respondents to our Day Trader survey were: Real Tick III, CyberTrader, eSignal, myTrack, and QCharts. Other software used included: Datek Streamer, TradeStation, Quicken Quotes, PCQuote, WindowOnWallStreet, and A.T. Financial. Other software to consider include: MetaStock, Professional and DTNIQ. Some of the information available from a trading software package is shown in figures 5-1, 5-2, and 5-3.

FIGURE 5-1. *Intraday chart screen.*

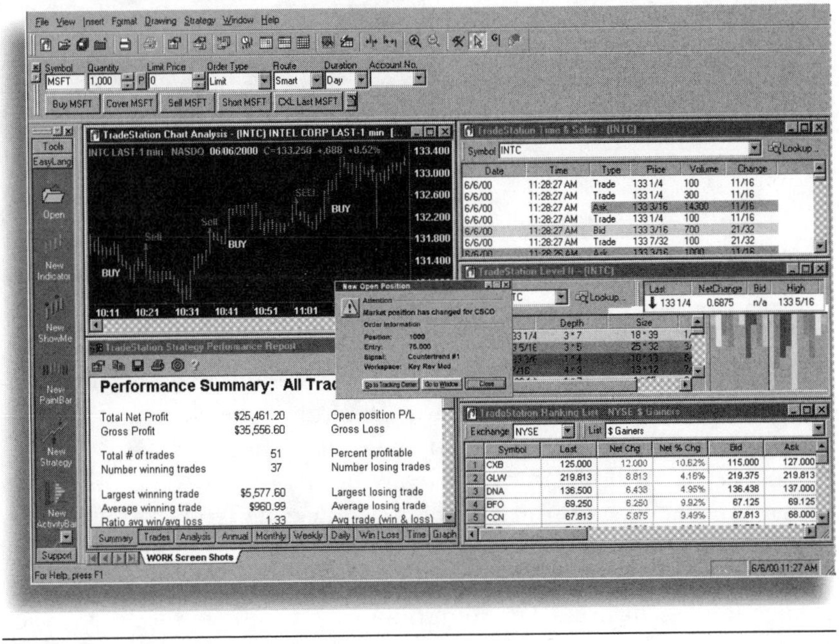

Source: Omega Research

FIGURE 5-2. *Nasdaq Level II screen.*

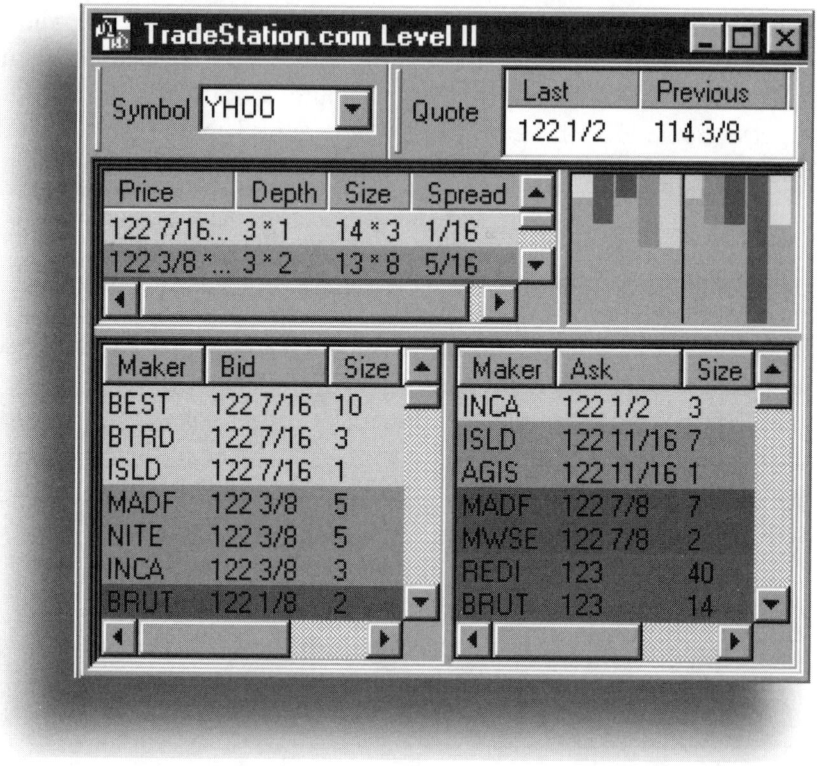

Source: Omega Research

Desk and Chair

Make sure you have a large enough desk to house your PC, screen(s), and printer. Your keyboard should be at a comfortable height. If you are buying a new desk, then consider an ergonomically designed style that will provide you with a comfortable and adjustable unit. Keep reflections from lights or sunlight away from the screen or you will experience glare. Place a glare screen on your PC, if necessary.

Since you will be sitting for many hours, it pays to spend money on a comfortable chair. You'll find many office chairs advertised for $99 to $250. Once you sit in most of these you'll know why they are priced so low. You need a chair that is ergonomically designed, where you can change the height from the ground, the arm height and location, back support, tilt, and so on.

FIGURE 5-3. *Time and sales screen.*

Time	Type	Price	Volume	Change
13:49:33	Tick	127 7/8	100	+1 3/16
13:49:33	Tick	127 7/8	200	+1 3/16
13:49:33	Tick	127 7/8	100	+1 3/16
13:49:33	Tick	127 15/16	200	+1 1/4
13:49:33	Tick	128	500	+1 5/16
13:49:31	Tick	128	100	+1 5/16
13:49:29	Bid	127 7/8	2000	+1 3/16
13:49:28	Tick	127 13/16	200	+1 1/8
13:49:28	Tick	128	100	+1 5/16
13:49:27	Tick	127 13/16	200	+1 1/8
13:49:27	Tick	127 13/16	200	+1 1/8

Source: Omega Research

I use a Herman Miller "Aeron" chair, which I bought about five years ago for about $750. It not only looks brand new but was the best investment I ever made. It is extremely comfortable and totally adjustable (see figure 5.4). Another popular chair is the "Executive" (manufactured by BackSaver). Before you buy any chair make sure you test it out first.

Conclusion

Trading from home can be an outstanding experience. But it depends on the individual and the type of personality you have. If you decide to trade from home, you must get everything in order. This can be a daunting task for some. One way of not having to go through the proc-

FIGURE 5-4. *Herman Miller Aeron chair.*

Source: Herman Miller, Inc.

ess is to consider trading at a day-trading brokerage office, if one is nearby. Chapter 7 covers all that you have to know. If you go that route, remember that you won't have to buy a new PC, set up a special place for it at home, or buy trading and quote software. All that is provided by the firm. Good luck no matter what you decide to do.

6

IT'S ALL ABOUT CONNECTIONS

Gibbons Burke

When stock trading first swept the country, the only way to get a quote on your stocks was to visit a broker's office. In the earliest days, the broker had a telegraph line to the exchange with a "ticker" device that would print a tape showing the quotes as they came across. That was the broker's added value—they were a source of news and quotes, and they had a secure line to the exchange for placing trades. A young man would stand at the ticker calling out quotes to a bunch of other young men stationed at one or more chalkboards in the room, and they would record the changes to the prices on the appropriate board. Quotes were provided free in exchange for customer business.

For nearly a century this system remained essentially unchanged. Halfway through the century the ticker box and chalkboards were replaced by electric displays, but quotes were readily available only by going to the brokerage office, which was usually set up to accommodate customers who wanted to watch the Big Board.

Today, every investor has the equivalent of a Western Union telegraph machine wired to their house. The Internet has wired the world with a way to get quotes anywhere anytime. As an active online trader you have many options available for connecting to sources of trading information and trade brokerage; however, there are some essential considerations in making your selection:

Copyright © 2001 Gibbons Burke. All rights reserved.

■ *Speed*—Can you handle the amount of bandwidth required to sustain your style of trading? If you are a position trader, then your requirements will be less than those of a day trader following Level II screens for half a dozen stocks.

■ *Reliability*—Your Internet connection is your trading lifeline.

■ *Cost*—If you are an active trader you must weigh cost against the amount of money you regularly put at risk. Saving money on your Internet connection can result in large losses.

Getting Connected

Getting connected to the Internet is one thing—staying connected is another. In this chapter various options are reviewed for choosing the right type of Internet connection. You should consider obtaining the fastest connection available to you within your means. In most cases this will mean Digital Subscriber Line (DSL) or cable connections. However, whatever you choose, it pays to be prepared for your main connection to be down. You should keep an account with a dial-up provider as well, so that you can get connected via alternative means if necessary. You should have an alternative if the route to your quote service provider or broker through your fast connection is snagged.

It is important to know that the Internet is composed of a loose confederation of companies, government agencies, universities, and nonprofit organizations. The path between any point A and point B can cross an infinite variety of connection points. The return path from B to A may be completely different. The quality of that chain of connections is only as good as the weakest link. The fastest DSL connection to the Internet will be only as fast as the slowest "hop" between you and the server you are trying to access.

The Internet is a relatively new communications infrastructure. It has not matured to the point that it is as reliable as your telephone dial tone or local water supply. There will be a day when it is that reliable. If you choose to rely on the Internet for your source of market information, then you need to be prepared to deal with the problems that can occur so that your trading is not interrupted.

The first step in the process is getting a connection to your quote provider. There are a variety of ways to connect to the Internet (refer to table 6-1):

TABLE 6-1. Connection Options

The need for speed Connection	Monthly Cost	Equipment	Speed (upstream/downstream)	Advantages	Disadvantages
Dial-up	$0–$35 + phone line	Modem—$50	56 Kbps (30 Kbps practical real limit)	Easy, inexpensive, "transportable"	Slow; unreliable
ISDN	$30 plus metered time charges—$100	Router $300–1,500	2 @ 64 Kbps + 16 Kbps (?)	Combines voice & data over same lines	Unreliable—frequent disconnections; metered access rates
DSL	$40–$100	Router $200–800	384 Kbps–1.5 Mbps / 128 Kbps	No speed degradation with users in neighborhood	Speed degrades with distance from central office; Regional Bells slow to install
Cable	$40–50	Cable Modem $100	30 mbps / 128 kbps–10 Mbps	No interference with your phone or TV viewing	Speed degrades as other people in your neighborhood get the service.
Wireless—Ricochet	$29.00	Ricochet modem $160 Wireless modem $150–520	28.8 Kbps	Total mobility within a few areas	Slow
Wireless—Bell Atlantic	$40–65		9600 Kbps	Available in more areas than Ricochet	Slower
T1	$1,000	Router	1.544 Mbps	Extremeley fast	Very expensive
T3	?	Router	45 Mbps	Extremely fast	Very expensive

- Analog telephone dial-up (modem).
- Digital telephone (ISDN, xDSL).
- Digital cable.
- Ground-based wireless.
- Satellite wireless.
- Hybrid solutions (WebRamp).

Analog Telephone (POTS) Using Modem Dial-Up (56,000 bps)

Telephone modems have been around for a long time. When I first started using them they could send and receive information at 110 bits per second (bps) with an accoustic device connected to your terminal by placing the handset into a cradle. Plain old telephone service was designed for voice communications, so only a narrow range of audio frequencies are carried to save cost. This physical network—the copper cabling—hasn't changed in any real technological sense since Alexander Graham Bell. Modems convert digital data into an audio signal that can be carried by this equipment, and the bps rate measures how much information the modem is able to carry across the connection.

Improvements in modem speed began to arrive steadily as the modem companies learned to squeeze more and more data through the voice channel using data compression and multiple tones—quantum jumps to 300 bps, 1200 bps, 2400 bps, 14.4 Kbps (kilobits or thousand bits per second), 19.2 Kbps, 28.8 Kbps, and now 56 Kbps. 56Kbps may be the ultimate upper limit for analog transmission over what the phone company has long called, in technical terms, POTS (Plain Old Telephone Service). Actually, the practical physical limit for an analog line is more like 30 Kbps, no matter what the modem manufacturers would like you to think.

When two modems connect—for example, when your computer dials your Internet service provider—they engage in a "handshaking" ritual where they test the quality of the connection. The two modems establish how fast they can talk to each other and which modem languages they both understand in a negotiation process that you hear as those crazy noises in your PC speaker when you are connecting.

The word *modem* is a contraction of "MODulation-DEModulation," because that's what it does—it takes digital data from your computer and turns it into a modulating sound wave carried by the phone line, which is then demodulated by the modem on the other end and turned back into digital data. Sometimes two 56Kpbs modems may speak different dialects of crazy noise, so may not often achieve the peak data transfer rates. This digital to analog to digital process and the handshaking that goes on in maintaining the connection means that analog connections are by nature slow compared to a direct digital connection, my next topic.

Most ISPs provide dial-up service as the base option, and have 56Kpbs modems waiting to take your dial-up call. Costs range from as low as free to $40 per month. There seem to be several major services who provide a basic flat-rate unlimited time package for $19.95 to $21.95 per month. When considering which pricing plan to choose, be sure to get a flat-rate plan for unlimited amounts of time.

Unlimited Access Plans

Following is a list of the major U.S. providers of dial-up bandwidth with their monthly fees:

Earthlink.net	$19.95
AOL.com	$21.95 ($19.95 if you sign up for a year)
ATT.net	$21.95
Altavista.com	Free (advertisements)
CompuServe	$19.95 ($17.00 if you sign up for a year)

In Europe, free Internet access is common, because telephone service is metered on local calls. In the United States, free dial-up Internet access is available from www.altavista.com, and others, but you must install a special piece of software, which will monitor what you look at on the Web and then deliver advertisements targeted directly at your particular interests. They will also disconnect you if you don't do anything on your computer for twenty minutes, so is probably not suited for trading purposes.

Dial-up service is useful for several reasons. It is easy to use—modems are commonplace. It is transportable—you can dial into an ISP from just about anywhere. Many of the major service providers, such as CompuServe, AOL, Earthlink, and ATT, provide international access numbers, so the Internet is a local call away. Local calls in Europe can be expensive, and ISPs may charge metered rates for access overseas.

Digital Telephone—ISDN (64 Kbps–128 Kbps)

Analog data transmission methods work hard to squeeze as much information as possible through a channel that wasn't designed for the purpose, and the outcome isn't good. Recognizing this, phone companies started planning for a new service to replace POTS called integrated services digital network (ISDN), which used the existing copper wiring in people's homes. The new service was introduced in 1988 with the great expectation that it would completely replace POTS within ten years. The promise was great—ISDN is made up of two 64 Kbps channels for a total combined bandwidth of 128 Kbps. There is an additional 8 Kbps control channel to boot. In addition, POTS service is provided over the same connection—you could have a telephone conversation while connected to the Internet. Because ISDN is digital it is free of the "latency" of an analog connection. Even though 128Kbps is roughly twice as much as 56Kbps, ISDN can achieve speeds five times faster than the fastest analog modem.

ISDN was slow to be deployed and is often unreliable. It requires a special "router" device, which can cost between $400 and $800, into which you plug your telephone, fax, and computer. While many people are currently using ISDN, it has effectively been leapfrogged by the newer DSL and cable technologies for connecting to the Internet, although for now it may be more widely available.

ISDN service often requires you to pay your ISP extra charges for a higher level of service, because the ISP must buy an ISDN modem and connection from the phone company to provide your connection. Second, when you use more bandwidth, they have to make sure they have that bandwidth on their connection to the Internet.

Digital Telephone—xDSL (7 + Mbps)

Like ISDN, digital subscriber line (DSL) also uses the exiting copper wiring of the POTS telephone network, but it can achieve much higher data transmission speeds. It's almost like having a local area network connection to the Internet—it can potentially achieve 7 million bits per second (megabits or Mbps) speeds over the twisted-pair copper wire network already in place in most homes and offices. To put that in perspective, Ethernet local area networks can carry data at 10 megabits or 100 megabits, depending upon which flavor you have.

However twisted-pair copper cable has its limits—your PC must be located no farther than 18,000 feet from the "DSLAM" router at the telephone company's central office. Beyond that distance the data carrying capacity of the twisted pair degrades significantly. Additionally, the performance of the connection will depend on your distance from the central office. So many users are physically out of reach type of service. You can check availability of DSL at your particular home address with many of the DSL providers, such as your local phone carrier, or nationwide Internet providers such as Earthlink.net.

DSL service is relatively inexpensive, ranging from $39 to $99 per month depending upon your provider and the type and term of service you contract for. Home users are typically consumers of data, and so many opt for asymmetrical DSL (ADSL)— this means that they are provided, say, 128 Kbps of bandwidth for data leaving their PC versus 5 Mbps on the incoming side. This would not be ideal for hosting a Web site where other users are pulling down data from your computer but is fine for trading purposes, because most of the data traffic is incoming market information. A special router is required, which can range from $200 to $800.

Besides ADSL, there are a few flavors of DSL, such as R-ADSL, ADSL Lite, VDSL, HDSL, IDSL, and others, depending on your particular location. The technology has not settled into a single standard. A good source of information about the varieties of services available can be found at: http://www.xdsl.com/content/backgroundinfo/overviews/default.asp.

Digital Cable

The connection options discussed so far use twisted-pair copper wires of the existing telephone network to connect you to the Internet. Another method that is growing in popularity employs coaxial cable used by cable television networks to beam hundreds of television channels to your home. Currently there is a battle growing between the cable companies and the telephone companies to wire up America for high-speed Internet access. Bandwidth of a cable connection is claimed by companies such as @Home to be a hundred times faster than a 56Kbps dial-up connection.

Unlike the telephone system, which has always been designed for two-way connections, the cable network was intended to broadcast—information flowed one way across the cable. Because of this the cable companies have had to build out an additional network of "headend" connection points neighborhood by neighborhood. Everyone in your neighborhood connects through a central point. What many have experienced with cable connections is that when they first are hooked up, they have blazing speed, but as others in the neighborhood get hooked up and start using the Internet heavily, the performance of the connection degrades. Pacific Bell, the largest provider of DSL services in California, has aired some aggressive television advertisements hammering the cable industry on this point.

Ground-Based Wireless

For active traders on the go who find themselves away from a telephone jack for dial-up access, wireless connections can enable them to stay in touch with the markets anytime, anywhere.

Several companies offer wireless modems that allow you to connect to the Internet via the airwaves. Right now, the service availability is very limited, and connection speed is slow (9600 bps to 28.8 Kbps), but the convenience of being able to stay in contact with the markets no matter where you are makes this a compelling choice for active traders.

Ricochet (www.ricochet.net) offers a solution in the San Francisco, Washington, D.C., and Seattle areas based on a proprietary wireless technology on an area of the radio spectrum that is license free. Their network is composed of Microcell Radios, which are shoebox-size devices mounted on utility poles and street lamps every quarter to half mile in their coverage areas. Access speeds up to 28.8 Kbps are possible. Service is $29 per month for unlimited access; the Ricochet external modem costs $159.

Another solution offered by Bell Atlantic (http://www.bam.com/wireless/internet1.html) piggybacks on the cellular network to provide 9600 bps connections anywhere on the Eastern Seaboard for a flat-rate access for $40 to $65 per month. It uses the Airtouch AirCard PCMCIA modem designed for laptops.

Apple Computer now offers the Airport (http://www.apple.com/airport/), a mobile Internet connection station for the home or small office that allows up to ten Apple iBook and PowerBook laptops, and iMac and G4 desktop units to be networked together using a wireless network. It is fast for a wireless network: 11 Mbps that uses the 2.4 gigahertz frequency spectrum. This wireless network lets you take your iBook, PowerBook, or PC laptop wherever you want to and stay connected no matter where you are, and the entire family can use the Internet connection at the same time.

The Airport uses the IEEE 802.11 standard for direct sequence spread spectrum (DSSS) wireless networking developed in collaboration with Lucent. This open standard technology means that you can include other computers in the network as well. Lucent offers a WaveLAN (http://www.wavelan.com/) PCMCIA card, which can be used to connect PC laptops into the wireless network. A Macintosh is still required to administer the Airport base station, which is much less expensive than the Lucent equivalent.

This technology may become the basis for a nationwide wireless infrastructure that would allow you to roam anywhere and be connected to the Internet seamlessly.

Satellite Wireless

If you are a trader truly on the move, roving beyond a fixed regional area in a mobile home, or even on board a yacht out at sea, the best way to stay connected might be to use satellite Internet connections to stay in touch. Satellite-based ISPs might be a good alternative high-speed access method for those located in areas where DSL is not available and there is no cable service. Some systems use satellite for inbound (downstream) data flow but use a telephone connection for outbound or upstream data.

Some systems for mobile satellite connections allow a mariner to keep a connection to the Internet using a gyro-stabilized satellite dish, which, reportedly, can continue to function in all but the heaviest seas and worst weather conditions. These systems will be correspondingly expensive, but they are available for traders in the seagoing cruising class.

Hybrid Solutions

Someone once said, "Diversification is the only free lunch on Wall Street." This means that the best way to reduce your risk exposure is to diversify your investment portfolio among a number of stocks to reduce the adverse effect if one or more goes sour. The same logic can be applied to the information and execution risk in your trading. If you have only one way to be connected to the Internet—through one Internet service provider—and that ISP is having a bad day, your portfolio could have a bad day too.

At bare minimum, as a trader you should have at least two ISP accounts. Use the one you like best, but be ready and able to connect using the secondary one if the first one gives a sign of trouble. Even if your ISP is fine, the route that they choose to send your data over the Internet may develop traffic snags. Choose for your second ISP one that uses different paths over the Internet, so when one ISP has traffic on its routes, your other ISP should be able to bypass the traffic.

There are some useful tools for diagnosing this sort of problem. Windows comes with two of them: "ping" and "tracert." Ping measures the time it takes for a message to travel from your PC to the destination server. Tracert traces the route between your PC and the destination server and lets you know how much there was at each "hop" along the route. These tools are discussed in more detail in the following sections.

The ultimate in speed, flexibility, and reliability may be achieved by combining two or more simultaneous connections. This approach can increase your bandwidth and allows you to reduce the risk that you will not be able to trade if one of your ISPs develops trouble or traffic on the Internet gets bad. In areas where high-speed digital access via DSL or cable modem is not available, for example, you can get a router for $250 that allows you to connect to the Internet via three different dial-up modem connections to three different ISPs. The combined bandwidth of the three dial-up connections is a vast improvement over one dial-up connection and can approach the speeds of ISDN. But connecting to three different ISPs gives you an additional measure of reliability you can't get with a single digital connection, because a single ISP is a point of failure that, if it breaks, gives you no recourse.

Ramp Networks, Inc. (http://www.webramp.com/) manufactures the routers that allow you to pool bandwidth. Their WebRamp black boxes also include an Ethernet hub with four jacks, so you can plug in multiple PCs to share the Internet connection.

Obviously, the more telephone lines you use and the more ISPs you pay, the costs are going to be higher. However, at $20 per month per ISP, it's not a lot compared to the cost of not being able to get out of a losing trade. Additional telephone lines are not really that much more if you don't get all the gizmos on the line the phone companies want to sell you. This is truly the most robust way to connect to the Internet for trading until the Internet itself is more robust.

Staying Connected

Once you get connected to the Internet, the next big challenge is how you can stay connected so that the money line to your quote source and your broker stays operational. A basic understanding of how the Internet works will be useful in diagnosing problems when they occur. Unreliable connections may go relatively unnoticed using a Web browser, but if you are relying on a real-time streaming quote feed, you will notice very quickly when there is a problem communicating with your quote server.

The Internet is a network of networks—a patchwork quilt of computers tied together in a loose cooperative but also competitive confederation of service providers. The route that your information takes over what is called the "backbone" of the Internet from your computer to another computer can vary with the time of day the Internet service provider you use, and the ISP used by the computer on the other end. Rarely do the packets of bits of information sent back and forth between two computers travel nonstop, unless you are directly connected to the destination computer by a cable. Information is handed off in a bucket brigade chain between your computer and the destination computer over a series of "hops" or connection way-points—points between the source and the destination. In this chain of communication your connection to the destination is only as good as the slowest link in the chain, no matter how fast your connection to the Internet may be.

Like Little Red Riding Hood, the path to grandma's house can be filled with hungry wolves. Many problems can occur along the route. The information will travel across backbone networks owned by competing companies. The job of each computer along the line is to route *packets* of data to the next place in line. Sometimes the "pipes" connecting different backbone provider's networks can be saturated with traffic. When that happens, data packets can be dropped—lost in the online version of Davy Jones' locker, requiring the originating computer to re-send the lost packet. Your quote on JDS Uniphase arrives late, and you could miss a trade.

One day the Internet will be much more reliable than it is today, but it is not yet developed into a mature, stable technology. When it does mature, then your connection to any server in the world will be as reliable and trouble free as the telephone network. But it is helpful to remember that the telephone network is over a hundred years old. The Internet is in its early twenties, and though the pace of growth and innovation is fast, there is work yet to be done.

Given that the Internet is what it is, as a trader who depends on this technology to trade profitably you will need some tools to survive. Strategies and tactics to overcome the problems when they arise are necessary—the alternative is to stop trading when things get bad. The first step is to have a basic understanding of what is going on under the hood. This knowledge will enable you to properly diagnose problems when they appear and give you the ability to overcome them so you can continue trading.

Understanding the Medium

At the most basic level there are seven key places where trouble can affect your trading day. These problems can occur at any point along the chain of connections from your computer to the destination computer. Whenever you experience a problem you should start your investigation at the point where you have the most ability to do something about the problem: your PC. You have the most ability to deal with the situation the closer it is to your computer. The farther away the problem is, the more difficult it will be to correct. Possible problem locations are:

1. **Your computer.** There are occasions when your computer cannot keep up with the incoming data; getting behind in processing that information can cause your programs to update slowly or crash. If you are monitoring several hundred stocks in real time and simultaneously

running Java-based programs on a Web browser, you can overload your processor's ability to handle the load.

2. **Connection to the Internet.** This is of great importance, obviously, because it is the point of failure that is most likely to fail. The first consideration is whether your connection is "fat" enough to carry all the information you are trying to squeeze through it. It is easy to overload 56Kbps modem connections—especially when downloading heavy Web pages.

3. **Your ISP's network.** Your ISP may have a network of connections spanning the country, and your information will have to traverse all these connections to get to where it is going. The fewer connections there are the better, because there are fewer possible points of failure. Each connection adds some *latency,* because packets of information may have to spend some layover time in the connecting router. Worse, packets of information may be dropped by an overloaded router and lost.

4. **Your ISP's "peering" connection to the destination computer's ISP.** How traffic is routed between different Internet backbones is a complex Byzantine world involving commercial politics on a grand scale. It is in the interest of each ISP to provide "peer" connections with as many other ISPs as possible to better serve their customers, but these relationships are developing organically and sporadically. Here is where perhaps the Internet is the least mature and changing the most rapidly. What this means for you is that, if your ISP pairs well with the destination computer's ISP, you will experience good connections. If the pairing is bad, or worse, uses a third intermediate ISP, your connections may be less reliable.

5. **The destination ISP's network.** Like your ISP, the destination computer's ISP may have its own network of intermediate router "hops" across which your information will have to travel. Again, the fewer the better, but in many cases this is out of your control. Without that network, your information "can't get there from here."

6. **The destination ISP's connection to your destination computer.** This is similar to your computer's connection to the Internet. If the destination computer is a popular Web server or an overloaded real-time data vendor, it may be saturating the connection, causing latency and packet loss. Another source of problems here can occur when your destination server is the target of a denial of service (DOS) attack by an Internet Terrorist. These vermin attempt to disrupt the operations of

the destination computer by flooding their servers with requests for information. This can not only overload the destination computer's ability to serve the information but also saturate the connection to the Internet.

7. **The destination computer.** If the destination server is not able to serve the demands made upon it, its clients' service can become unreliable or slow.

Clearly, there are many places where things can and do go wrong when you are using the Internet to get information vital to your trading process. But understanding how things are connected together can help you determine where the problems are happening and what steps you can take to work around them. The following tools can help you determine where along the chain the problem exists.

Diagnosing the Problem

ping

The most elemental tool in the Interneteer's toolbox is ping, named after the sound made by the sonar device used in submarines (and destroyers) to locate underwater objects by sending out a burst of sound into the deep and timing the echo of the sound reflected back to the sender. Similarly, an Internet ping sends a small data packet to the destination server, which immediately echoes the packet back to the originating computer, which measures the time it takes the information to travel across the Internet route and back. The ping serves three functions: (1) determining that the destination is reachable over the Internet; (2) measuring the amount of time it takes; and (3) determining that the destination computer is "alive" and responsive. All three are useful bits of information.

Ping originated as a standard Unix operating system command but has been assimilated by the Microsoft Windows environment, which comes equipped with a ping command in the DOS command window. All you have to do to use this command is to type: ping [*server name or IP address*].

For example, if you were to type "command" in the Start-Run menu command and then type, ping herndon-r01.quote.com

at the DOS prompt in the window will appear showing the ping report to one of Quote.com's real-time quote servers:

Pinging herndon-r01.quote.com [209.143.250.12] with 32 bytes of data:

Reply from 209.143.250.12: bytes = 32 time = 89ms TTL = 116
Reply from 209.143.250.12: bytes = 32 time = 89ms TTL = 116
Reply from 209.143.250.12: bytes = 32 time = 81ms TTL = 116
Reply from 209.143.250.12: bytes = 32 time = 87ms TTL = 116

Ping statistics for 209.143.250.12:
    Packets: Sent = 4, Received = 4, Lost = 0 (0 percent loss),
Approximate round trip times in milli-seconds:
    Minimum = 81ms, Maximum = 89ms, Average = 86ms
ping herndon-r01.quote.com

If you are using a Macintosh computer, you need to download an excellent piece of shareware called Anarchie or Mac TCP Watcher, which are both made by Stairways Software (www.stairways.com).

The Windows version of ping has a command line option that is useful for determining packet loss over the path between your computer and the destination computer by pinging continuously. It will count the number of pings sent out that didn't return: ping −t [*server name or IP address*].

Ping is useful for several functions. You can use it to quickly determine if you have a connection to the Internet and whether your networking is operating properly. Sending a ping to a server that has a good chance of being operational is a good way to do this. For example, you can type "ping www.yahoo.com" if you can't get to Yahoo's Web server, chances are you won't be getting through to your broker. Another good way to check your connectivity is to ping your ISP's Web address.

traceroute

The traceroute command does what it sounds like it does—it traces all the hops in the path between your computer and the destination server. It tells you how much time it takes to travel to each way-point in turn (compared to ping, which measures the total round trip travel time to the destination only).

As with ping, the traceroute command had its origin in the UNIX operating system. It too has been implemented in the Windows environment, but its name was shortened to tracert because DOS can only handle command names of eight or fewer characters. To use the traceroute command in a Windows DOS prompt type: tracert [*server name or IP address*].

Here's what the route looks like when you use this command to ping a trade server for one of Quote.com's QChart servers from a hotel room in London:

#	Min	Ave	Max	IP Address	Machine Name
1	0.122	0.132	0.149	193.149.64.1	max1.msn-uk.pipex.com
2	0.123	0.153	0.211	193.149.64.254	msn-gw1.msn-uk.pipex.com
3	0.126	0.155	0.211	158.43.198.1	fddi5-0-0.london.pipex.net
4	0.122	0.167	0.210	158.43.193.233	pos1-0.cr1.lnd6.gbb.uk.uu.net
5	0.123	0.178	0.221	146.188.5.41	pos11-0-0.gw2.lnd1.alter.net
6	0.125	0.154	0.208	146.188.2.221	422.atm6-0-0.cr1.lnd1.alter.net
7	0.196	0.203	0.218	146.188.4.209	167.atm3-0.br1.nyc5.alter.net
8	0.197	0.199	0.203	137.39.30.117	431.atm4-0.gw1.nyc5.alter.net
9	0.196	0.207	0.218	146.188.177.238	151.atm3-0.xr1.nyc1.alter.net
10	0.197	0.208	0.223	146.188.177.145	195.atm8-0-0.br1.nyc1.alter.net
11	0.202	0.252	*	206.132.150.129	s5-0-1.ar2.jfk.gblx.net
12	0.196	0.206	0.223	206.132.253.97	pos3-1-155m.cr1.jfk.gblx.net
13	0.199	0.206	0.221	206.132.253.86	pos4-0-622m.wr1.nyc2.gblx.net
14	0.212	0.218	0.228	208.178.174.125	pos7-0-622m.wr2.wdc2.gblx.net
15	0.204	0.213	0.226	206.132.113.102	pos2-0-622m.cr1.iad3.gblx.net
16	0.206	0.212	0.220	206.132.253.50	pos3-1-0-155m.hr2.iad.gblx.net
17	0.209	0.216	0.229	209.143.250.14	herndon-r03.quote.com

This route shows all the waypoints in the path between my computer and the computer named herndon-r03.quote.com. If I dial-up tomorrow or an hour from now, the path may be different. If I trace the route to a different computer the route may be completely different.

The first column in the report shows the hop number. The machine listed in the first line of the report, or the first hop, is the computer to which your PC is directly connected—your on-ramp to the information superhighway. You can see that the destination computer, in this case, is seventeen hops away from my computer. Each hop consists of a machine called a router whose job it is to route packets towards their destination. Many of the routers serving the Internet are made by Cisco—one reason why its stock has been doing so consistently well. They are building the backbone of the Internet.

The next three columns show the time in seconds (sometimes this is displayed in milliseconds) it takes the ping packets to travel from your computer to that hop. Shown are the fastest, average, and maximum times taken in multiple samples. In this case, the average round-trip travel time between my computer and the destination is 0.229 seconds, or 229 milliseconds. That's not bad, and more importantly there are no points along the line where the travel time jumps up significantly from the previous hop. This is a good connection.

The next column shows the Internet protocol (IP) address of the machine at each hop. Every computer connected to the Internet has a unique address such as this. We humans don't do as well with numbers, so for every IP address there is usually (but not always) a machine name associated with this address. This name has to be looked up using the Domain Name Service (DNS), a look-up service for machine names and IP addresses.

The times on the first hop are important. This is the first link in the chain, and if it is clogged, it doesn't matter if the other ones are free and clear. Your communications will be as fast as the slowest chain allows. If the chain is dropping packets at the first connection, then your communications will be unreliable up and down the line, and may mask other problems down the line.

Packet loss will be indicated by an asterisk (*) in one of the times listed, such as you see on hop 11. That means that one of the pings sent to that hop went missing. This is a potential sign of trouble at that hop—perhaps the router at that hop is being asked to handle more traffic than it can handle. When this happens, packets are dropped, and communications through that router can slow down—much like a highway traffic jam.

If you spot a condition like this anywhere in the chain, you will see packet loss starting with that hop (and it may cause packet loss to appear at subsequent hops) as well as a significant increase in the ping times (increased latency) starting with that hop. You can generate more detailed statistics on the packet loss at that hop by using the "ping − t" command to ping that hop continuously for a longer period.

The packet loss or latency problem can be dealt with in a number of ways depending on where it is taking place along the chain of connections. If you see packet loss or high ping times to the first hop and you are using a dial-up connection, try disconnecting and dialing again—you may have hit a bad modem at your ISP or your telephone line may have developed noise. You can try dialing an alternative dial-up number at your ISP, or try a backup ISP (you do have a backup ISP, don't you?). If the condition persists after you reconnect, you might try restarting your computer—sometimes the internal networking gizmos on your PC can cause trouble.

If you are using a fast connection like ISDN, cable modem, or DSL you don't have much choice except to try reconnecting. If that doesn't help the problem, be prepared to use a dial-up connection to a modem-based ISP instead. Your connection won't be as blazingly fast, but it may save the day until your fast service gets its house in order.

If the packet loss occurs in one of the hops near your ISP, then you can try a different local number for your ISP or use your backup ISP to route around the problem. You can also try to report the problem to your ISP. They may be able to get the problem corrected, but often this is a vain exercise.

If the problem appears nearer to your destination computer you may have luck getting them to fix the problem. But the best solution is to try to connect to a different server at your quote vendor. Quote.com, for example, has servers in many different locations on the Internet, and you can change the server you are connected to by pressing the Ctrl-Alt-N keys simultaneously in the QCharts program. This may result in a connection to a server at a different location, which will avoid the snarled traffic.

In the Unix world "traceroute" is a standard command. In the Mac world, Stairways.com's Anarchie (shareware) and WhatRoute (free) are the best tools to perform traceroute—the Mac OS does not come with these tools built in.

Better Tools

Ping and traceroute are common, basic Internet tools for diagnosing your connections. Better tools exist. One of my favorites on the PC platform is called Ping Plotter, a $15 shareware program for Windows available at www.nessoft.com. Ping Plotter provides a visual display of the traceroute plot above, but where traceroute typically runs a scan once and then quits, Ping Plotter will continuously monitor the connection between you and the destination computer. It also does a much better job at tracking packet loss statistics for each hop. Instead of an asterisk, Ping Plotter will display the percentage of pings that were dropped.

Other advanced tools available for Windows users are NeoTrace and Visual Route, both of which are available at shareware downloading sites such as CNet's www.download.com and others.

The usefulness of this chapter will be short-lived as we are in a rapidly changing environment. As the technology for networking all the computers on the planet matures it will become faster, cheaper, and increasingly reliable. People will look back on these words and laugh at the idea that serious traders had to worry about such mundane tasks as tracing the path that data takes between computers. We look back with amusement at the early automobile enthusiasts for whom starting the car meant cleaning the spark plugs first or at the very least, required a trip to the front of the car to crank it by hand.

But the fact is that the information superhighway is not a paved concrete throughway—it's still a gravel road with plenty of potholes and not many signs. Until the day comes when Internet service reaches that level of reliability, these tools can be useful to maintain your connection to the source of information that allows you to make your living trading.

TEN STEPS TO SELECTING A TRADING FIRM

Day trading firms (direct-access firms, as they are more commonly called) have sprung up like weeds in the past two years—there are about sixty or so. Most of the newer ones are small and have only one or two offices with well under a hundred traders. Others are much larger and have hundreds of traders.

The focus of this chapter is provide the you, the potential "retail" day trader, with the critical information you need to obtain from any firm that you plan to do business with. Your "due diligence" will enable you to make an intelligent decision as to which firm best meets your needs. You wouldn't buy or lease a new car with doing your home-work—comparing car models, prices, leasing programs, crash data, re-pair records, and so on. The same approach should be used in selecting a trading firm.

Once you've made the commitment to becoming a day trader, your first key decision is to determine whether to trade at home (remote trading) or physically at a trading firm, if one is nearby. This is an important decision, since your trading results will be impacted to some extent by which environment you select. If you are not within commut-ing distance of a trading firm or you don't want to spend time fighting traffic, then you'll have to trade at your home or your office. Also, if you like to be on your own without distractions, then the home office environment is usually best.

But if you like the comradeship of being surrounded by other trad-ers and you have the opportunity of being monitored by a "live" mentor in real time, then a trading firm may be for you. Additionally, trading at a firm means that you won't have to buy any computer equipment or trading software, since it is all provided by the firm for a fee or free with a minimum number of trades per month.

This chapter covers the key criteria you should consider when selecting a trading firm. You should attempt to obtain as much of the information mentioned in this chapter as possible before making a final decision. However, be aware of the obstacles you may face—the trading firm may not want to provide you with all the information that you are requesting because of three main reasons. First, they may not have gathered the information and are not about to. Second, it may be confidential. Third, it may be too embarrassing for them to provide it to you. Nevertheless, be persistent and ask the right questions. Since no trading firm wants to pass up the opportunity to snag a "cash cow" (potential day trader), they may surprise you and provide more information than you thought they would.

Step 1: Surf Trading Firm Web Sites

The easiest and quickest way to get information on trading firms is to go to their Web sites to see what they have to offer and if they have a location nearby. Some firms have only a few locations, while others have many offices across the country and continue to add offices at a rapid pace. A list of some of the largest firms with their Web sites is provided in table 7-1. Keep in mind that most firms are looking for only "retail" day traders, while others are much more selective and are looking only for "professional" day traders with experience who trade the firm's capital, not theirs, and who share in the profits. Some firms cater to *both* retail and professional traders. The listing of representative firms shown in table 7-1 is based on their major emphasis as of July 2000.

Methodically work your way through the firm's Web site, clicking on all relevant sections to see what information is provided. Normally, you should expect to find the following items on each firm's site:

- *About us*—Description of the company and biographies of the principal officers.
- *Products*—Detailed description of the different products and their features.

TABLE 7-1. *Trading Firms (July 2000)*

Firm Name	Contact Information
Retail Trading Firm Focus	
All-Tech Direct	www.attain.com
Andover Trading	www.andovertrading.com
Broadway Trading	www.broadwaytrading.com
Carlin Financial Group	www.carlingroup.com
Castle Securities Corp.	www.castleonline.com
Datek Online	www.datek.com
Marketwise Securities	www.marketwise.com
Momentum Securities	www.soes.com
Navillus Securities	www.navillus.com
On-Line Investment Services	www.onli.com
On-Line Trading	www.onlinetrading.com
On-Site Trading, Inc.	www.onsitetrading.com
ProTrade	www.protrade.com
Remote Trading International	www.remotetraders.com
Self Trading	www.selftrading.com
Summit Trading	www.summittrading.com
Tradescape	www.tradescape.com
Van Buren Securities	www.vbsecurities.com
Yamner & Co.	www.yamner.com
Professional Trading Firms	
All Star Equities	not found
Bright Trading	www.stocktrading.com
Lieber & Weissman Securities	(800) 261-9557
Mt. Pleasant Brokerage Services	(803) 884-9191 no website
VBSecurities	(888) 781-9400

- *Software*—Detailed description of the trading software offered and its features.
- *Demo screens*—Sample software screens that are available using their software.
- *Remote site details*—Hardware, with software requirements delineated.
- *Training programs*—Description and pricing of their training program, if offered; testimonials may be provided as well.
- *Commission schedule*—What the firm charges for its listed and Nasdaq trades, extra fees for using specific ECNs, and whether volume discounts apply.

- *Miscellaneous fees*—Other fees charged by the firm in addition to commissions for using their equipment and software, wire transfers, and so on.
- *Account opening forms*—These forms can typically be downloaded, signed, and forwarded to the firm with a check or a wire transfer.
- *Account minimums*—Indicates the minimum amount of starting capital (usually $25,000 but can range from $10,000 to $75,000), annual income, and net worth.
- *Links*—Web connections to vendor partners (e.g., ISPs and real-time data and charts) and other trading-related sites.
- *FAQs*—Frequently asked questions and answers, including list of offices and new offices planned.
- *Contact*—How to contact the firm via phone and e-mail for further information.
- *News and press releases*—A few firms provide recent news stories and press releases about their product and services or acquisitions of other firms.
- *News and quotes*—Delayed stock quotes and late breaking news in varying degrees of detail.

As you view each firm's site you'll notice distinctive differences among them. Compare each site's overall quality, the speed of obtaining the information, the ease of navigation, and the depth of the content. Your overall assessment of the site will provide a first impression of the firm—good or bad.

Step 2: Obtain Complete Information from Specific Firms

Start compiling information on the trading firms that appear to meet your needs. There may be only one or two firms with offices in your city or none at all. Eliminate all other firms from consideration if you are planning to day trade in the office of a firm. (Those traders that live in the New York metropolitan area and a few other major cities in Connecticut, Florida, California, Georgia, and Illinois may have the luxury of having up to three or more companies to choose from because of the population density.)

Call all nearby firms to obtain any additional information that is not provided on their Web sites. Ask for brochures, more detailed price lists, account opening forms (all forms and agreements may not be provided on the Web site), and newspaper and magazine articles (that mention the firm or profile successful traders). You may have to specifically ask for news articles if they are not mentioned or provided on the Web site. Make sure you have the firm's full name, address, phone numbers (regular and 800 number), Web site, e-mail address, main office location, and addresses and phone numbers of the office(s) in your area.

Don't forget about using the Internet to obtain additional news articles related to "day trading" and "direct-access" trading by going to www.cnnfn.com, or http://finance.yahoo.com, or www.askjeeves.com, where you can type in a question such as "Where can I find information on day trading?" In many news-related stories, day-trading firms and their traders' success stories are highlighted. On the darker side, do not forget to go to the regulatory sites to determine if a company is involved in any legal entanglements or has been cited as not living up to specific regulations. Visit the SEC (www.sec.gov), North American Securities Administrators Association, Inc. (www.nasaa.org), the National Association of Securities Dealers (NASD) (www.nasd.org), and the General Accounting Office (www.gao.gov).

Suitability Requirements

One way to tell if a trading firm is looking out for your best interests or theirs is to find out how they determine if a potential client is suitable for day trading. Some firms take this responsibility very seriously and do more than a cursory review of your application information—trading experience, investment experience, risk capital, and trading objectives. Other firms take your money without regard to your background or training. Therefore, if the information about suitability is not mentioned on their Web site, forms, or literature, then directly ask, "What are your requirements for accepting day trading clients?" The more stringent their requirements the better.

If the firm does not have suitability requirements, then ask them why not? Ask the firm what are its minimum criteria for allowing a person to open an onsite or remote day-trading account. They should be evaluating the following factors:

- Net worth.
- Annual income.
- Number of years of investing experience.
- Knowledge of the securities markets.
- Familiarity with basic order types (limit versus market order).
- Risk capital available (to lose without causing a problem).
- Requiring a passing grade on the firm's day-trading pretest (if they have one).
- Taking and passing a training course given by the firm.
- Other criteria.

Two important and revealing questions to ask are: How many potential clients has your firm rejected as unsuitable for day trading in the past twelve months? What percent of all new clients is this?

Performance of Firm's Day Traders

Query each firm on the following statistics to obtain a feel for the overall success of the traders using the firm:

1. Number of remote traders and onsite traders in all their offices.
2. Number of trades made per year by remote traders and onsite traders.
3. Percentage of the remote traders that made a profit in past twelve months.
4. Percentage of the onsite traders that made a profit in twelve months.
5. The average (median) profit in dollars of remote traders who made a profit in twelve months.
6. The average (median) loss in dollars of remote traders who lost money in twelve months.
7. The average (median) profit in dollars of onsite traders who made a profit in twelve months.
8. The average (median) loss in dollars of onsite traders who lost money in twelve months.

9. The number of onsite traders that closed their accounts in twelve months.
10. The number of remote traders that closed their accounts in twelve months.
11. The percent of day traders (for past twelve months) *trading at their offices* that have been with the firm for the following length of time:
    [%] Less than one month
    [%] Two to three months
    [%] Four to five months
    [%] Six to nine months
    [%] Ten to twelve months
    [%] Less than two years
    [%] Less than three years
    [%] Three years or more
12. The percent of all day traders (for the past twelve months) *trading remotely using the firm's system* that have been with the firm for the following length of time:
    [%] Less than one month
    [%] Two to three months
    [%] Four to five months
    [%] Six to nine months
    [%] Ten to twelve months
    [%] Less than two years
    [%] Less than three years
    [%] Three years or more

Most firms will probably not have this data, and if they do they may not want to release it for competitive and regulatory reasons—it may prove that day trading is not as profitable as it is made out to be in the firms' marketing materials. A few firms may have this data and may provide you with some statistics that are not embarrassing to them.

I tried to obtain this data, as well as other detailed information, from many of the larger day-trading firms as part of a questionnaire that I developed for publication in this book. Unfortunately, not one of the firms provided me with any of the information that I requested. Therefore, I urge you, as a potential customer of a trading firm, to request this information. Hopefully, over time, the more potential clients (e.g., new traders) that ask for the data, the higher the probability is that the firms will provide it in the future. Moreover, if regulatory authorities were able to require the firms to gather and publish this information, that would be a very positive step.

Remote vs. Onsite Trading Experience

Ask the firm, based on their experience, what are the advantages and disadvantages of trading in their office versus trading remotely. Moreover, ask the firm whether they believe that day trading at their office is superior to day trading remotely for the novice (if you are a beginner) day trader and the experienced day trader. See if their answer makes sense to you. Ask them to back up their answer with facts and figures, and possibly references from both camps. Perhaps the firm favors trading on their premises because they've found that more trades are made. This, of course, is not in your best interest as a potential customer.

Account Opening Kit

Find out whether or not you can open an account directly on the firm's Web site rather than printing the forms and sending them in. A few firms may be able to do this online by the time you read this book, since a bill has been passed by Congress approving electronic signatures, which gives this electronic signature similar legal status to a penned signature.

In any case, you would have to complete the following forms to open an account depending upon your unique trading requirements:

1. *Account administrative form*—Basic background information, annual income, total net worth, bank reference, investment objectives, investment experience.
2. *Nasdaq and NYSE agreements*—Each exchange has its own rules and regulations that are standard.
3. *W-9 form*—You provide your Social Security number, name, and address and sign the document that indicates the information is truthful.
4. *Margin agreement and shorting agreement*—These indicate the margin rules and shorting rules.
5. *Risk disclosure*—Typically similar wording to NASD risk disclosure (see chapter 14, "Regulatory Findings on the Day-Trading Industry").

Be aware that items 2 and 4 can be long contracts in tiny print that are written in legalese and technical jargon. *Make sure that you understand what you are signing.* If you're not sure what it all means, then have someone who is familiar with the forms explain them to you. One approach is to e-mail your questions to the firm and ask for a clarification via e-mail. Another approach is to ask a professional investment advisor or financial planner or other knowledgeable person not affiliated with the firm to explain them to you.

Possibly, the SEC, NASD, or attorney general of your state could direct you to knowledgeable and objective sources. Unfortunately, these forms are not written in "plain" English. This is the fault of the industry and regulatory authorities. Hopefully, there will be sufficient pressure from you and other traders to force regulators and exchanges to simplify them. Many mutual fund families have simplified their prospectuses due to the regulatory and public outcry.

The risk disclosure document is clearly written and easy to understand. Read it very carefully. If you do not believe the contents of the disclosure statement or you think that it is not important, then you've made a tremendous error in judgment. The odds are that you will fail as a day trader if you don't take all the necessary steps to minimize the risks involved.

Capital Requirements

Each firm has a minimum starting capital requirement for opening an account. Most firms require $25,000, a few want only $10,000 to $15,000. But some want $50,000 or more. The more capital in your account, the more stock you can buy or sell short. You must meet the firm's minimum requirement to start trading. The best way to fund the account if you want to start trading quickly is to wire in the funds from another brokerage, mutual fund, or bank account. If you fund the account by check, most firms will require a five- to ten-day "hold" for check clearing purposes. Make sure you understand at the outset that *under no circumstances should you be day trading with money you can't afford to completely lose—known as "scared" money.* This money should not be earmarked for paying bills, saving for a house, paying for a college education, or saving for retirement. And certainly don't add more capital to the account if you lose your initial stake—that could lead to a total financial disaster.

Margin Requirements

Since most day traders use margin to the maximum each trading day, you should be very familiar with how margin works. If you're not, then you may be shocked one day to find out that you have been charged a fee for carrying your positions overnight or have been wiped out beyond your initial capital if your stocks tank the next day.

Margin rates are established by the Board of Governors of the Federal Reserve System, as set forth in Regulation T. Margin refers to the amount of money borrowed from a brokerage firm to purchase securities. Initial margin requirements were first set in 1945 and have ranged between 50 percent to 100 percent over the years.

Currently, the initial margin requirement is 50 percent. This means that when you buy and hold a stock overnight, you must put up 50 percent of the cost of the purchase. This 50 percent can be funded by selling a stock that same day, with borrowing power you already have in the account, or by sending in a check. If you day trade and you use margin during the day, but close all your positions by the end of the day, then you do not have to put up any new money unless your stocks have gone down so much that your equity is below 25 percent of the value of your stocks.

The New York Stock Exchange and the National Association of Securities Dealers have a requirement that the equity in an account may not be less than 25 percent of the value of the securies. Once the equity in the account drops below that 25 percent, a brokerage firm will demand that the equity in the account be raised to anywhere from 30 percent to 40 percent. This is done with a margin call, demanding that a certain amount of money be added to the account through cash or additional marginable securities. The amount of equity demanded by the brokerage house is governed by their own in-house rules. The only way to know this figure is to ask the brokerage house.

If for any reason the customer cannot add the cash or marginable securities demanded by the margin call, the firm will liquidate (sell) sufficient securities to cover the shortfall and bring the equity up to the 30 percent to 40 percent. If the proceeds are insufficient, then the person must come up with additional funds.

Here is an example of margin calculations. If you deposit $25,000 in your day-trading account on day one, then the firm can loan you another $25,000 to buy securities. If you buy and hold 1,000 shares of stock at $50, you have used all your available funds for that transaction on that day. The firm will charge you margin interest on the $25,000 you have borrowed.

Assume that on the next day the stock drops to $30 on a bad earnings report and closes at $30. The margin loan is still $25,000 but the account equity has fallen to $5,000 ($30,000 market value minus $25,000 margin loan). Since the minimum maintenance margin is 25 percent, the account equity cannot fall below $7,500 (.25 × $30,000). Therefore, assuming that the brokerage house requires you to bring the equity up to 35 percent, not unusual, a maintenance margin call goes out to the customer for $5,500 to bring the account equity to $10,500, which is 35 percent of the $30,000 value of the securities. If the customer does not bring in immediate cash or marginable securities, then the firm would sell enough securities so that the $5,000 would represent 35 percent of the value of the remaining securities: $5,000 is 35 percent of $14,285! So the brokerage firm would sell $15,715 in stock. And if they do not hear from you on time, they have the right to sell whatever they want to.

Margin is one of the Fed's tools to minimize speculation in the securities markets. In 2000, margin requirements were discussed frequently at the Fed's Open Market Committee meetings because of Fed Chairman Alan Greenspan's belief that equity prices, in general, were in the stratosphere and that margin debt was at an all-time high in the Spring of 2000. The more money investors can borrow from the brokerage house, the more speculative their position. If margin requirements were increased, investors would be in a less precarious position if their stocks tanked.

The current initial margin requirement is 50 percent and has been at that level for many years. The margin interest is benchmarked to the broker call loan rate, which is currently 8.25 percent (July 2000). This is the rate charged to brokers and dealers by banks for securities lending. Day-trading firms vary widely in the interest rate that they actually charge for their margin loans. Some firms add an extra one percent point or more to the broker loan rate. You should ask each firm about their margin interest rate and whether it is variable depending upon the dollar amount of their loan to you. Many firms charge a lower rate for a larger loan amount. Remember that if you never carry over a position to the next day, then you don't have to be concerned about this entire discussion of margin. (At the end of every day you know how much money you made or lost. Every purchase has been sold.)

But, if you are ever going to carry a position overnight and owe the brokerage house money, you should be thoroughly familiar with the all of the above. You must understand the entire process: the interest charges, the potential for margin calls, the need to come up with cash or marginable securities, and in the worst case the potential losses as a result of a liquidation to meet the margin call.

Some day-trading firms, especially the professional firms, allow you to borrow huge amounts during the trading day. Needless to say, by the end of the day, your account has to meet the 25 percent maintenance. With just $25,000 of your own money, you can buy as much as $250,000 worth of stock. While this creates the opportunity to make a killing if you are right, it also creates the risk of losing the entire $25,000. For instance, you could buy 2,000 shares of a stock at $125 per share. If it goes up 10 points you will be ahead $20,000. If it goes down 10 points, your $25,000 has been cut to $5,000.

The beginning trader should never use more than 50 percent margin.

You should know just what the firm's policy is regarding lending money to their customers. Get all the details, especially if they charge for intraday loans. Find out what their interest charges are for overnight loans. Get the figures in percentages and dollars for specific amounts.

The most important thing is for you to have a thorough and complete understanding of the firm's margin requirements.

Money Market Account

Ask the trading firm what interest rate they are paying on their money market account. Why is this important? As a day trader your money should be in cash each night. Therefore, you want to receive a competitive interest rate. Some firms pay a percentage point or more *below* the best rates available. For example, one firm could be paying 6.12 percent (average seven-day yield) on its money market account, while another firm could be paying 4.75 percent or even 3.5 percent. Obviously, the more capital in your account, the more interest income you are losing. Thus, check with the firm and consider the impact of a low interest rate on your overall income for the year. You can get the current average money market rates at many financial Web sites, as well as specific money market rates in the *The Wall Street Journal* once a week, and in other daily publications.

Account Monitoring

Potential and new traders should find out whether the trading firm monitors the accounts of traders (onsite and remote) real-time to keep the trader out of a self-destructive mode. Monitoring means that the firm is tracking each account's cash position, buying power and margin positions trade-by-trade tick-by-tick throughout the day.

It is critically important, especially for a beginning trader, to be alerted to a potentially precarious financial situation (e.g., negative account balance, negative buying power, margined out, and so on) as it is occurring. Determine whether your terminal or software will notify you of the situation with a message or alert or whether a supervisor will discuss the situation with you in a discrete manner if you are trading onsite. Ask whether the firm has the right to stop you from trading your account under any circumstances.

At the minimum the trading firm should be reviewing all accounts at the end of the day for their financial status, compliance to margin requirements, and for any unusual or problematic situations. New traders should be monitored very closely, especially in the beginning, so that they don't self-destruct. Any firm that you contact that doesn't provide tight supervision of your account—to protect you from yourself—should be eliminated from consideration, in my view.

Step 3: Review Services Offered

Carefully review each trading firm's services and product offerings. This information is usually available on the Web site. Contact the firms to obtain any brochures with accompanying inserts describing their offerings in more detail. If this information is not detailed enough, then e-mail or phone the firm for clarification. Highlight the critical information in the brochures and print out key information from their Web site for further analysis.

Services

Most firms fully describe their services on their Web site and certainly in their brochures. The major service offered is, of course, "direct-access" trading. A firm's client focus usually follows one of three models:

- Model 1: Providing the service only to "retail" traders.
- Model 2: Providing the service to "retail" and "professional" traders. These traders work for the trading firm with the firm's capital. Some firms also provide the service to "institutional" traders who work for other financial organizations.
- Model 3: Provide the service to only "professional" (licensed and regulated) traders.

Additionally, most "retail" trading firms offer not only onsite trading capabilities but also remote trading. So, if you begin trading onsite at the firm and later decide it is not for you, then you can easily switch to trading from home using the same software. This means that you won't have a new software learning curve.

In addition, most firms offer a training program for the beginning trader, and some offer multiple training programs and "boot camps" for traders needing additional training or more advanced training. The key questions to ask about the training programs are provided later in this chapter. And a more detailed discussion of training programs in general is provided in chapter 3, "Basic Training."

Hardware

One of the major benefits of trading at a firm is that you do not have to buy any computer hardware. The firm provides the computer set-up, sometimes two to four side-by-side 17-inch or 19-inch screens. The software has been installed and tested and is ready to go. The computer is directly hooked up to a high-speed telecommunications network that provides streaming price quotes, real-time tick-by-tick intraday charts, Nasdaq Level II, time and sales data, and news. Moreover, market orders on active stocks are executed in less than 5 seconds.

Make sure that the brokerage firm has redundant systems that back up their main system in case of intermittent failure, a systems failure, or power outages. Having an open position in these circumstances can prove costly if you are unable to make a move. Also, the firm will usually not reimburse you for any losses during these occasions. Make sure you read your agreements regarding these matters. Ask the firm to provide information on their down-time over the past six month time frame. Also, ask the references or other traders at the firm about any outage experiences.

Trading Software

Real-time Quotes, Chart, and News

All trading firms provide the features of their trading software, including sample screens and reports. Be aware that each firm offers specific software, which you'll have to master to maximize its use. Some software is very complex and not easy to set up initially.

Some firms have simulated trading screens. Real Tick III (Townsend Analytics, Inc. is the vendor) is a very popular software package used by a number of trading firms. And there are many competitive products that capture real-time data. This includes dynamic streaming quotes, customized tickers, extensive intraday and historical charting (tick-by-tick, minute by minute, bar charts, Candlestick charts, and Point & Figure charts), price and volume alerts, technical indicator studies, Nasdaq Level II (lists all the market offerings on the bid-and-ask sides), and time and sales report (listing of all sales executed with the time, price, and number of shares, as well as bid and ask data). Also, most firms' software offers customized desktops. Make sure to ask the firm whether they use an internally developed software package or another vendor's package. If the latter, ask for its name and obtain a brochure that describes all its features.

Additionally, the software provides the ability to pull up the most active stocks by exchange, the new highs and lows for the day and for the year, the stocks most up and most down, the percentage most up and down, and the indices, futures, and options. And much more real-time information is available to traders for their review at any time of the day.

All firms offer multiple news services from such vendors as Dow-Jones Business News, BridgeNews, Reuters, and Bloomberg. Moreover, other sources of information may be provided, such as JAG Notes, First Call earnings estimates, Zacks Research System estimates, COMTEX Business News, and Wall Street Wire.

Portfolio Tracking

Each firm's software provides the ability to track and display your positions in real time. Some software is much better than others. Typical information provided includes:

1. Current value of securities in account.
2. Current amount of margined securities.
3. Total profit and loss year-to-date.
4. Total profit and loss for the day.
5. Total profit and loss for each position year-to-date.
6. Total profit and loss for each position for the day.
7. Buying power (how much cash and margin is available to buy or sell short at a moment in time).
8. Listing of positions open with number of shares, price paid, total value, profit or loss up to the second.
9. Confirmation screen showing all trades for the day with time, shares, and price.
10. Open orders.

Step 4: Order Handling, Fees, and Commissions

Order Execution

The order execution screen should be a seamless mouse-click away so that you can rapidly enter the ticker symbol, number of shares, limit price (if any), and other critical data. Many systems have the ability to preset these parameters ahead of time. You just click the mouse to execute the trade if everything is in order or make a quick change as necessary. With direct-access execution, market orders in active stocks are "filled" within seconds (two to twenty seconds or less).

Access to all equity markets should be provided, including NYSE, Nasdaq/AMEX, ECNs (e.g., Island, ATTN, Archipelago, REDI, SOES, Instinet, Selectnet), and other market makers. A few firms offer "intelligent" or "automatic" order routing to obtain the best available price from all market makers or exchanges in its system. This is an important feature that should be carefully reviewed for its advantages. Ask each trading firm if they offer this feature and how it works. For firms that are not currently offering it, ask if they are planning to offer it within the next six months.

Also determine the firm's after-hours trading capability, trading liquidity, and how the firm handles those orders. After-hours trading is not something that should be high on a new trader's list of features because of the lack of liquidity in many issues and the higher spread between the bid and the ask prices. Eventually, this situation will be ameliorated.

Payment for Order Flow

One subject that you should be familiar with is payment for order flow. Traditional brokerage firms and many online brokers usually route your buy and sell orders to favored market makers, who rebate a few cents per share back to the firm to compensate them for the order. This rebate can be considered an additional cost to you. You should ask any firm that you are going to do business with either on site or remotely if they receive payment for order. If they do, ask them how much they receive and whether or not it affects the "best" execution you can get. Most of the trading firms that offer direct access do not receive any payment for order flow. Therefore, it is a moot point in these cases.

Monthly Service Fees

All firms charge a monthly fee for onsite trading that covers the equipment, software, and real-time data feeds. Usually firms offer various service plans, with the more sophisticated services costing more. A range of $100 to $400 per month is typical in the industry. Most firms rebate all or a portion of the fee if a minimum number of trades monthly is executed. Review the firm's pricing packages to see which one is best suited for your needs. Remember that you can change plans at any time, especially if you trade at a higher threshold level.

Miscellaneous Fees

Some firms charge miscellaneous fees for such services as:

- Outgoing wire transfers.
- Handling fees on transaction confirmations.
- Returned checks.
- Mailing confirmations to your home.

Ask each firm for a complete fee schedule. You don't want to be surprised to find a $1.00 or $2.00 added to each transaction for "handling," which eats into your profits. Fortunately, most firms do not play these add-on games.

Commission Structure

Each firm has a published commission structure for the Nasdaq/AMEX and NYSE. In most cases, the commissions are different for the two exchanges. Most firms post their commissions on their Web site. The majority of commissions range between $12.95 to $20.95 per trade, depending on the number of shares bought or sold and the volume of transactions. A number of firms have tiered pricing—the more trades made, the higher the chance of reaching a higher threshold and a less expensive price. For example, one firm may charge $20.95 (for up to 1,000 shares) for a Nasdaq stock for 200 trades a month, but the firm drops its commission to $18.95 for over 200 trades. Some of the deep discount brokers charge $5 to $10 a trade, but keep in mind that these are strictly brokers and may not offer direct-access trading.

Also, the firm may charge a higher price for limit orders than market orders. This charge ranges between $1 to $3 per order. Most firms charge an additional fee for routing the order to a specific electronic communications network (ECN), but some firms may offer their own routing or a particular ECN at no additional charge. This fee ranges between $0.005 to $0.015 per share for Nasdaq issues.

Be aware of not just commissions but the opportunity cost—the hidden charges that jack up the cost of doing business. If you do not use direct access, then you may be paying a higher price for your execution. Direct access provides lightning fast trade execution at competitive prices.

Step 5. Psychological Counseling

As you'll see later, all of the experienced traders that we interviewed (chapter 12, "Interviews with Traders") consider the mental or psychological aspects of trading to be 90 percent or more of the formula for trading success. Once you read chapter 8, "Trading to Make Money," and chapter 9, "Your Mind's Money Machine," you'll gain a clear vision of how your psychological makeup impacts your trading. Since the vast majority of new traders have a rough time making profitable trades, especially in the first few months of their trading careers, onsite psychological counseling at no cost is definitely a service that should be on your list of "must haves."

Find out what a trading firm offers in the area of psychological counseling by obtaining answers to the following questions:

1. Do you provide psychological counseling?
2. Are all traders eligible to obtain the counseling from day one? Is counseling offered to onsite *and* remote day traders? (If you eventually decide to trade at home instead of onsite, perhaps these sessions will no longer be provided to you, even if you could go to the firm's offices to obtain the help.)
3. Who pays for these sessions?
4. How often can sessions be attended?
5. Do you have a resident psychologist on staff in your main office and in the office you want to trade in?
6. If you don't have a resident psychologist, does one come to your office regularly?
7. Are one-on-one sessions available? If yes, who pays for these sessions?
8. Does your firm offer group psychological counseling sessions? If yes, how often, and what is the typical agenda?

Step 6. Day-Trading Training Program

Almost all the trading firms offer training programs for new day traders, offer courses through affiliate companies, or are developing courses to meet the need. The curriculum content, length, cost, and methodology of presenting the training varies widely. Obtain any brochures, course outlines, and other written material and Web site information. In addition to the course offerings of day-trading firms, there are many other training courses. Information about these courses is provided in chapter 3, "Basic Training."

You should obtain complete information on each firm's training programs. Some of the key questions to ask are:

1. Does your firm offer prospective day traders any type of training program?
2. Does your firm require that a prospective day trader take your training program?
3. Is the person required to pass the course before being allowed to trade at your firm? If not, why not? If yes, can the person

retake the course as many times as necessary without being charged an additional fee?

4. After new traders complete the training course, is a supervisor assigned to work with them in their first few weeks to watch over their shoulder or mentor them during live trading hours? Please explain.

5. Is the training program cost 100 percent recoverable from future commission dollars, if the trader trades onsite or remotely at your firm?

6. Does your firm offer a 100 percent refund, if the trader feels that the course did not meet the advertised goals? Explain your policy.

The other important questions to ask are included in chapter 3, "Basic Training." Make sure you include those questions in your evaluation process of each firm's capabilities.

Step 7. Visit the Trading Firms' Offices

Once you've reviewed all the information that you've gathered from the trading firms near your home, the next step is to visit them. Call the firms to schedule a tour of their facilities. Make sure to schedule the visit during market hours so you can get a feel for the office environment and clientele. You can probably set up a few tours for one day of about one to one-and-a-half hours each. If the firms are near each other, you may be able to tour three firms in one day—at 10:00 A.M., 1:00 P.M., and 3:00 P.M., for example.

Here is a checklist of what to look for on your tour:

■ The overall ambience of the trading room—be aware of the proximity of the traders to each other, the noise level, the lighting (dark or bright), the floor layout, different rooms for different types of traders (e.g., scalpers, trend followers, swing traders, and professional traders), camaraderie of traders, the overall cleanliness, smoke-free environment or not, air-conditioning level or heating level, depending upon the season—a too hot or too cold room could impact your critical decision making.

■ The caliber and sophistication of the PCs used, including the

RAM and hard drive size, number of screens provided, their size (at least 17 inches) and resolution of the screens, screen glare, and so on.

■ The comfort of the chair—since you'll be sitting in one all day you want a chair with lumbar support that has adjustments. Sit in the chairs provided, try to adjust them, and ask the traders how comfortable they are by the end of the day.

■ Spend time at a terminal and have the guide provide a five to ten minute demo of the software's capabilities.

■ The speed at which traders get their market orders executed (should be seconds).

■ The demographics of the traders—age, sex, dress code.

■ The friendliness, knowledge, and honesty of the tour guide—perhaps an indication of the management style and professionalism of the firm.

■ Who at the firm you are introduced to. For example, are you ushered into the CEO's office (or other senior officer) who asks you a few questions or are you handed off to marketing and sales people, who try to convert you into a client?

■ Availability of refreshments, restrooms, and lounges.

■ Ask to speak with a few of the traders after the close of business, if they are willing to spend time with you. Ask them their opinion of the firm—good points and bad points.

Based upon this tour and your detailed information gathering process you should have a clear idea as to whether you want to trade at home or at a firm. Your decision does not have to be final. You can always decide to go either way. If you don't like the environment you've selected or the trading results you are getting, you can make a change at any time.

Step 8. Reference Checking

One aspect of selecting a day-trading firm that you may overlook in your analysis of a firm's capability is the critical step of reference checking. This misstep could be devastating. Why? Picking the wrong firm could set you back not only financially but also experience wise.

All day-trading firms are looking to grow their revenues. Their main earnings engine is trading commissions. The more day traders that use their firm and remain there, the more profit they make. Of course, the firm also gets revenues from monthly fees and training programs. But for many firms, the commission dollars are the bulk of their revenues. According to newspaper reports of the day-trading firms (the vast majority are privately held firms), they generate substantial profits.

Therefore, one of the best ways to confirm a firm's advertising claims and information (that it has provided in hard copy and on its Web site) is to speak with current clients. Contact the firms that you are interested in and request twenty references—a mix of customers trading less than six months, customers trading at the firm over one year, and customers who decided to take their business elsewhere or just quit or got wiped out. Ask for names, phone numbers, and e-mail addresses of these customers. An upfront firm will provide you with references in all three categories. (You may not be given the names of the last category of customer—but those individuals would probably be the most enlightening.)

Ask each of the references detailed questions such as the following:

1. What were the main reasons you decided to trade at the firm?
2. What other firms did you review?
3. What was your second and third choice of firms?
4. Did the firm's advertised service capabilities actually work in practice?
5. How truthful was the firm in spelling out the "risks" of day trading?
6. How upfront was the firm in detailing all commissions and fees?
7. How long have you been trading on site at the firm?
8. Did you take the firm's training course? If no, why not? If yes, why?
9. If you did take the course, how would you rate it from the standpoints of overall quality, instructor quality, real-life situations, usefulness, cost, and any other criteria you'd like to mention?
10. Would you highly recommend their course to beginning traders?
11. Did most of the individuals taking the course with you have a positive experience?

12. How valuable was the course in preparing you to day trade?
13. How would you rate the firm in the following areas on a scale of 1 to 5, with 1 being the highest rating:
    Execution time of market orders.
    Execution time of limit orders.
    Quality of trading software.
    Quality of charts, technical indicators.
    Ease of making a trade.
    Completeness and usefulness of portfolio management tracking.
    Currentness of account information, intraday, including buying power, margin, and so on.
    Accuracy of trade confirmations.
    Percent of time system was down and trades were not processed in the past twelve months.
    Ability to electronically monitor your account and point out poor trading decisions.
14. How good is the trading software, and what software does the firm use?
15. How long did it take you to master the software?
16. What are the most important factors that distinguish this firm from others that you are aware of?
17. How comfortable to use is your workstation, including your chair?
18. Do you or other traders usually experience eyestrain or headaches at the end of the trading day?
19. What are the best things about this firm?
20. What are the worst things about this firm?
21. Do you have any other comments about the firm that could impact my decision to trade at the firm?
22. Can you provide me with the names of any other traders who currently trade with this firm or who have left the firm because they were dissatisfied?
23. Do you plan to close your account and go to another firm in the next six months? If yes, why?
24. Of the traders that you knew who closed their accounts, what were their reasons?

If you get a mixed response from the references of a particular firm, then ask the firm for additional references. If a firm has hundreds of traders, for example, they should be able to easily give you fifty references or more. Firms that have operating problems or difficulty keeping clients will hem and haw and not give you references. This in itself is an indication that there is a problem. Steer clear of any firm that does not provide as many references as you request in a timely manner.

Other Sources of Information

As a potential trader or as a beginning trader you should attend a trading expo, visit vendor booths, and strike up conversations with other traders about their experience with different firms. For example, the International Online Trading Expo was held on February 18–20, 2000, in New York City. There were over 5,000 traders and potential traders in attendance who jammed the exhibit hall packed with more than a hundred exhibitors. The attendees had two days of tutorial sessions from expert traders and trainers. The latest national expo from this firm was in Ontario, California, on August 18–20, 2000, where thousands of traders and traders-to-be attended. For more details on this expo, refer to chapter 3, "Basic Training."

OmegaWorld 2000, sponsored by Omega Research, was held in New York City on June 8 to 11, 2000. Attending were system traders and newbies who were looking for the latest trading strategies and systems to use on their Omega TradeStation and Option Station software. There were over sixty speakers, top trading and investment experts including six keynote speakers who talked about the different aspects and strategies of trading. The exhibit hall was packed with products and services for traders. And of course there was a full day of preconference workshops. For more information on this event, refer to chapter 3, "Basic Training."

Internet

Gomez.com tracks full-service and online brokers in a number of different categories, as well as provides the hyperactive investor with specific firm rankings. The categories measured include: overall score; ease of use; customer confidence; onsite resources; relationship services; and overall cost.

Unfortunately, this site doesn't specifically rank day-trading firms.

However, one site that provides a wealth of objective information on day trading firms, trading software and other useful information is www.sonic.net/donaldj. Make sure you check this site out. It is updated as new information is received.

Step 9. Take a Training Seminar

Before opening an account at a firm, your first step should be to take one or more training courses or seminars to provide you with detailed knowledge about the in and outs of the markets, technical tools, psychology, money management, risk, and other critical factors. These courses are offered by most trading firms as well as by many vendors. Since you have read chapter 3, "Basic Training," you know what you have to do.

Step 10. Open an Account at a Trading Firm

Your last step, after completing your education program (which may include multiple courses and months of preparation) is to complete the trading firm's paper work—account forms, exchange documents, margin agreements, and so on—and send the firm a check or wire transfer to open an account. Once all the paperwork is completed, which could take a week or two, you are ready to begin trading on site. But before you make one trade, you'd better have a solid education, as detailed in chapters 3 and 4, a game plan in writing, and a trading strategy that you have confidence in and that you have tested either with paper or simulated trading. And make sure that you are psychologically prepared, that you understand the critical importance of money management, and that you are aware of the "trader" status for filing your taxes. Onward to Part Three, which covers these three critical issues.

PERSPECTIVES— TRADING PSYCHOLOGY, MONEY MANAGEMENT, AND TAXES

CHAPTER 8

TRADING TO MAKE MONEY

John Piper

There are no good or bad ideas about markets; there are only useful ideas. This chapter focuses on what is useful, how to make money as a trader. Since I'm a full-time trader of futures and options, making money is my business, and I stand or fall on my results.

Keep in mind this key point: The whole money-making process takes place within our own heads. If you think about it, no two people who trade for their own account at a trading firm take the same trades. The reason for this is very simple. Each of us perceives the market differently. One trader may look at the market in terms of price spikes, others look at it in terms of moving averages, others in terms of fundamentals, and others in terms of first hour breakouts.

What this means is that we each perceive the market differently, based on our experiences in the market and our methodology. But we are all looking at the same thing, the market, in all of its many manifestations. When we trade, we trade our perceptions of the market. The whole game is inside our heads. That is where we win or lose. So the first useful idea is "to get our heads straight." There is no alternative. Until we learn to deal with those unruly instincts, emotions, and thoughts, we are not going to make money consistently. Consistency is the name of this game.

We all have different personalities, and that is why we all have dif-

---

Copyright © 2001 John Piper. All rights reserved.

ferent trading personalities. There is no right or wrong way to do it, but there are definitely some ways that will suit each of us and some that will not. So how do we make money in the markets? What do we do?

That is the wrong question. It is not about *doing*, it is about *being*. To trade successfully, you have to become a successful trader. Indeed, success is the exact opposite of doing. I find that the less I do, the more I make. This may sound flippant, but it is precisely true, and it makes a point that is essential to success.

The Triune Brain

Apparently, the brain can be divided into three layers. The inner part of the brain deals with instincts and biological drives. The second part derives from our basic mammalian heritage and involves emotional activity. The outer part makes us specifically "human." It involves fundamental reflective thought processes and imagination.

The human brain has evolved over millions of years, and the instinctive part is by far the oldest, emotions came next, and the thoughtful part is relatively recent. In real terms what this means is that our instincts are very much hard wired. It is not a question of thinking but direct action. Think about this in trading terms. Whatever we may think about markets is not going to be relevant; if an instinct cuts in, we will act before thought starts to come into it.

The Three "Yous"

Emotions are problematic, because we can mistake them for thought; and thought is hardly ideal in many ways. But the point is crucial. You are invariably your own worst enemy, but it is not just one "you" that you need to worry about, it is three "yous"—the instinctive you, the emotional you, and the thoughtful you. Generally speaking, each part is programmed to do the wrong thing at the wrong time.

To give a few simple examples: When markets plunge we may instinctively want to sell. But the successful trader wants to buy when the price is low, while the instinctive trader may find he or she simply cannot do it. Emotionally, we all like to take a profit, but the successful trader must let the profits run.

Emotionally, no one likes to take losses, but the successful trader must take losses quickly. Most traders lose because they have not got on top of their own instincts and emotions.

Many of you use system trading and have experienced the problem of not taking system signals and of taking trades that are not part of the system. This has a lot to do with errant instincts and emotions. Another factor involved in these problems is conflicts within yourself. For example, one trader came across an excellent system—80 percent success rate with two-minute bar charts and very small drawdowns, but hundreds of points of profit each month. Unfortunately, he couldn't trade it.

This trader had a strong belief that "mechanical systems do not work." It is therefore hardly surprising that he could not trade the system. He also had many fixed ideas about market action and what sort of action would follow in certain situations. The system kept giving signals that contradicted his beliefs. Before you can make money, you have to deal with these sorts of issues.

But first you need to know about them. I traded in the early years with no clear system, and every trade I took I thought was in line with my methodology—a rather loose one, to be sure. It was only when I started to use a precise system that I began to realize how much trading I had been doing that had nothing to do with my methodology at all.

Now, I do not trade a precise methodology, although I follow a general pattern. But I believe it is an essential part of a trader's development to do so, because it is only by having a strict line to follow that we can see when we are *not* doing so. It is rather like those stagehands dressed all in black at the theatre. Against a black backdrop you cannot see what they are doing. Make the backdrop white, and they become very obvious.

By using a precise system, we are using a white backdrop, and those stray emotions and instincts become very clear. Once we know they are there, it is not so difficult to work out what is happening inside ourselves and to do something about it. Not always as easily done as said, but there are people around who can help if we find it too difficult.

Journey of Self-Discovery

While you are going through this journey of self-discovery—the most important part of the process—you will also be developing a feel for the market and working towards discovering your own system. You must discover *your* system—mine won't do it for you.

We each have different personalities and therefore different *trading* personalities. We need to design a system that suits us, and the best way is to do so is from scratch—where trading software that can test systems can be so useful. But many traders have no clear idea of where to start.

I use extremely simple systems, because I believe complexity is not helpful. But it depends upon the individual trader's personality. What I think is unimportant. It is what you think that is important to your system. This is a critical point, because during our lives each of us has built up a belief system, and it is going to be very difficult for any of us to do anything that conflicts with that belief system. So, if you have a belief that moving averages are not a good way to trade, then you will have trouble trading a system that uses them. But we should not simply be complacent about our beliefs, since some of them may need changing.

Many people engage in what might be called bad habits, including smoking and excessive drinking. Doing so is partly a result of a belief system. Stopping such habits requires a change in that belief system. Many people believe that they cannot enjoy themselves unless they have a drink. It is very difficult for such people to stop drinking. It is easy to demonstrate that they can enjoy themselves without having a drink, but it may take some time.

Some beliefs may be far easier to change. The trader who did not believe in moving averages may change his mind if he sees good results from such a system. So it is not necessarily simply a matter of developing a system that suits you; a large part of it is personal development.

As I have said, the whole trading experience is in our own heads. It is obvious that we decide when to trade and when not to trade, but once we realize that there are various parts of us competing for command, namely the three parts of the triune brain—thought, emotion and instinct—it is clear that there is more to it. Instinct has an immediate access to our action centers; otherwise, survival instincts would simply be too slow.

The Trading Pyramid

Emotion and Thought

Emotion comes into play, and then thought enters the picture. Thought is comparatively slow. This is another reason why we have to become traders. Trading successfully must become a habit. It is just like riding a bicycle. When we start on the bicycle it is all in our thinking, and we wobble along and fall off. Then we train ourselves to ride the bicycle automatically. Winners must do the same with trading. Most of my trades are done automatically these days. I have trained myself to ignore stray emotion and instinct, or maybe I have trained those emotions and instincts. I am not sure which.

To use an analogy, think about crossing a road. We stand on the side of the road and look around. We analyze the situation. We wait until it is safe, and then we cross. This is similar to what traders do. They want to get across the road to the profit waiting on the other side. But they define "safe" in many different ways. In the markets many fail to get across that road. Even experienced traders cannot cross the road safely every time. In the real world, trucks do not just suddenly appear and run you down, but they do in the market.

So the whole trading experience takes place inside our own heads. And this is where we can win or lose, nowhere else. People talk about the "holy grail" in trading. You will not find the holy grail in software, systems, and books, you will only find it by looking in a mirror!

Commitment

Building your system involves a feedback loop, and if we look at the "Trading Pyramid" (see figure 8.1), we can see how the various levels interact. In this manner the pyramid itself becomes alive, and the model becomes immensely useful. This model was developed so that traders could have a gauge of the various skills they need in order to succeed. The base of the pyramid is *you*, because it is your personality that determines how you will trade and make money. The next level is commitment. Commitment is absolutely essential in a trader as this is a tough business. Without commitment you will not make much progress.

Discipline

This brings us to discipline, the next layer of the pyramid. You need discipline to control instincts and emotions; you need discipline to follow your system rules; you need discipline to operate your stops. I do not believe there is any magic in trading techniques. The magic lies in the trading skills we bring to our approach, not in the approach itself.

FIGURE 8-1. *The trading pyramid.*

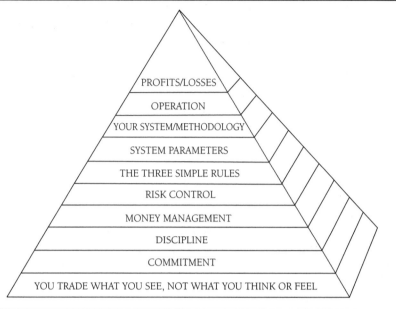

Great traders are not great because they have discovered a winning approach. They are great because they bring the winning approach to their system. It is how they use that system that makes the difference, and one of the key aspects of this is money management.

Many traders lose because they put themselves under too much pressure. They want to make lots of money right away. They trade too many contracts and immediately get scared. Remember, scared money never wins. I know this because I have been there myself. A well-known trader in the United Kingdom said that winners know more about losing than losers do, because they keep on doing it until they succeed. Losers don't have the stamina. They give up too early. Winners keep on trying. But you have to learn from your mistakes.

Money Management

If you do not operate effective money management, then you will get wiped out, guaranteed. If you don't believe it, then look at some simple statistics. If you are using a system that has a 50 percent hit rate (winning rate), you should understand what this means statistically. Most traders have no idea about this. Out of every two trades, one is likely to be a loss.

Out of every 4 trades, we are liable to get a string of two losers.
Out of every 8 trades, we are liable to get a string of three losers.
Out of every 16 trades, we are liable to get a string of four losers.
Out of every 32 trades, we are liable to get a string of five losers.
Out of every 64 trades, we are liable to get a string of six losers.
Out of every 128 trades, we are liable to get a string of seven losers.
Out of every 256 trades, we are liable to get a string of eight losers.
Out of every 512 trades, we are liable to get a string of nine losers.
Out of every 1,000 trades, we are liable to get a string of ten losers.

Interestingly, most traders abandon a system that hits a string of four or five losers. But it is bound to happen. This example could be extended indefinitely. You have got to understand simple statistics, otherwise you will spend your entire life switching from one system to another. What you really need to do is to become an expert in *your* system, but that takes time. A big part of this is money management.

You have to be ready for that killer run of ten or more losses. If you are not ready, then you are a fugitive from the law of averages, just waiting for the statistical certainty to wipe you out. Most traders overtrade, both financially and psychologically. Pressure in both these areas is a killer.

Risk Control

Next we have risk control. This is also critically important. All the best traders manage risk very aggressively. If you don't get it, it will surely get you. Every market approach has a certain logic and that logic has to do with risk.

If the approach is too risky, it will kill you. A tightrope walker does not, contrary to popular belief, learn to balance on the tightrope. He or she learns to live with imbalance. So traders and investors must learn to live with risk.

Three Simple Rules

This brings us to three simple rules. I often call these "secrets," because they are well hidden, hidden in full view where everyone can see them—thus not realizing their value. The three are:

1. Cut your losses.
2. Let profits run.
3. Trade selectively.

Put simply, if you do not cut your losses, they will wipe you out. If you do not run your profits, they will not cover your losses. If you do not select only the best trades, and your system may do this for you, then the dross will drag you down.

System Parameters

Now we come to your system parameters, which determine how you want to trade:

- What instruments?
- How frequently?
- How much risk?
- Which markets?

Many traders have trouble with this and seem unable to grasp what may suit them out of the vast range of possibilities. But it is really a simple choice of how you want to trade. There does need to be an "edge," an idea of what might work, what may allow you to make money.

You will now be seeing how the pyramid works in practice. Each layer is essential to the succeeding layers. Your system parameters are unlikely to make much sense unless they follow the three simple rules. These follow those from money management and risk control. But you need discipline, before you can operate these. Before that you need commitment even to want to operate the discipline, and so it goes throughout the pyramid. But the pyramid is more than just a series of levels, each of which relies on all the levels below.

There is also a range of feedback loops within the pyramid. For example, if you are having trouble trading your system, then perhaps the parameters need adjusting. Maybe you should have more regard for discipline. It is much easier being disciplined about something you like to do. So make your system more to your liking, and that will help the discipline. All the way through the pyramid there are similar feedback loops that can help you win. The action takes place in your mind, but the pyramid gives you a model by which to work.

Your System Methodology and Operation

The next level is your system, the result of all that has gone before. Then comes the operation of your system, a huge subject all on its own. This is when the fun really starts. You have to trade your system, but if everything else is in place, it won't be a problem. (Actually it will, because there are things you won't know about yourself until you start to trade.) Then the pyramid really comes alive, because new feedback loops come into being between the various levels.

For example, you may find you have difficulty sticking to the rules of your system. This may be a discipline problem, or it may be that the rules do not suit you in some way. Part of the solution may be varying the rules, part may be to become more disciplined. The final level is your profits and losses. These determine whether your pyramid is well constructed. A well-built pyramid produces profits. One that is not produces losses.

We all look at the markets differently, and we all have different trading personalities. In trading, nothing is good or bad, right or wrong. It is all about being useful, and we define that as making money. As an example, some traders like to buy upside breakouts, which occur when price takes out prior resistance. These traders make money consistently by doing so.

Others like to fade such breakouts, which means to sell them, and they also make money. How can this be? Simply because these traders have learned all about risk control. Their losers do not lose much, but their winners win big. That is the secret of all successful trading. It is simply a matter of developing a methodology that becomes a winning habit and that makes the most of your personal strengths and minimizes the effect of your personal weaknesses.

Whenever I look at a new system or at a new trade, I always look at the potential downside. If you always ensure that the losses are small, then you will do OK. For the monies I manage I write option premiums and then hedge, if need be, using options and futures. My aim may be considered modest. I look to make 3 percent to 4 percent per month; that is around 50 percent per annum, and that is net of losses. But I find that my approach keeps losses down to a minimum. This is why I write option premiums. This works fairly well, but it is not so much what I do as how I do it.

So what are the key factors determining overall success in the markets? Everyone who is involved with markets wants to come out a winner. Four essential areas separate the winners from the losers. These points are as applicable to investors as they are to traders. My track record allows me to say that these factors are essential.

There is nothing revolutionary here. Most of this is well known to investors and traders. Indeed, it is too well known, because remember, the best place to hide a secret is where everyone can see it. That way most people do not realize its worth. I have covered this before, but some ideas are worth repeating. These four factors are more than simple rules *for* success. They also mark the path *through* success. Here are the four:

1. Cut your losses.
2. Run your profits.
3. Trade selectively
4. Maintain good balance.

Profits and Losses

It is the balance of your pyramid that determines whether you win or lose. If you construct a pyramid bearing a close relationship to the leaning tower of Pisa, then that is not good news. The market will provide far less support than does the ground in Pisa. But if your pyramid sits squarely and is robust, you will win!

There are four stages of development that we all go through in any endeavor to reach success: novice, intermediate, expert, and master. Novice traders and investors come to the market without much of an idea of what they are getting involved in. They have a view that they will have an easy ride, producing lots of lovely profits. Invariably they will get a rude awakening—what we might call a reality shock. This is when they learn to cut their losses. And it is this lesson that marks the move to the intermediate level. I believe that intended losses should never exceed more than 2 percent of a portfolio. Remember that in fast market conditions it is simply not possible to exercise that level of control—this applies to most trading strategies. Some traders get away with risking up to 5 percent, but most of the major winners adopt an approach risking less, not more, often just 1 percent.

Adopting such a strategy has two immediate benefits. First, the probability of a killer wipe-out is much reduced. Second, the pressure is off. Now the investor or trader can relax and operate his or her strategy successfully. But although the novice has taken some big steps forward, there is still a long way to go. Now he or she must learn to run profits—this is item number two on our list. Big profits are essential so that you can pay out your losers and still come out on top. This point may not be obvious to investors as we near the end of the biggest Bull Market ever—a Bull Market that has already taken out all the historic precedents. But two things are certain: one is that this Bull Market will end. Indeed, it may already have done so. And the second is that the points I am making here will be essential if you are to win in the market that comes afterward.

Running profits may seem easy, but remember that novices have received a battering from the market and are usually nursing some big losses. They may have learned to cut losses but now they are cutting them too fine—effectively stifling all their trades. They have to overcome their fear. Already we can see how balance is important. The novice phase may be characterized as "greedy"—this is off balance one way.

The intermediate level may be characterized as "fearful"—that is off balance the other way. The investor or trader has to overcome his or her fear to get onto the next phase, to become expert. This is not easy. When I started to trade in the late 1980s, it took me around eighteen months to get into the intermediate phase, leaving some heavy losses behind me. I reckon it took the best part of five years to overcome the fear that I had built up because of those losses. Consider five years as fairly typical. Some do it quicker, but others taker longer.

Once traders transcend these problems, they start to make good money—this is stage three. At this point they will have developed a useful strategy (in the sense that it works, it makes money) and will be well on the way to becoming expert in the application of that strategy. When someone is expert he or she begins to understand something about trade selectivity—which trades do not offer a good risk and reward profile and which ones do. This ability, built on years of hard work and experience (the only way to succeed in any serious endeavor), leads to much larger profits. Now the trader is truly doing well. But this is not the end of the road. He or she is now making good money but still has something to aim for. That something is balance, and here we enter an entirely new panorama—stage four.

Investment and trading are life experiences. The individual has to evolve and transcend his or her own limitations to succeed in this field. The same applies to any sporting competition, to mountain climbing, or to anything that involves peak performance. To operate at such levels one has many self-imposed limitations that have to be overcome. Indeed, not only self-imposed ones!

If one of your competitors makes it to a higher level of achievement, then so must you, if you are to remain competitive. This is definitely the case in the market, and this is where balance comes in. At the highest level, investment and trading is purely a reflection of the trader's or investor's personality. Any imbalance will produce losses. But perfect balance is not possible. We have to learn to live with imbalance. The ideal is to retain the same state whatever life throws at us— whether we are admiring a beautiful mountain view, whether we are stuck in a ten-mile traffic backup, or whether a market crash has just cost us 20 percent of our portfolio. Now that's tough, but it's true balance! But if you can do that, then you are a master.

Keys to Success

I have traded full time for over a decade, and I believe success is dependent on four key factors:

1. *Discipline.* To win you must develop a methodology. To make this work, you must make it your own. By this I mean you must personalize your methodology to suit you. But you still need the discipline to follow it.
2. *Relaxation.* Unless you are relaxed, you will take too many trades, and then you will lose. To be relaxed means you must not put yourself under too much pressure, so make sure your gearing level is comfortable.
3. *Humility.* The market is the great humiliator. If you start humble, then the market does not need to humble you. A good kick is sometimes necessary, but in financial terms it is not desirable. Also, if you are full of yourself, then you will have no room for

anything else. You need to pay attention to the market if you are going to win.

4. *Balance.* Balance is the final aim. We may never achieve it, but it gives us something to strive for, and that is why it is so valuable.

Notice how these four topics tie in with the four steps I mentioned earlier. It takes discipline to cut losses, and it takes relaxation to run profits. It takes humility to stay focused and to select trades appropriately. Finally, it takes good balance to be a master. (Refer to figure 8-2.)

Low-Risk Opportunities

Trading is a business, and as with all business you want to risk a little to make a lot. Many of you are in business. You may sell telephones, repair washing machines, or design kitchens, but the same thing applies. You keep your risk low, and often you can virtually eliminate risk in a well run business. This is not possible with trading, but you can and must keep risk low. Traders are interested in spotting and taking advantage of low-risk opportunities.

Traders need a system. You should either develop or purchase one. It is much better to develop your own system, although some traders need help with this. But there is a very good reason why traders need a system. It is to detect all those instincts and emotions. The system tells you what you ought to do. Your instincts and emotions will make you do something different. So when you take a trade that has nothing to do with your system, you start to see the real you. You start to understand that there is something else at work, and that something else is not focused on making money. Similarly, you will find yourself not taking system trades, and again it will be emotions and instincts getting in the way. The system also provides ready-made low-risk opportunities, cutting losses, and running profits.

FIGURE 8-2. *Keys to success.*

■ Cut your losses	→ Novice	→ Discipline
■ Run your profits	→ Intermediate	→ Relaxation
■ Trade selectively	→ Expert	→ Humility
■ Good balance	→ Master	→ Balance

Nine Ways to Make Money

Every trader is interested in making money. Based on my trading experience here are nine ideas that work:

1. Reduce position size.
2. Find a trading mentor.
3. Use stops that have meaning.
4. Understand the logic of your trading approach.
5. Let profits run.
6. Be selective.
7. Don't predict.
8. Don't panic.
9. Stay humble.

Reduce Position Size

It may seem odd that reducing position size is the number one idea for making more money, but it is so. Many traders put themselves under excess pressure. By doing so they are prone to make bad decisions, and they lose money. So don't do it; reduce position size to a level at which you are comfortable. Then you can make sound trading decisions and make money. Many traders count "overtrading" as their worst mistake—and they are right. Here is the cure to that problem. Part of this is psychological and part is financial. But the financial aspects impact on the psychological.

It is a statistical fact that a system with a 50 percent hit rate—and many good systems have worse hit rates than that—will hit a string of ten or more losses every thousand trades. You have got to account for these statistics in your trading. This is important, so I will illustrate it. The chance of one loss is 0.5; of two losses is 0.5 times 0.5, or 0.25; of ten losses is 0.5 to the tenth power, or 0.001, which is 1 in 1,000. And the more trades you do, the bigger the strings you are likely to hit. But that big string may hit you in the first twenty or thirty trades, you just don't know. That is how the odds pan out. There is no luck in successful trading, but there is a lot of luck in each individual trade. If you overtrade you are challenging the law of averages, and the losses will get you. No wonder you are under psychological pressure. You subconsciously know the risk you are running even if you do not admit it to yourself. So reduce position size and make more money!

Options have a lot of positives. They also have a lot of negatives. But if you find that trading futures is not doing it for you, then consider options. For example you can often sell an out-of-the-money option for over 100 points on the Dow. Yet how many of your futures trades yield profits in excess of 100 points. If the answer is few, maybe you should consider trading options. Writing an out-of-the-money option for over 100 points is similar to trading futures for a profit of that amount. The difference is time frame, because to bag the whole option price, you first have to write the option and, second, you have to hold it to expiry. This is very different from a short-term futures trade. There are many more factors that may affect the market over the life of the option than may be applicable over a fairly short-term futures trade. But some traders find options are more amenable to what they want to achieve, and this is the key point: you need to use a vehicle that ties in with your trading personality.

But there are many more options strategies than merely writing naked options. Near expiration an option may give a much better risk/reward ratio than trading a futures contract. Indeed, you may be able to buy an option for no more than you would normally risk on a futures trade, and the potential rewards may be very similar.

Find a Trading Mentor

Trading is a very difficult business, not the least because it is a zero-sum game. No, cancel that—it is a negative-sum game. Every time you enter the game you pay a fee. That fee is called commission, and you pay that after you've paid all the other costs involved—price feeds, computers, software, and so on. It is no surprise that a lot of traders lose. If you need help with your trading, then find someone who has experience to help you. Ideally, this will be a local trader, and many are prepared to help, because trading is a fairly lonely business with little meaningful human contact. Helping another trader can be rewarding. Otherwise you may need to find a professional trader who is willing to help, but you may well expect to pay a fee.

Use Stops That Have Meaning

Not all traders use stops. If you don't use stops, everything becomes a lot simpler, because you get wiped out fairly quickly. Actually, that is not true for everyone, but it is true for some, if not many. If you are using an approach that utilizes stops, then try to ensure that your stops have some significance. Otherwise you tend to be throwing money away. I don't trade stocks, but examples would be below key support, or above key resistance, or beyond price spikes.

Understand the Logic of Your Trading Approach

Every approach to the market involves risk. As traders we must control risk. Indeed, as a tightrope walker learns to live with imbalance, so traders must learn to live with risk. But risk can kill us. It can also make us wealthy. Understand the logic of your approach and the risks you are taking, because that risk will come home to roost. In one sense the market is a generator of random sequences, especially if you follow a precise algorithm. If your approach has a weakness, the market will find it in one of those random sequences. For example, we reviewed earlier the statistics of a 50 percent successful system. If you operate such a system and risk 10 percent on every trade, then that system will wipe you out, because eventually you will hit a string of ten losers. That is the logic of that approach.

Let Profits Run

Unless you let your profits run, you will never cover your losses—let alone come out on top. You must also cut your losses. Traders can learn to cut losses quite easily, but the lesson to run profits seems a little more difficult to learn. This is not surprising. First, it is the direct opposite of cutting loses. Cutting losses is an active function requiring careful monitoring of what is happening. It requires action. Running profits, in contrast, requires inaction. Action is the last thing required if you want to run your profits, because the only action you can take is to cut the position. Therefore, you can add to existing positions. This can be a good idea because it gives you something to do—a task to perform—thus occupying time you may otherwise spend closing out profitable positions.

Doing nothing can be tough. But there are other factors. In this society we are used to quick gratification. We want our goodies, and we want them *now*. The same goes for trading profits. Once we see them, we want them—but we cannot have them if we want to let profits run. In the book *Emotional Intelligence*, by Daniel P. Coleman, the marshmallow test is outlined. An infant is left in a room with a marshmallow and told that if she does not eat it, she will get another one. (Apparently this simple test is a far better guide to future success than any number of intelligence tests!) This is exactly what traders must do if they want to let profits run. So don't eat that marshmallow, and you will get two!

Be Selective

There are so many keys to success. This is the one that separates those who make lots of money from those who just get by. If your selection process is working well, then you will eliminate a portion of losers, and that makes a big difference. But how do you do it? The only way is through hard work and experience. Traders need to develop their own selection system and become expert in that system. Once expert, they can select trades—but many traders dismiss this. It is all too easy to miss the best trades. But the good trades run on and thus allow alternative entry points. Clearly this is an option to be handled with care. If something is working, don't fix it. It is also true that trading is an evolutionary process. Traders tend to go through changes, and so do the markets. When this happens, traders have to change as well. There are some trades that make no sense—for example, entering near the close unless there are very solid reasons.

Don't Predict

Market action is not predictable. A trader does not predict action—he or she takes calculated risks. You risk a little to make a lot. Define the opportunities you want to take and then test the concept on paper. If it doesn't work on paper, it will not work in the real world. A good system may get it right only one-third of the time, but it will make money. Trying to predict what will happen is a losing game. Every successful trader I have ever spoken to agrees with this. One of the big problems with prediction is that you can become emotionally attached to your prediction and ignore market action that denies it. This can lead to big mistakes. It is better to develop your approach and let that make the money for you.

Don't Panic

This is critical. Panic is mother to losses. Part of this is not putting yourself under undue pressure. The more relaxed you are, the less likely you are to panic. This again comes back to reducing position size. But another part of this is fully rehearsing your trading approach and the various actions the market may take. If you rehearse all the possibilities, and visualize your feelings as they occur, then you will be prepared when they happen. If you are prepared, you will not panic. But part of it is temperament. Some are more prone to panic than others. Becoming familiar with the trading environment is clearly a big help, and those who cannot cope with that environment are quickly weeded out.

Stay Humble

A person who is full of him- or herself has no room for anything else. Such a person will not listen or learn. A trader who is not humble may not listen to the market and will get wiped out. We have all heard stories of macho traders who took on the market and were turned into mincemeat. Humility is an essential for trading success.

9

YOUR MIND'S MONEY MACHINE

Oscar Goldman

The dream is alive. It was a cold day in New York as I looked out at over three hundred hopeful faces that I was about to address, full of anticipation of hearing about the magic of the minds of the world's top trading pros. I could tell, based on experience, that this crowd of mostly beginners knew that they were missing something; they just didn't know what it was. It reminded me of the time that I began trading, about nine years ago. I had a dream of becoming one of the world's top traders.

I could almost taste the success, the money, and maybe even the fame. Little did I know that shortly after I began trading, the dream, for a period of time, would be shattered. The reality of my ignorance and lack of experience would appear in the form of painful losses again, and again, and again, until eventually the dream faded and I became aware of the *real* reality rather than my original interpretation of it. It was only at that point that the deep wounds of loss started to heal, and the winnings started to accumulate, and again the dream was alive.

The words that you are about to read in this chapter could have a dramatic effect not only on your trading future but also on your future in general; not only on the trading part of your life, but also on your life in general. I have found over and over again, after coaching hundreds of people and speaking in front of thousands of people across the country,

Copyright © 2001 Oscar Goldman. All rights reserved.

that life and trading go hand in hand. If one is off, it seems to affect the other dramatically.

I recognized that I had only one chapter, and therefore only a few pages, in which to create something that would leave a lasting impact and therefore create lasting results. I have written a chapter that should take you sixteen or more weeks to finish. No, I am not insinuating that you are a slow reader, but you are about to read a chapter unlike any you have read before. Allow me to explain.

Several months ago I started writing a weekly column addressing the psychology of trading that reaches 3 to 5 million people a month on the Internet. The response was, and continues to be, absolutely phenomenal. I receive hundreds of e-mails from faithful readers applauding the impact that the contents of that column have had not only on their trading but on their lives in general.

Those weekly columns were meant to be a continuing series that would take the trader through a consistent process to become a winner. So, because of the response and impact, I have decided to share with you the first sixteen weeks of this continuing series. It is highly recommended that you go through this process one week at a time to allow your system to absorb and process the material. You have heard many times that discipline is a critical factor in being a world-class trader, and this is going to be one place that you need to exercise that discipline, one week at a time.

If you are like the multitudes of people who are currently reading this material, then you will find yourself looking forward to constant improvement. Over time you will start to realize that your dream is not only alive, it's about to become a reality. So, here we go with the beginning of your journey to becoming a very successful trader.

Week One
The Beauty of Beginnings

Do you remember your first kiss, your first car, your first pet, or the first time you fell in love? Of course you do. What do all these experiences have in common? They were all new beginnings. There was no reference to the past. There was only looking to the future—to the possibilities, the adventure, the exploration, the great passionate feelings, the freedom. Please stop reading, and close your eyes for a moment. Really remember those beginnings and feel those feelings, and smile.

Fellow trading warriors, welcome to a new beginning, one that will never end. This week, and every week from this point on, you will grow to understand the meaning of that statement, a beginning that never ends. If you go through this material every week as a new beginning, you will find that not only your trading results will change but also your whole life will change.

One thing that you must be clear about is that this is not going to be just another few pages of empty reading. In order for you to make a dramatic change in your results, you are going to have to take dramatic action. You approach trading as a whole person (you, your history, family influence, thought process, belief system, and so on). So, you must deal with the whole person in order to give yourself the results that you want.

No, I am not going to be your "therapist"; however, I am going to be the best coach you have ever had. Please note that I said "best," not "easiest." I am going to be a combination of Mother Theresa and Gen. Norman Schwartzkopf. I am going to help you, support you, kick your butt, and hold you accountable. If you are committed to creating the results that you want out of your life, then you will be able to join me a few months from now to celebrate your arrival in the "winners circle."

I would like to close out this first week by reminding you of who you are. If you're the kind of person who finds it easy to follow through on difficult decisions, then you will find yourself rocketing to new highs. If you are one who is uneasy when making difficult decisions, then you will find new freedom as you develop the skills to change that unease to confidence in order to reach new highs. In either case, please stop and look at the thought process that you follow in your mind in order to make decisions.

Write something about that process in a new journal that you designate strictly for the work that we will be doing. You must do this before next week. Once you have done that, congratulate yourself on taking the first step in becoming the most successful person you have ever been. Until next week, I want to welcome you to a most exciting beginning that will never end.

Week Two

A consistent man believes in destiny, a capricious man in chance.
—Benjamin Disraeli

Welcome to week two. I hope you are as excited as I am about beginning this journey. If you have not done last week's work, please stop and do so at this time before continuing. This process, as with anything in life that has lasting effect and value, will start with a foundation and build on that foundation week after week. So, I am going to ask you at this beginning stage to get into the habit of reading these pages on a weekly basis and rising to the challenges that are placed in front of you.

The trickiest part of rising to any challenge in the beginning is simply making the decision to do so and recognizing that most beginnings involve a little discomfort on the way to the payoff. Learning requires change from the old way to the new way, from the program that is producing current results to the program that will produce the desired results. Before you experienced the pleasure of your first kiss, you most likely had to go through the discomfort of risking rejection. Before you experienced the freedom of your first bike ride, you had to go through the pain of falling. So, the point is that we must make a decision to get to the goal, the payoff, and the win, no matter what initial discomfort we are likely to encounter.

Here is your first challenge. Take the notebook or diary that you designated for this work and the exercises that we will be doing here, and title your first page "Declaration of commitment to my future." The first entry on that page will be as follows:

> I, [your name], have made a commitment and a decision to follow through with the exercises, and will do everything within my power to live up to the challenges that are presented in this chapter. I recognize that I am doing this for myself and for the people I care about [please list the names of the loved ones in your life]. I can and will create the future that I desire.

Date and sign this declaration.

If you want great results from the work that you will be doing here, you will commit to reading this declaration once or twice a day.

If you desire extremely great results, then you will make a copy of this declaration and give it to your loved ones. If you follow through with this first challenge, then I applaud you and congratulate you on a much more satisfying, brighter future. If you are one of the people who thought the first exercise might be silly, or wonder what this has to do with trading, then I am going to suggest that you find some writings on the subject of discipline and/or rent the first *Karate Kid* movie, and in the meantime be content with the results that you currently have and do not come back to these pages until you have followed through on the first challenge and exercise. Now, go back and reread the declaration and recognize that you hold your future in your hand; feel a sense of power and peace, recognizing that you will no longer leave anything up to chance. Make it happen, and look forward to next week.

Week Three

> The beginning of a habit is like an invisible thread, but over time we repeat the act, we strengthen the strand, add to it another filament until it becomes a great cable and binds us irrevocably, thought and act.
>
> —Orson Swett Marden

Welcome to week three of becoming the person you really are. I am assuming that you have done your "homework" so far, and you should be proud of the fact that you will continue to do so. One of the most critical elements of success, trading or otherwise, is to make a decision (see last week's exercise). The second most important element for success is to develop a habit of being successful. We all know that we are creatures of habit. The brain, unfortunately, does not distinguish between good habits and bad habits. It just simply does what it's told.

So, what does that mean to you, to your life, and to your trading? It simply means that you must come to grips with the fact that you are a creature of habit. That you are a result of those habits. You also must come to grips with the fact that if you do not like certain results that occur in your life, then chances are you have developed some destructive habits. Please recognize that it is not easy to admit to ourselves that we are doing something that does not work, that it is *our* actions that are causing *our* discomfort.

So, your first assignment for this week is to admit to yourself that you are a creature of habit. It is constructive, once you have made that realization, to actually utter those words out loud: "I am a creature of habit." It is even more helpful to confide in someone the fact that you are a creature of habit.

If you have stayed with me this far and actually followed this thought process, then you are ready for the good news. The good news is that you have a choice. You have the ability to choose and to develop empowering habits. Again, remember that the brain does not distinguish between one kind of habit or the other—it just simply does. So, the big question is: How do you make the switch? How do you become the kind of person who consistently develops great habits? And, in fact, *thrives on great habits?*

The answer is very simple—it starts with just one little habit. The whole reason that you wrote out your declaration of success last week, and you read it once or twice a day, was for you to start developing a good habit so that your brain starts getting used to forming a simple habit with a positive result. Now you realize why I was adamant about having you follow through on last week's exercise and why it's critical for you to continue to build your habits week after week.

Your accomplishment for this week is to decide on something that you have been wanting to do. Make it simple. It could be as little as exercising 5 minutes a day, reading a few pages a day, eating a little less each day, or loving someone more every day. For the next seven days, you absolutely must become passionate about wanting to do that thing. Get excited about building that foundation, recognizing that this is where it all starts.

Finally, I want to remind you that as you are joining me this week, the third week in a row, you are already developing a good life-changing habit. Good for you. You are already winning. With that in mind, go out and make this a "great habit" week. You may choose to share what you are doing with other people, enroll and encourage them in developing good habits, invite them to go through this process with you, and if you really want to go all out, you can start a "good habit club." Have fun with it, and let someone know how well you are doing. Do it big, and look forward to next week.

Week Four

Welcome to week four. I hope this finds you well and wealthier. We are going to do something different this week .

In the following paragraphs, you will find some great pearls of wisdom that I have gathered over time. I highly recommend that you print, save, read, and reread them on a regular daily basis. Doing this will not only help you become a better person, but also prepare you for future lessons. I am glad that you are a part of my life and look forward to connecting with all of you next week.

- I've learned that I can get by on charm for about fifteen minutes. After that, I'd better know something.
- I've learned that I shouldn't compare what I can do to the best *others* can do.
- I've learned that I cannot make someone love me. All I can do is be someone who can be loved.
- I've learned that it takes years to build up trust and only seconds to destroy it.
- I've learned that I can do something in an instant that will give me heartache for life.
- I've learned that I am responsible for what I do, no matter how I feel.
- I've learned that either I must control my attitude or it will control me.
- I've learned that regardless of how hot and steamy a relationship is at first, the passion fades, and there had better be something else to take its place.
- I've learned that heroes are the people who do what has to be done, when it needs to be done, regardless of the consequences.
- I've learned that true friendship continues to grow, even over the longest distance.
- I've learned that just because someone doesn't love you the way you want them to doesn't mean that person doesn't love you with all he or she has.
- I've learned that maturity has to do with the type of experiences one has had and what one learned from them, and less to do with how many birthdays one has celebrated.
- I've learned that it isn't always enough to be forgiven by others; sometimes one must learn to forgive oneself.
- I've learned that my background and circumstances may have influenced who I am, but I am responsible for who I become.
- I've learned that it takes me a long time to become the person I want to be.

Keep loving, keep laughing, keep learning, and look forward to next week.

Week Five

Where Is God's perfection?

Welcome to week five. How are you doing? Are you excited about being a "great habit" machine? Doesn't it feel good to set a goal and reach it? The idea now is to continue doing that, and continue reaching new highs until you have become the perfect trader. Yes, I did say the perfect trader. At this point a lot of you are probably asking, "Is it possible to become the perfect trader?" And the answer is yes. Stay with me now. Before we go on, however, we have to answer the question, What *is* the prefect trader?

I am going to ask you an even more important question. But before I do, I must warn you (now that you have been with me for five weeks and, I believe, are ready to move on) that I am about to take you to a realm of training and understanding that few coaches in this industry ever dare to go or understand. So once you have identified what (in your mind) the perfect trader is, the even bigger question is, Are you perfect enough to *become* the perfect trader? The answer is (regardless of what your brain tells you) a resounding *yes.*

Now that I have your attention, I am going to explain what I mean by sharing a story with you that a great friend of mine shared with me. It will expand our definition of perfection and, therefore, our capabilities.

In Brooklyn, New York, Chush is a school that caters to learning disabled children. Some children remain in Chush for their entire school career, while others can be mainstreamed into conventional schools. At a Chush fundraising dinner, the father of a Chush child delivered a speech that would never be forgotten by any who attended.

After extolling the school and its dedicated staff, he cried out, "Where is the perfection in my son Shaya? Everything God does is done with perfection. But my child cannot understand things as other children do. My child cannot remember facts and figures as other children do. Where is God's perfection?"

The audience was shocked by the question, pained by the father's anguish, and stilled by his piercing query. "I believe," the father said, "that when God brings a child like this into the world, the perfection that He seeks is in the way people react to this child." He then told the following story about his son, Shaya: One afternoon Shaya and his father walked past a park where some boys Shaya knew were playing baseball. Shaya asked, "Do you think they will let me play?" Shaya's father knew that his son was not at all athletic and that most boys would not want him on their team. But he understood that if his son was chosen to play, it would give him a comfortable sense of belonging.

Shaya's father approached one of the boys in the field and asked if Shaya could play. The boy looked around for guidance from his team-mates. Getting none, he took matters into his own hands and said, "We are losing by six runs and the game is in the eighth inning, I guess he can be on our team, and we'll try to put him up to bat in the ninth inning."

Shaya's father was ecstatic as Shaya smiled broadly. Shaya was told to put on a glove and go out to play short center field. In the bottom of the eighth inning, Shaya's team scored a few runs, but was still behind by three. In the bottom of the eighth inning, Shaya's team scored again, and now, with two outs and the bases loaded with the potential winning run on base, Shaya was scheduled to be up. Would the team actually let Shaya bat at this juncture and give away their chance to win the game? Surprisingly, Shaya was given the bat.

Everyone knew that it was all but impossible because Shaya didn't even know how to hold the bat properly, let alone hit with it. However, as Shaya stepped up to the plate, the pitcher moved a few steps to lob the ball in softly so Shaya should at least be able to make contact. The first pitch came in, and Shaya swung clumsily and missed. One of Shaya's teammates came up to Shaya and together they held the bat and faced the pitcher waiting for the next pitch. The pitcher again took a few steps forward to toss the ball softly towards Shaya.

As the pitch came in, Shaya and his teammate swung the bat and together they hit a slow ground ball to the pitcher. The pitcher picked up the soft grounder and could easily have thrown the ball to the first baseman. Shaya would have been out, and that would have ended the game. Instead, the pitcher took the ball and threw it in a high arc to right field, far beyond the reach of the first baseman.

Everyone started yelling, "Shaya, run to first. Run to first." Never in his life had Shaya run to first. He scampered down the baseline, wide eyed and startled. By the time he reached first base, the right fielder had the ball. He could have thrown the ball to the second baseman, who would tag Shaya, who was still running. But the right fielder understood what the pitcher's intentions were, so he threw the ball high and over the third baseman's head.

Everyone yelled, "Run to second, run to second." Shaya ran towards second base as the runners ahead of him deliriously circled the bases towards home. As Shaya reached second base, the opposing shortstop ran to him, turned him in the direction of third base and shouted, "Run to third." As Shaya rounded third, the boys from both teams ran behind him screaming, "Shaya, run home." Shaya ran home, stepped on home plate, and all eighteen boys lifted him on their shoulders and made him the hero, as he had just hit a "grand slam" and won the game for his team.

"That day," said the father softly, with tears now rolling down his face, "those eighteen boys reached *their* level of God's perfection."

If you are like me you will start to realize as you read this story that it is in *imperfection* that perfection is created, that you have everything you need in order to get everything you want. You just have to recognize what it is you have and know that it is exactly what you need. Most so-called pros will give you the false belief that you need something outside of yourself in order to get what you want or become the best trader that you can be.

The truth is, it's how you use and mold what you have that allows you to reach the goal. In preparation for the journey that we are about to take in discovering and molding what truly makes you perfect and the perfect trader, prepare yourself and your soul by thanking God for the perfection you are about to discover. Share this story with as many people as you can. Make a difference in your life by making a difference in theirs, as you look forward to next week and the next step in your process/journey.

Week Six

Things do not change, we change.

—Henry David Thoreau

Welcome to week six. I am sure that many people had a strong response to last week's story. Many might have shed tears while reading

Shaya's story. They were not tears of sadness but of joy, of having looked into your heart and recognized the joy of seeing perfection in your imperfections. As I mentioned to you last week, we have started a journey that very few people take. This is where I sometimes lose some readers simply because they're not willing to look at their imperfections long enough to discover perfection. I hope, pray, and count on the fact that you are going to be one of those who will go the distance and realize your God-given perfection. I can assure you that when you start to get a glimpse of that reality, not only will you become a great trading success but you will become a success, period.

The first and most critical element to any kind of success in any aspect of life on any level is the ability to see the truth. Although this may sound simple, and ought to be simple, it usually is not. Let me explain what I mean. Whenever we are faced with a decision, usually we are presented with three realities (even though we may not see all of them at the same time). There is *our* reality, there is *other people's* reality, and there is *real* reality. In other words, we see things either through our own eyes, through other people's eyes, or simply through the eyes of truth.

I submit to you that most of us spend most of our time seeing our own interpretation of things or other people's interpretation of things, rather than seeing things as they truly are. I submit to you that one of the biggest reasons that failure happens—in trading and/or in life—is because we spend most of our time trying to have the world (and markets) fit the picture we have painted rather than seeing the picture's true colors. I submit to you that we spend most of our time trying to prove that we are right rather than *being* right (you will need to really spend some time thinking about this one).

So, if you can identify with this truth, then you must be thinking about how to get to a place of seeing The Truth most of the time, if not all the time. Please recognize that this is a process. It will take some time, and I will have to take you through some "breaking" (will explain next week). In the meantime, here is what you need to do this week to start retraining your eyes, your brain, and your soul.

Let's start with your eyes, which will lead you to your brain and soul. You will need to start seeing things as you have never seen them before. No, I don't mean seeing them in a different light or from a different perspective. I mean seeing them as if you had just been given eyesight for the first time. I hope that you felt the impact of that statement. If you didn't, then you were seeing or hearing your interpretation of that statement, rather than the impact of the actual statement. So let me ask you again. How would you be, how would you respond, how would you feel if you had just opened your eyes and started to see things for the first time? Do you *realize* the fascination that you would have? Do you realize that if you were seeing a fat person and a muscular person for the first time, you would not have those definitions? You would just simply be fascinated by the differences of your experience. You would not have a negative response to one over the other. You would simply see them as is—you would simply see the truth.

If you really take some time (several to many hours) to understand, meditate, assimilate, and implement this truth, then you will begin to understand the *impact* that truth *will* have on your trading results as well as your life's results. If you get the impact of how incredibly powerful this truth is, then you should have a fantastic week being totally fascinated by everything around you; your kids, your mate, your pets, your car, traffic, the trees, the sky, and so on and so forth.

So, when you are done reading the last few words of this week's column, please close your eyes and when you re-open them you will see a totally new world. You will see The Truth about things as they are, you will look forward to discovery, you will look forward to next week.

Week Seven

> Many ideas grow better when transplanted into another mind than in the one where they sprang up.
>
> —Oliver Wendell Holmes

I want to start off this week's lesson by letting you know how very proud I am of you for having come this far. It takes courage to become the real you—and you are courageous. It takes work, and you are doing the work. There are great rewards in store for you, and you will get them. So, let's get to work. I mentioned the word *breaking* last week. And I also mentioned that I would be sharing more about who I am, as you continue to share with me who you are. I need to explain breaking before I can walk you through it. I am going to do that by sharing a personal story with you, and although this is not easy, I will do it for two reasons. One is for you to get to know who I am; the other is so that you understand that what I teach usually has been experienced first and doesn't just come out of a book, so I hope you're paying attention.

I started out in the business world at a very young age. I was very creative and very entrepreneurial. By the time I was sixteen I was making more money than my father and the school principal combined. By the time I was eighteen I had bought my first apartment building. By the time I was twenty-five I had a net worth of well over a million dollars. That was the good part.

The unfortunate part was that I started to associate who I was with how much money I was making. My whole self-identity became attached to my financial net worth. Between the time I was twenty-seven and twenty-eight I experienced the definition of extreme pain and of "breaking." First, I lost all of the money, which was devastating due to the fact that my whole self-identity was tied to the money. Next, I lost the only romantic relationship that I had been involved in up to that point, which had lasted six-and-a-half years. Then, as if that wasn't enough, the only person that I could really talk to, the only remaining comfort, my only best friend, was killed in a car accident. The pain was unbearable.

I had gone from having everything to having nothing. There were no answers. I was totally empty and totally hopeless. I did not want to go on. It was from that place of brokenness, and by the grace of God, that the Master Potter started to mold a different man, a much wiser man.

I share this personal trial with you not only to give you my personal example of breaking but also to remind you of some of the trials that you may have gone through, to remind you that some of your biggest lessons arrive shortly after your biggest trials and tribulations. So, why is that? And is there another way? Why did the Israelites have to be in the desert for forty years before they could reach the promised land? Why do our children have to be disciplined sometimes in order to be taught? And why do we have to incur a lot of losses in order to get to a place of mastering the art of trading or the art of living? This is where I tie this week's lesson to last week's lesson.

Last week we talked about the three kinds of truth. And the truth is that life has a way of hitting us hard as long as we are holding on to our interpretation of the truth or other people's interpretation of the truth. In fact, life has a way of hitting us hard, and continuing to do that until we are totally broken and totally nonresistant. At that point, life gifts us with the truth. That is when you start to see the power of wisdom, the power of God working in your life. You will need to think about this and meditate about this a great deal in order to get the full impact. You will need to go back and rethink your trials in order to possibly rediscover the true reasons for their occurrence.

In a previous paragraph I asked two questions: "Why is that?" and, "Is there another way?" The answer to the first question is that you must break the old ways and interrupt old patterns in order to begin anew. It is impossible to get pure water by filling a cup that has some contaminated water in it. The best way is to start with a new cup, an empty cup. So, become a new container. The answer to the second question, Is there another way? is a very profound *yes,* which I have already given you if you were reading between the lines. (Just the way life does it, between the lines.) The simple truth is we would not need to experience breaking and the pain that comes with it if we did not resist. Your children would not have to endure the pain of discipline if they simply accepted your direction. And you would not have to endure as much agony regarding your trading if you simply accepted the truth about trading, which I will expand on next week.

So, in summary, you may want to do a few things. First, you need to to make a decision to break and throw out the old pottery in order for something new to be molded. Second, you need to celebrate the empty space that allows for a new beginning. Third, you need to rejoice in the abundance, the exhilaration, the satisfaction, and the peace that come from filling up your new container. So, go back and put it all together, revisit all of the past weeks from the beginning, be proud of what you have become, and get excited about the fact that we are about to bring the future into the present. Rejoice in who you are, you have paid the price—now get ready to reap the rewards, look forward to the future, look forward to next week.

Week Eight

How To Become Much Better Than Very Good

Welcome to week eight. So, are you an empty container? Have you gone through a house cleaning? Are you ready to be filled with all the right stuff? If you have done the work (see last week's work on "breaking"), if you have thought and meditated, then you will understand why military training happens the way it does throughout the world and since the beginning of time. It is exactly the same philosophy that is implemented in martial arts training. Have you ever thought of why that seems to be the case? Would you also agree with me that that kind of training seems to produce a tremendous amount of discipline and mastery?

You must recognize that the martial arts masters, teachers, and coaches do what they do (breaking) for one extremely important reason—*survival*. You see, they recognize that the student's life depends on their training. To not leave any room for error they must go through the reprogramming and/or "emptying" process in order for the student to get exactly what he or she needs. So, if you are willing to be taught—then you will learn the lesson. So, let's start your training.

Reaching true mastery isn't a matter of attending weekend seminars or becoming a little better at what you do. Whether you want to become a skilled pianist, a master trader, or a great parent, you must commit to the discipline of practice, practice, practice. Once you view mastery as a journey and acknowledge that the trip may be difficult and slow at times, you'll have the stamina and the good sense to go beyond the setbacks that emerge along the way. Throughout history, most people have assumed that life's superstars were "gifted" people, that they were just born talented. The truth is, most people have *become* talented simply because they have worked very hard at it.

A 1994 article in *American Psychologist* reported that teachers at a conservatory were asked to rate which student violinists were likely to become world class musicians, which were likely to become good professional musicians, and which would be just average. Those who were classified as potentially great had practiced 10,000 hours, those in the middle range had practiced 7,500 hours, and the mediocre had practiced 5,000 hours.

Just simply practicing, however, will not guarantee that you will reach the level of mastery. The trick is to practice your skill correctly from the start (refer back to the martial arts example). What that means is, if you set out on the wrong track you will *never* achieve your *full* potential. Let me give you an example. Many people start playing tennis with poor form—holding their shoulders high and their wrist stiff without stepping through the swing. Over time they'll get better at the game, but they'll never become as good as they could be unless they use the right technique. So, putting all of this together, you will probably come to the conclusion and understanding of why it is critically important that you find the right teacher. It is the shortest distance from where you are to where you want to go. It is exactly the reason why all professional athletes have coaches even though they are very good at what they do. Without a coach to guide you along your path, you'll waste time and energy. The ideal coach is someone who has achieved what you want to achieve and who is willing and able to share what he or she has learned, preferably one on one when possible. This is a master teacher, coach or mentor.

Choosing a coach has to be taken very seriously. You are literally putting your future, your improvement, your mastery into someone else's hands. Trust and respect must be in place. Before committing yourself, do your homework—verify the person's integrity and expertise. If I had my money on the line as a trader I would want to see a proven, profitable track record before I allowed and trusted anybody's coaching. So, once you have done your homework, there is nothing more valuable and cost effective than having a coach or mentor.

In summary, as you continue your journey, you must make a commitment to practicing (never giving up) until you become a master. Second, you must make absolutely certain that you are learning the right material in the right form. Third, and most critical, you must spend the time, turn every rock, do whatever it takes to find your coach and mentor. It is wise for me at this point (as I know many of you will be asking) to address the issue of one-on-one coaching with me, which I will only do with those of you who are totally committed to being among the best traders. Otherwise, I will be more than happy to recommend others with whom you can work. However, whether you are coached by me or someone that I recommend, if you have been getting everything that I have taught so far and are serious about your results, then it is critically important that you follow through on this issue. We are about to start rocking and rolling, so stay committed, be alert, put on your armor, follow through, and look forward to next week.

Week Nine

"I can see that pleasures are to be avoided if greater pains be the consequence, and pains to be coveted that will terminate in greater pleasure."

—Michael Day Montaigne

Welcome to week nine. How many of you have skipped over a word that you didn't understand while reading something rather than stop and take the time to look it up? In other words, how many of you have opted to take the easy way out? The truth is, a lot of us are guilty of that. In fact, we spend most of our lives trying to decide between what we would like to do versus what we end up doing. If we were to put that decision-making process under a microscope we would come to the conclusion that everything we do in life comes down to what we consider to be pain and pleasure.

The problem is that most of us face our decisions about what is going to cause pain or pleasure in the short term instead of the long term. Yet, in order to succeed (see the opening quote) and acquire most of the things that we value and desire requires us to be able to break through the wall of short-term pain in order to have long-term pleasure. We must put aside the passing moments of fear and temptation (greed) and focus on what is most important in the long term—core values and personal standards, as well as *long-term* profits. You must also remember that it is not actual pain that drives us but our fear that *something* will lead to pain. It is not actual pleasure that *drives* us, but our belief—our internal sense of certainty—that taking a certain action will somehow lead to pleasure. We are not driven by the reality but by our *perception* of reality.

So, what ends up happening by our trying to avoid pain and gain pleasure in the short term is that we end up creating long-term pain for ourselves. Let me give you an example. When we first start trading we start with the fantasy of phenomenal short-term gains. Yet we lose track of everything life has taught us about how one arrives at phenomenal gains. We forget the truth about the fact that in order to achieve phenomenal gains, one has to make an investment of capital, time, and education.

But to make this investment would require a bit of short-term discomfort, which a lot of people will end up pushing aside, thinking only of the immediate gratification of the phenomenal gain. Of course, they end up experiencing nothing but long-term loss and long-term pain. Not long ago I went to a trading seminar and ended up sitting next to an orthopedic surgeon who was just being introduced to the subject of trading. He had heard from a lot of his friends about how they had made a lot of money in the stock market, specifically with dot-com companies. So, of course, he wanted to get in on the action.

On top of that, he was actually dissatisfied with being an orthopedic surgeon, so he immediately started creating the fantasy that he could replace the income from his practice (about half-a-million dollars a year) by simply becoming a day trader.

I tried to convince him that he was playing Russian roulette, but he would not hear any of it. He had already attached so much pleasure to the idea of replacing his income that he would not look at the possibility of having to go back to school the way he did to become a doctor in order to be able to duplicate that income. He only wanted to focus on the payoff, not on the price that has to be paid.

Friends, it is time that you come to an understanding that everything you do in life is done based on your perception of what creates pain and what creates pleasure. It is also time that we start looking at your internal structure, your internal mechanism that determines your definition of pain and pleasure. We will do that as we continue our work here, but in the meantime, the lesson for this week is to commit to attaching a great deal of pleasure to long-term goals, to attach a great deal of pleasure to the process and the journey. It is the only way to get to a place of experiencing the pleasure of attaining a goal that keeps on paying off.

I have prepared you over the last several weeks for this moment. You have been coached in writing down your commitments, in seeing the truth, in becoming an empty container, and in stopping to take an inventory (go back and read last week's lesson, and do it if you haven't) in order to be ready to make the transition that we are about to make now—the transition from fantasy about profits to the reality of profits in every aspect of life. You are now ready to accept the truth that a price has to be paid, and you are now ready to pay that price. So, create a great deal of pleasure for having come this far, and for having the courage to see the truth. I assure you that having come this far puts you in the top 5 percent of the human race, of people who know what it takes and are willing to do what it takes. I can honestly say now that I am honored to be your coach, and I look forward to meeting you in person one day, as we both look forward to next week.

Week Ten

Creating Lasting Change

Welcome to week ten. It's been almost three months since you started reading this column. You should, at this point, be noticing some lasting changes in your life. Maybe you're approaching things from a different angle, maybe you are experiencing the benefits of a new habit. Whatever it is that has changed should be making you a different person than the person you were. If you can honestly say that that is the case then—terrific—we'll just keep building on that. But, if you cannot honestly say that part of your core belief system has shifted or changed, then I would say something is missing, and therefore the information that follows will be helpful.

For changes to be of any true value they have to be lasting and consistent. You've all experienced change that lasts for a short period of time only to feel let down and disappointed in the end. In fact, many people attempt change with a sense of fear and dread, because unconsciously they think that the change is going to be temporary. A prime example of this is someone who needs to start an exercise program, but finds him- or herself putting it off primarily because he or she unconsciously believes that whatever pain is endured in order to create the change might only bring a short-term reward. I'd like to share with you three powerful principles of change that, if implemented consistently, could have a powerful and lasting effect on your life.

The first principle is the principle of raising your standards. Anytime you sincerely want to make a change, the first thing you must do is raise your standards. You need to increase what you demand of yourself. You need to write down all of the things that you will no longer accept in your life, all of the things you will no longer tolerate, and most importantly you need to write down all that you aspire to become. A number of years ago, after doing a lot of self-work and internal change, I decided that it was time to move on to be the person that I had become and leave behind everything that represented the person that I was. This included the place where I lived and the people that I surrounded myself with. And although it was difficult, I realized I could no longer tolerate people who were "stuck" to be in my life. It's time that you get rid of dead weight—yours and others.

The second principle involves changing your belief system. If you raise your standards but don't really *believe* you can meet them, then it will be hard to even try. You will be lacking the sense of certainty that allows you to tap the deepest capacity that is within you and moves you forward. Our beliefs are like unquestioned commands, telling us how things are, what seems possible, and what seems impossible, what we can and cannot do. They shape every action, every thought, and every feeling that we experience. As a result, changing our belief system is critical to making any real and lasting change in our lives. We must develop a sense of certainty that we *can* and *will* meet the new standards we have set for ourselves before we actually *do* it. An example of people who raised their standards and then believed they could reach them are heroes like Abraham Lincoln, Mohandas Gandhi, Martin Luther King, Jr., Walt Disney, and Mother Theresa. Empowering beliefs—the sense of certainty that you can—is the force behind any great success throughout history.

Finally, the third principle is one of developing a different set of strategies. In order to keep your commitment to the new standards you have set for yourself, you need to develop a new set of strategies. A great core belief that you can develop for yourself is a belief that if you set a higher standard and absolutely believe you can achieve it, that you will simply *find a way*. You will do whatever it takes to find the best strategy. And remember that the easiest way, in most cases, of finding the best strategy is to find someone who already has a great strategy in place and just simply duplicate that strategy.

So, in summary, I encourage you to raise your standards to a level that excites you, that compels you to a new beginning, then absolutely believe you can and must achieve. Then do whatever it takes to determine what the best strategy is and/or finding someone who has the strategy in place. Then follow it until you reach your goal. Keep your feet on the ground. Keep reaching for the stars, and look forward to next week.

Weeks Eleven and Twelve

Seven Steps to Success

Welcome to weeks eleven and twelve. So, did you find something in your life that you want to raise the bar on? Maybe trading, or maybe something else? If you did, then did you stop to analyze your belief system about that particular aspect of your life? Did you also consider changing your strategy? If you have actually implemented these three steps regarding an aspect of your life, then you are truly getting what this is about—the fact that it's about doing and being rather than just reading. So, before you continue on with this week's work, stop and either congratulate yourself or do some soul searching about how committed you are to doing the work that is outlined here. I will remind you again and again that the road to success is a "road less traveled"; however, it offers a much better view, so let's move on.

Allow yourself two weeks to do the work that follows, as I think it's going to be necessary for you to take the extra time to do the work properly. We are going to start looking at seven areas of mastery that create an incredible life. I've mentioned before that in order to become very successful at any one aspect of your life, you have to have balance in other aspects of your life. So, over the next thirty days we are going to look at balance and mastery in the following seven categories: emotional mastery, physical mastery, mental mastery, financial mastery, relationship mastery, time mastery, and spiritual mastery.

Emotional Mastery

Emotional mastery is the most critical of all the categories. Mastering your emotions will speed up the process in mastering the other categories. Think about it. The reason you want to become a great trader, or make a lot of money, is not because of the fact that you enjoy accumulating a lot of little green pieces of paper but rather because of how you are going to *feel* by becoming a great trader and accumulating a lot of money. It will give you more freedom, and it will allow you to do things for yourself and people that you love.

Virtually everything we do is done to change the way we feel—yet most of us have little or no training in how to do this quickly and effectively. It's amazing how we often use our mind's ability to work ourselves into an emotional mess, forgetting about the multitude of talents and abilities at our disposal. Too many of us leave ourselves at the mercy of outside events over which we may have no control, failing to take charge of our emotions—over which we have *all* the control. How else can we explain the fact that while the United States has less than 5 percent of the world's population, its people consume more than 50 percent of the world's cocaine supply. We spend billions of dollars on alcohol consumption, and over 20 million Americans a year are diagnosed as clinically depressed and consume $750 million worth of the antidepressant drug Prozac.

We will go through the process of discovering why we do the things we do and the triggers for the emotions we experience most often. You will be able to develop a step-by-step plan to show you how to identify which emotions are empowering and which are destructive, and how to use both kinds to your advantage, so that your emotions become a powerful tool rather than a great disability.

Physical Mastery

It's not worth having anything you've ever dreamed of unless you have the physical health to be able to enjoy it. Do you wake up every morning feeling energized, powerful, and ready to take on the world? Or do you wake up feeling tired and resentful at having to start the day? Are you going to become an example, or are you going to become a statistic? One of every two Americans dies of coronary disease, one of three dies of cancer. We mindlessly cram our bodies with high-fat, nutritionally empty foods, and we poison our systems with cigarettes as we sit passively in front of our TV sets. You must learn how to take control of your physical health so that you not only look good but feel good. Trading is a very demanding physical activity. If your body is not capable of handling the physical strain, this will affect your emotional ability. You must look at creating a body that radiates energy and vitality.

Mental Mastery

Your brain is the most powerful organ in your body, and just like the strongest muscle in your body, it must be exercised on a regular basis in order to grow. Otherwise it slowly decays and eventually stops working. Science has shown over and over again that in order to stay mentally alert we have to push our brain. One of the best ways of combating Alzheimer's disease and memory loss is to continue to learn new subjects. If you take care of your brain, it will take care of you. So, you must get into a habit of feeding your brain daily, just as you do your body.

We will cover the remaining categories of mastery and balance in the next segment, two weeks from today. In the meantime, what are you going to do with what you've just read and the categories we've discussed here? Is this going to be the last time you read this material, or is it going to be the first of fourteen times (once a day) that you read it? Are you going to leave it on the screen, or are you going to print it out? Are you going to start looking at the different aspects of your life and do something about them? Or are you going to passively watch as time and life pass you by? If your answer is, *"yes*, I am going to do this, I am really going to 'get off my ass' and do this, I am going to look at these categories and develop a plan of improvement, a plan of work, a plan of mastery," then I applaud you for being one of the few, the chosen, the proud, the achievers. It is with pride that I look forward to continuing to work with you as we look forward to the next two weeks.

Weeks Thirteen and Fourteen

Welcome to weeks thirteen and fourteen. How have you been in the last two weeks? Did you take time out to do an inventory of your life, as suggested a couple of weeks ago? Did you particularly stop to look at the emotional, physical, and mental categories of your life? Have you ever thought of reaching mastery in those three categories? Did you think about it in the last two weeks? Are you starting to get a clue at this point that if you want an incredible life—incredible in every aspect of it, not just trading—you're going to have to take the time to think about it and get into the habit of making it happen?

If you have not heard me say this before, then it's time that I reminded you that trading is the ultimate contact sport. Let me repeat that again—*the ultimate contact sport*. What that means is that you have to become a tough, lean, and clever machine. In order to do that you absolutely must develop all aspects of who you are. So let's continue with more of the categories that we need to reach mastery in.

Weeks Fifteen and Sixteen

"As the fletcher whittles and makes straight his arrows, so the master directs his straying thoughts."

—Author Unknown

Welcome back. Are you beginning to feel a sense of mastery, now that you have been working on and mastering five essential parts of your life? Doesn't it feel good to know what it is that you need to be working on? Today we get to touch on the last two of the seven categories of mastery. Again, it is recommended that you work on and explore and develop each one of the two categories per week. Therefore, spend the time to really explore, dissect, and look at each category of mastery in detail. As you know by now, the more you put into this, the more you'll get out of it. So, let's keep going.

Time Mastery

Masterpieces take time. It took Michelangelo many years to paint the Sistine Chapel. It took the Egyptians many decades to build the pyramids, and it took God six days (that's many millenniums for you and me, in man's time) to create the universe. So, you've heard before that masterpieces take time, you know that it's true. Yet, for some reason, we seem to have lost track of that truth, we seem to have forgotten that masterpieces take time. We seem to have deteriorated into a people who want immediate gratification, who want things to happen yesterday. But as you know by now, it doesn't matter what we want if it doesn't fit with reality.

It doesn't matter if our reality and our timing don't fit with the reality and timing of the way things happen. What needs to happen will happen, in the time in which it needs to happen. It doesn't matter if you want to become a great trader in less than five years, even though you've just started. It doesn't matter that you hear that it's possible to take $10,000 and turn it into a million dollars in less than a year. The only thing that does matter, the only thing that is true (and therefore, anyone telling you anything else is simply lying to you) is the reality that if you want to become a world-class trader *it's going to take time.*

So now you know why, from the very beginning, I told you that this was going to be a long, continuing process. Now you know why I take you through the steps, one step at a time. You're going to have to come to grips with one of two realities about time. Either you use time wisely and in your favor, or you try to hurry it and miss it, or completely lose it. Just like with everything else you've learned so far, you need to stop and consider mastering the commodity of time. You need to stop and figure out how to live in, maximize, and get the most out of each moment, recognizing that it will never come back. You need to be wise enough to look at past time to consider how to invest and maximize future time. So, take time to get time.

Spiritual Mastery

In all the time that I have been trading, reading the hundreds of books that I have read on the subject, and talking to thousands of people all over the world about trading, never once did I hear anyone formally address the subject of one's spiritual belief system as being an integral part to success. So, it would not at all surprise me to have some of you wonder why I am going to become the first person to formally address the subject. I am going to make it real simple for you to understand.

Either you work and function as a total human being, with emphasis on *being*, or you don't. You are either tapping into the ocean of unlimited wisdom or you're not. I think that you would all agree with me that if one had the choice of tapping into unlimited wisdom, yet looked the other way, one would be considered foolish. So, although it might be hard for your mind to grasp, the idea that I am relating to you is that if you truly want to become a world class trader, you need to build on a foundation of mastery as a total human being. And if you're going to become a total human being, then you need to build on the spiritual foundation that this country was built on. You need to rediscover your Creator. You need to rediscover God.

So there, I've said it. We have covered seven categories of Mastery, the seven pieces of the puzzle, the seven keys to the world's treasures. No wonder they call seven a lucky number. Now you have a decision to make. Are you going to continue in the never-ending process of Mastery in the seven categories? Are you going to continue the work and continue receiving the rewards? Or are you going to look the other way and pretend that it never happened?

One thing is certain: if you've come this far, you will never be able to blame anyone else for your state of being any more. Now you know where to look if something is missing in your life. The answer will always be in one of the categories.

In summary, I hope and pray that you stay on the road less traveled, away from the masses, the ignorant, and the bankrupt. I hope that you will join me, becoming the best that you can be, on this journey that never ends. No end to emotional satisfaction, no end to physical health and well-being, no end to mental ability and intelligence, no end to relationship understanding and satisfaction, no end to magnifying and enjoying time, and no end to giving to and receiving the God who created it all. Most of all, I pray that there will never be an end to this relationship that I have developed with you, as we both continue on this fascinating and joyful journey. Until next time.

10

MONEY MANAGEMENT

Ryan Jones

There is no question that today's trader is more equipped with knowledge, ideas, trading strategies, indicators, and the ability to combine these elements into his or her trading than ever before in the history of this industry. Yet, it is amazing that the statistics of profitable traders versus unprofitable traders remains relatively constant year after year. These statistics are bleak at best. Upwards of 80 to 90 percent of all traders lose money by year's end. Traders may trade to make more money than they would investing in conventional investment vehicles. Yet the percentages indicate that few make money trading, and most don't accomplish that goal.

There are many reasons and many theories as to why these facts remain true. One reason is that people who get involved in trading have very short-term goals. They are falsely led to believe that the short-term goal of getting rich quick is valid and even realistic through day trading, because day trading itself is extremely short-term in comparison to standard investment vehicles. However, if one is going to successfully trade in these markets, one must have a longer term outlook. That doesn't mean that the time period that a trade is held onto should be longer, but that the overall plan and expectations should be based on a longer time period, not a trade-by-trade, day-by-day, or even week-by-week period.

Copyright © 2001 Ryan Jones. All rights reserved.

There are two basic aspects of trading. The first is when to get in and when to get out of which markets. This aspect is covered through indicators, oscillators, moving averages, price action patterns, trading systems, software, newsletters, hot lines, fundamental reports—and the list goes on. It encompasses exit rules such as where to place stops, where to place profit targets, trailing stops, and whatever other means are used to decide when to exit a trade. This aspect covers all types of trading, including day trading, long-term trading, break-out trading, trend-following trading, and others. Sadly, most traders emphasize solely this aspect of trading. I believe that a trader emphasizes this one aspect as a result of his or her inability or unwillingness to address a longer term trading plan.

The second aspect of trading deals with something that all traders, without exception, make a decision on every time they make a trade. That aspect deals with how much of their account they are going to risk on that trade. Sadly, most traders spend very little time understanding what effect that decision is going to have on the overall performance of their account. Most traders have heard suggestions thrown out by their brokers or have read books that make a suggestion but with little disclosure about what the pros and cons will be. If you are in that boat, the next section is for you.

Percentage of Risk

If you happen to be in the camp that does not regard money management principles as a highly important and powerful aspect of trading, consider the following example:

A coin flipping game is offered in Las Vegas. The rules are that a coin is going to be flipped in the air 100 times. If the coin lands heads up, you will lose $1.00 for every $1.00 you bet. But, if the coin lands tails up, you will win $2.00 for every $1.00 you bet. (Obviously, if this game were really offered in Las Vegas, the coin would not have a tails side, but that is beside the point.) Regard this coin as having an equal chance of landing heads or tails with each flip. You are given $100 total to bet on the coin-flipping game. You may bet as much or as little as you wish on each flip ($1.00 minimum increments). However, being the savvy trader that you are, you are going to apply some sort of money management rules to maximize your return over the 100 flips. These are the choices you have.

You may risk 10 percent of the account balance on each flip of the coin.

You may risk 25 percent of the account balance on each flip of the coin.

You may risk 40 percent of the account balance on each flip of the coin.

You may risk 51 percent of the account balance on each flip of the coin.

As your account balance increases, the size of your bet will also increase. As the account balance decreases, the size of your bet on the next flip will also decrease. If you choose 10 percent and the next flip of the coin is a winner, you bet $10 on that flip and therefore you win $20. Your account balance is now $120, and you bet 10 percent, or $12, of the new amount on the next flip. If the flip is a loser, you lose only $12, and the account balance is $108. Round down and the next bet will be $10 again. This one is a winner, and you are up to $128. And the cycle goes on for 100 flips of the coin. Which of the options would you choose? Does it make a big difference?

If you chose:

10 percent, your account would have grown to $4,700 after 100 flips!

25 percent, your account would have grown to $36,100 after 100 flips!

40 percent, your account would have grown to $4,700 after 100 flips!

51 percent, your account would have decreased down to $31 after 100 flips!

This assumes that the flips would have had a fifty-fifty chance of coming up heads (or tails) regardless of order. The question was, "Does it make a big difference?" and the answer is a resounding *yes!* Increasing the percentage at risk on each flip by only 15 percent (going from 10 percent to 25 percent) increased the total return by 668 percent! Increasing the percentage from 40 percent to 51 percent (11 percent, you turned an absolute no-lose situation into a losing track record. We'll get back to this example later.

Benefits of Proper Money Management

The bottom line is that money management plays a huge role in the overall success of traders. It will play a huge role in how successful you are as a trader in the next five years. What can proper money management do?

1. Keep you from being wiped out.
2. Allow you to approach system trading with a plan and the ability to continue trading even if the system fails miserably.
3. Increase your profits five- to tenfold (500 percent to 1,000 percent) without increasing the overall risk of the account dramatically (many times it decreases the overall percent at risk in the account).
4. Protect those profits should the system end up failing miserably.

Consider the following example:

One trader traded a relatively inexpensive stock trading service for one year. During that one year, the trader's account reached $27,000 in profits. The following year, the service only made $15,000. The total profit of the trader was $42,000.

Another trader also traded the same hotline for the first year. However, this trader applied conservative money management principles to the trading. The first year, his profits reached $63,000 instead of only $27,000, which is an increase of 233 percent over the profits of the first trader. The second year, however, total profits were $113,000 instead of only $15,000, bringing the total profits for the two years of trading up to $176,000. This computes to a total increase of 419 percent more profits for the second trader.

The third year of trading for the hotline took a terrible turn. It lost $15,000. Trader number one was at $27,000 in profits for the three years of trading. Trader number two, however, was at $102,000 in total profits. This means that trader number one gave back *all* (100 percent) of the profits gained during the second year of trading, while the second trader gave back only 65 percent of the profits gained during the second year. The second trader ended up with $75,000 more in profits than the first trader!

The question for this example is: Which trader do you want to be?

Fixed Fractional Method

We will begin our look at money management with the most common method, called the "fixed fractional" method. This method encompasses everything from risking no more than 2 percent or 3 percent of your account on each trade, to trading one unit (a unit can be one option, 100 shares of stock, or any other size of fixed standard) for every $10,000 in your account, to what is called "optimal f" (stands for optimal fixed fraction). We will take a brief look at each while pointing out the pros and cons of using such highly recommended methods.

The first method is risking 2 percent to 3 percent of your account on each trade. This is recommended to many day traders by many brokers and is also a popular money management method with money managers. It states that a trader will not risk more than 2 percent or 3 percent of the total account balance on each trade. For this example, the total current account balance will be $25,000. The next trade signal comes in IBM with $1.00 total risk per share. Since no more than 2 percent can be risked on each trade, a simple math calculation is performed to determine how many shares should be traded. That calculation is as follows: Total risk on trade divided by total percent of account at risk ($1.00 ÷ 2 percent or .02 = $50.00). In other words, to follow the rules of this method, you would place on 1 share for every $50 in the account ($25,000 ÷ $50 = 500 shares). Since IBM, at the time of this writing, is trading at 110, 500 shares would require a $55,000 account with no margin—with margin, a $27,500 account. It could not be placed. Obviously, if you didn't have enough to risk with 2 percent, you wouldn't have enough to risk with any higher percentage.

There are a couple of things that should be pointed out about using this method. First, it cannot be used without regard to any other factors. The main factor in the example is the price of the stock being traded, not the risk. If you had the same $1.00 risk with a $20 stock, obviously, you wouldn't have a problem placing the trade. The second is that this is not an efficient way to determine the size to trade on every trade. It does not take into consideration the overall goal or overall risk tolerances of the account. If the overall risk tolerance level in the account is only 10 percent, it would only take five losing trades in a row to reach that level. And, in day trading, if you have never suffered five losing trades in a row, wait, you will. If the overall risk tolerance level is 50 percent of the account, then it would take twenty-five losing trades in a row before you realize that overall level. And, if you have ever suffered twenty-five losing trades in a row, you should change your method.

The next method we will take a look at is "one unit for every $10,000 in your account" (again, a unit is any set standard determined by the trader). This method is widely recommended because of its simplicity and general ease of implementation. I find it interesting that so many traders are willing to use this for those two reasons. Hundreds, even thousands of hours and thousands, even hundreds of thousands of dollars are spent on where to get in and where to get out of which markets, but money management is reduced to a 3.5 second line of "one unit for every $10,000." Few traders know the actual effect this statement has on the overall performance of a method.

One (1) unit for every $10,000 in an account is just another way of saying that you are going to risk X percent of your equity on each trade. For example, if your largest potential losing trade is $1,500 and you trade one unit for every $10,000 in your account, you are risking 15 percent of your account on the next trade. The calculation for this is: largest loss divided by required equity per contract equals the percent at risk on every trade. If your largest potential loss is $1,000, then you are risking 10 percent of your equity on every trade. The problem with this statement is very similar to the prior 2 percent method. It is not taking into account the available capital for the trade. If one unit is 1,000 shares risking $1.50 per share, the risk is only $1,500, but it takes $110,000 to trade 1,000 shares of IBM without margin and $55,000 with margin. With only $25,000 in the account, you are supposed to trade only 2,500 shares. Obviously, not possible. The logical way around that is to make one unit smaller. If we make one unit equal to 1 share, we could trade a whopping 2 shares. If one unit equals 100 shares, then we would trade 250 shares, which still costs $27,500 without margin. Obviously, other factors have to be taken into consideration.

With this method of managing your money, I could stop there, and the point would be quite clear. But to drive home the argument, I will go to the next most commonly recommended money management method called "optimal f."

Optimal f

Optimal f is short for the optimal fixed fraction to be used on any given trading method and/or system. For example, I gave a coin flipping illustration where risking 25 percent of your account would have yielded more return than any other percentage possible. Twenty-five percent (25 percent) is the optimal f of that particular situation. Optimal f is not 25 percent for every trading situation. As a matter of fact, optimal f is different for every trading situation.

Notice that risking 10 percent of the account on the coin flipping example yielded the same amount of profits as risking 40 percent. Twenty-five percent (25 percent) is at the peak. This means that 11 percent yields the same as 39 percent, 20 percent yields the same as 30 percent, and 24 percent yields the same as 26 percent. It is a perfect bell curve. However, after 40 percent something begins to happen to that curve, because by the time you reach 51 percent, the positive expectation actually loses money. Everything under 10 percent still makes money.

This bell curve exists with every trading system, methodology, and performance record. Trading is not a controlled statistical game like flipping a coin. The win-loss ratio on each trade is different, and the odds of the next trade being a winner is not necessarily a fixed number either. Optimal f is determined by filing the past history of trades through a mathematical formula (which is not relevant for this chapter) to determine what the optimal f *was* for the previous trades. Notice that I said *was*. It is impossible to project what optimal f *will be* in the future. This becomes rather important when you realize that if you trade a fixed fraction that is higher than the optimal f, you could actually end up losing money. For example, if you calculate optimal f for the past 100 trades at 15 percent and trade risking 15 percent on every trade, the next 100 trades may have an optimal f of only 10 percent. If that is the case, you are trading too much risk. If you were to trade 21 percent, you would lose money. Going back to the 2 percent method, optimal f for trading may only be 10 percent, but based on the example given earlier of trading IBM or any higher priced stock, it becomes impossible to use optimal f. In addition, even if you could trade what *was* optimal f, drawdowns would be huge.

I think I have made a pretty good argument for finding a better solution to some of the most popular types of money management.

There are literally dozens of other reasons why any type of fixed fractional method should be avoided, but I do not think I need to continue to beat the proverbial dead horse.

Three Problems

There were three main problems that led me to do extensive research on the subject of money management. The first was the fact that the fixed fractional method was the only method available. The second was the fact that since I have a very low tolerance for risk, implementing a small fixed fraction such as 2 percent to 3 percent on each trade satisfied my low risk tolerance but set my alarm of impatience screaming. It would take forever for money management to have any real effect on my trading by using that method. The third problem and only other alternative was how to increase that percentage. This is why and how I developed the "fixed ratio" money management method.

Before I go any any further, I want to acknowledge for those extremely brilliant traders out there who are saying, "A ratio and a fraction are the same thing" that yes, generally, a ratio and fraction are the same thing. However, I want to make clear that the point of reference is completely different. At no time does the fixed ratio method reference the percentage being risked on every trade. It is a fixed ratio of something entirely different.

The fixed ratio method accomplished two things. First, it did not take long for the method to have a substantial effect on my trading and, in particular, my profits. And second, my risk level is now very tolerable, known, and controlled at all times. The formula for increasing and decreasing the number of units (or shares of stock) is as follows.

Starting with 1 unit:

Largest drawdown ÷ 2 = Variable input
Start account balance + (1 Variable input) = Account level that
    must be reached before the number of contracts is increased.
Largest drawdown = $5,000
Variable input = $2,500
Starting account balance = $25,000
Number of units traded = 1
Account level to increase to 2 units = $27,500

$25,000 + (1 \times \$2,500) = \$27,500$ (PLI, or Previous level of increase)

For trading a number of units greater than 1:

PLI + (Number of units traded × Variable input) = Account level required for additional increase.
PLI = $27,500
Variable input = $2,500
Number of units traded = 2
Account level to increase to 3 units = $32,500
$27,500 + (2 × $2,500) = $32,500

Essentially, what this method does is require that the same amount of profits be generated for each *increase in units* being traded prior to increasing to an additional unit. In the fixed fractional method, one unit was being traded for every X dollars in the account. For example, the 1 unit for every $10,000 in the account stated that, regardless of the number of units being traded, there would always be an increase once another $10,000 in the account was accumulated. Therefore, if you start out trading 1 unit with $10,000 in the account, you would go to 2 units once the account reached $20,000. One unit alone would have to pull in $10,000 to increase. But what happens when there is $100,000 in the account, and you are trading 10 units? You increase at $110,000. What 1 unit was required to produce in the beginning is now being required with 10 units. What took maybe thirty trades to produce the first increase in units now may only take three trades to produce. A $1,000 winning trade will now increase units from 10 to 11.

However, with the fixed ratio method, if it takes $2,500 in profits to increase from 1 to 2 units, it will take $25,000 in profits to increase from 10 to 11 units. (10 × $2,500 = $25,000). What took fifteen trades on average to increase from 1 to 2 units will take on average fifteen trades to increase from 10 to 11 units, and fifteen trades, on average, to increase from 99 to 100 units, and so forth.

The term "fixed ratio" comes from the fact that whatever variable input used is a fixed ratio to the largest drawdown. If the largest drawdown is $5,000 and the variable input used is $2,500, then the variable input is a fixed ratio of 2:1 to the drawdown. If the variable input is $1,000, then it is a fixed ratio of 5:1 to the largest drawdown.

General Rules

Before I break down this method further and illustrate its potential power, there are a few general rules of thumb to keep in mind. First, the higher the ratio, the more aggressive the method is. This, in turn, means that the lower the ratio, the more conservative the method is. More aggressive means more profits and more risk, and more conservative means less profits and less risk. Second, there is no "optimal r" or optimal fixed ratio that will yield more than others. There is no bell curve with this method. Finally, the lower the variable input, the higher the profits regardless of what relationship it is to the largest drawdown. For example, if the largest drawdown is $10,000 and a variable ratio of $5,000 is traded, it will not yield as many profits as a system that has only $5,000 in drawdowns, and a 2:1 ratio of $2,500 is used for the variable input. However, the total percent of the account at risk is relatively the same at any given time. Therefore, the lower the drawdown of a system and/or portfolio, the more effective the fixed ratio will be.

One of the most frequent questions I am asked when traders learn this method has to do with beginning trade size compared to increasing the first unit. The answer is that the initial *trade* size does not have to be the same as the initial *increase* size. Obviously, if the beginning trade size is 100 shares, the initial increase unit may only be 10 shares. If this is the case, the variable ratio should be determined by the drawdown expected with one unit equal to the increase size, not beginning trade size. If the expected drawdown based on 1 share totaled $50, the expected drawdown on one increase unit (10 shares) would be $500. As a result, you would increase from 100 shares (initial trade size) to 110 shares at $25,250. (1 unit × 250 + $25,000 = $25,250). The following would apply:

Increase another unit (10 shares) at $25,750. Total shares being traded = 120

Increase another unit (10 shares) at $26,500. Total shares being traded = 130

Increase another unit (10 shares) at $28,750. Total shares being traded = 140

Increase another unit (10 shares) at $30,250. Total shares being traded = 150

Increase another unit (10 shares) at $32,000. Total shares being traded = 160

Increase another unit (10 shares) at $34,000. Total shares being traded = 170

Increase another unit (10 shares) at $36,250. Total shares being traded = 180

Increase another unit (10 shares) at $38,750. Total shares being traded = 190

Increase another unit (10 shares) at $41,500. Total shares being traded = 200

Increase another unit (10 shares) at $44,500. Total shares being traded = 210

Increase another unit (10 shares) at $47,750. Total shares being traded = 220

Increase another unit (10 shares) at $51,250. Total shares being traded = 230

This method accomplishes several things. First, if offers the benefit of money management being applied almost immediately to the account. Since the beginning trade size was 100 shares but the increase trade size was 10 shares, the increase in shares came with only $2.50 per share profit! Secondly, if you have an average trade net profit of $2.50 per share, that means at the end of 100 trades, you will have made $25,000 in profits by trading a constant 100 shares on every trade without ever increasing. By increasing according to this application of the fixed ratio method, total profits in the account reach $146,000 trading 400 shares per trade. This is a 580 percent increase in net profits from the constant 100 share units. Meanwhile, if the $50 per share drawdown occurs, the constant 100 share account would drop by $5,000, or 10 percent. The account applying this level of the fixed ratio method would drop by almost $20,000, or 11.7 percent. This means that in order to increase the account profits by 580 percent, you are only taking on an additional 1.7 percent risk at this level! Forgetting percentages, the nonmoney management account would end up at $45,000, while the account applying the money management would end up at $151,000. That is a difference of $106,000 with the method only producing a total of $200 profit per share traded.

Increasing the trade size is something traders must do if they are going to start applying money management. Obviously, one of the worst things as far as profit potential is concerned is for the trader to not increase trade size as profits accrue. But what abut the initial risk of increasing trade size? For example, if the account increases to 110 shares at $25,250, what is the overall risk on the account if it suffers the $50 per share drawdown now instead of later on, after profits are achieved? If the account does not increase shares, the total risk would be for the account to drop down to $20,250. If the account increased to 110 shares and the very next trade was a loser of $1.50 per share, the account would drop to $25,085, which is below the equity level required to trade 110 shares. As a result, the number of shares on the following trade would decrease back down to 100 shares. If the remaining $48.50 drawdown per share were to take place, the account would drop down to $20,235 instead of $20,250. Total additional risk would be $15—not per share but *total*.

Obviously, there is much more to be considered. The examples given in this chapter are broad and for illustrative purposes only. When applying money management, there are three things that must be addressed, and they will be different for every trader. First, what is the goal of the account? Second, what is the total risk willing to be taken to achieve that goal? And third, what are the available resources to achieve the goal without violating the risk tolerance levels? With every trader, these things are going to be different. The more you understand money management, the more efficiently you will be able to apply it to your trading to accomplish your goals without violating your risk tolerance levels.

I would encourage every trader to learn more about this vital topic. Isn't it ironic that in the trading industry, 90 percent of the traders ignore money management *and* 90 percent of the traders lose money. Could there be a connection?

11

KEEPING YOUR TRADING PROFITS OUT OF THE GOVERNMENT COFFERS

Ted Tesser

This is the chapter about solutions. Inherent in the premise that there are solutions is the presumption that there must be problems. Which there are. In fact, there are several problems, not the least of which is that traders in this country are paying way too much tax on their profits to the federal and local governments. That is the first problem.

The second problem is that Americans today are not prepared for retirement by saving enough of their trading profits. The final problem can best be described by a plaque posted in a colleague's office. It read:

> *When you are alive, the Government will try to tax whatever they can.*
> *When you retire, they will tax whatever they let you save while you worked.*
> *And, when you die, they will take whatever they missed while you were alive*

Unfortunate, but true.

For those of you lucky enough to have built up wealth by trading and now want to pass it on to your heirs, the U.S. government has a nasty little surprise for you. The relative who will inherit the bulk of

Copyright © 2001 Ted Tesser. All rights reserved.

what you spent your whole life accumulating will be your greedy Uncle Sam.

Now, like I said, this is not a chapter about problems; it is one about solutions. And, as you can now surmise, the problems I will be providing solutions for are: most traders pay too much tax while they are trading. Most are not saving enough for retirement. Many traders who do retire will give most of that income back to the government when they retire. Some will have it litigated away by lawsuits, and what is left after they die will most likely not go to the ones they would like it to go to, but rather to a relative they would probably rather disinherit.

Among other things, this chapter will show you a way to disinherit the federal government. It will also show you how to keep the trading profits you work so hard to earn. And, I will ultimately show you, as traders, how to provide for an abundant retirement, a goal most of us have no idea how to achieve. These solutions are not difficult and can be easily implemented by virtually anyone willing to spend a surprisingly little amount of time to learn them.

Most traders spend all their time in front of a screen trying to squeeze the last point out of a trade. And they spend all their free time learning systems and methods to get them in or out of the market at precisely the best time to make maximum profits. You would be amazed at how little time it takes to learn how to keep the money you are trying so hard to make. This is a discipline that may not be as exciting and glamorous as that of making money, but it is ultimately is just as significant to your bottom line—therefore, infinitely more important than most people think. I will try to make this subject interesting and thereby somewhat understandable, so that at least you know enough to speak to a competent professional about it and help him or her implement the strategies that will truly make you quite wealthy—and keep you that way!

I will show you in this chapter how to make the ultimate trade— that of *ignorance for knowledge*. And, in choosing to make this trade, you, the trader and investor, will have chosen a path of abundance that will change your life forever. Hopefully you will find the time you've spent reading this chapter to have indeed been a profitable trade!

The Basics of Tax Planning

In my twenty-eight plus years in this field, the one thing I've always struggled with is how to minimize the effect of taxes for my clients. For the most part, the better they did, the worse their tax position became. This was because of the ruinous effect of capital gains taxes, income taxes, retirement taxes, estate taxes, gift tax, and all the other state and local taxes. You may not know this, but many people eventually give back about *90 percent* of their wealth to the government over their lifetime, when you consider all these tax liabilities.

It has gotten harder and harder for my clients to get positive rates of return after taxes. In order for them to maintain the same return in any given tax environment, it always seemed like my clients were forced to take many more risks with their capital to offset the impact of taxation. Before we get started here, let me say that some of the things I will be discussing in this chapter will be hard to believe. They're going to sound farfetched and too good to be true. Let me assure you that everything I recommend is clearly defined in the tax code.

Red, Gray, or Black and White?

There are several types of strategies that one can implement to avoid taxes and increase wealth.

1. The first type is strategies that are considered to be in the *red area* of the code. Strategies which are in the red are those that will clearly flag audits and, in fact, may subject the preparer and filer to tax-motivated transaction (TMT) penalties. None of my strategies will even approach this area.
2. The next strategy falls into the *gray area* of the law. These types of strategies are very aggressive. They are strategies that may at some point be challenged because of subjective and aggressive interpretations of the law. Again, none of my strategies fall into the gray area of the law.
3. Strategies that are *clearly black and white* interpretations of the law are the types of strategies I love to deal with. It is not worth the risk to me of subjecting my client or myself, for that matter, to the possibility of penalties, interest, and additional tax. I would much rather sleep well at night than implement a strategy that at some point may be challenged and disallowed by the IRS. Like in trading, it is then up to you to decide your level of risk

No Mystery

In reality, there are only two types of income tax strategies—those that involve *income* and those that involve *deductions*.

The first type we will look at are those strategies that involve doing something with your income. You can really only do four things with your income. You can:

1. *Transform it*, for example, into a lower tax bracket.
2. *Avoid it*, for example, turn taxable income into nontaxable.
3. *Decrease it*.
4. *Defer it* into another year or tax period.

On the other hand, you can really only do four things with your expenses. You can:

1. *Create them*, through paper losses (expenses you would normally have and now turn into deductions).
2. *Accelerate them* into the current year.
3. *Transform them* into more favorable deductions (such as: Schedule C deductions rather than Schedule A—we will talk more about this concept).
4. *Increase them*—make expenses that were previously nondeductible into deductible expenses.

My strategy consists of using all of these components to *eliminate* or *significantly reduce* your tax! Most traders feel that taxes are mandatory. In my experience I have found that they are not. You can actually eliminate or at least significantly reduce federal and state income tax. You can eliminate tax on your retirement plan. And you can also avoid the onerous estate tax.

By now you're probably saying to yourself, "That's insane." Well, I'm going to make an even crazier statement. The federal income tax, the retirement tax, and the estate tax are voluntary taxes. You can pay them if you want to, but if you wish to avoid them, you do not have to pay.

I am not talking about tax protestors—those who say that income tax is illegal, that the tax system was never ratified in the law. Take my word for it, income tax is legal. Furthermore, might makes right! If the government wants to tax you, it will. Fighting it, like fighting the market, is going to result in some unsavory consequences for you. Rather than fighting the government, I liken my strategies to *tax judo*. In other words, I use the government's own tax laws to help me to limit or eliminate tax.

A Paradigm Shift

In the sixteenth century, people believed the Earth was the center of the universe. They thought that all the planets revolved around the Earth. To think otherwise would have been heresy. In the late 1500s an Italian scientist named Galileo invented something called the telescope and thereby discovered that indeed the earth was simply one of the planets revolving around the sun.

Up until 1491, everybody knew the Earth was surely flat. If you sailed far enough to the world's outer reaches, you would fall off into space. That is until an Italian sailor named Christopher Columbus sailed from Europe to the West Indies and proved that the earth was in fact round.

Up until the mid-twentieth century, science was convinced that energy and matter were two distinct quantities. Along came a scientist named Albert Einstein who proved, through his theory of relativity, that energy and matter are, in fact, the same.

Up until 1997 there was no reference to trader status in the Tax Code. Although tax courts around the country and the U.S. Supreme Court had ruled that there existed a hybrid category (called the trader), both the IRS and most CPA practitioners would take the position that in order to be a business, traders had to have outside customers. Then came along the 1997 Tax Act, and Sections 475 (e) and (f), and the concept of individuals trading their own accounts as businesses was given written validity under the IRS Tax Code.

I have just illustrated two concepts called the *paradigm* and the *paradigm shift*. A paradigm is a set of rules or precepts through which the universe is viewed. It is a framework through which one makes sense of everything around them. A paradigm shift, on the other hand, is what occurs when something comes along to alter that set of rules or framework and hence an epiphany, or major change in consciousness, is attained.

Benjamin Franklin once said, ". . . in this world, nothing is certain but death and taxes"—the paradigm. I have always held that there is only one *sure thing*, and that everything else is negotiable (most of all, tax)—the paradigm shift. There are simple strategies available to all traders to eliminate or at least significantly decrease all income tax, tax on retirement accounts, and the ruinous estate tax. These strategies lie clearly in the black and white areas of the tax code. The best of these strategies utilize the reduction of income and/or the increasing of deductions.

Too Much Tax!

Whenever I give a seminar at a trading conference, I start out by asking what my audience's reasonable expectation of annual return on investment capital is. Depending on the audience, I usually get an answer of between 20 percent and 35 percent a year. This high expectation is probably due to the fact that the stock market has done exceptionally well over the past few years, and most people have grown accustomed to double-digit returns. In fact, in a recent *New York Times* survey, most of the people questioned expected to make at least 35 percent on their money per year over the next five years!

In actuality, over the past sixty-five or so years, the stock market has yielded about 12 percent annually (although many of my successful traders achieve significantly more). It doesn't matter what numbers you use, my illustration will make the same point. But for the sake of this illustration, let's assume that you could make 25 percent per year trading the stock market.

Let's also assume that you get out of college and you have no money; you get a job, get married, and start putting away money for retirement. In fact, you and your spouse each put away $2,000 per year into a mutual fund that earns 25 percent per year. That's all you ever do. You start at age twenty-one, and in a couple of years you and your spouse are making $100,000 jointly with a 7.5 percent increase in salary per year. You both work until you are age sixty-five, but save nothing but the $2,000 per year each, until you retire.

You may be surprised to find that by the time you retire, you and your spouse will have accumulated over $2.8 million—a tidy sum on which to retire! This is the power of compound interest and starting early in life. Now that makes two essential assumptions—first, that your interest accrues annually; and, second, that you pay your taxes annually, as well.

The next question I usually ask my audience is what they think the end result would have been if our fantasy couple had made one small adjustment to their financial plan. I ask them to assume that the couple continued to put away the same amount of money annually. They continued to achieve the same rate of return and to compound their investment income annually. Only now they were somehow able to avoid or defer paying tax on, but rather reinvested, this investment income during the period they saved the money.

I usually get a wide array of answers, but rarely do I ever get one close to the true increase in wealth that would occur. I usually get answers like twice that amount, four times that amount, and sometimes in a rare instance, ten or twenty times that amount.

But, in fact, none of these answers is even close! The true answer to this question is that if the couple were able to somehow avoid paying tax on the income, they would end up with approximately $367 million after the same period of time. This is an increase of over 13,100 percent of the amount they would have if they paid tax on the money!

Then, I really hit them with the kicker. This result does not even consider the possibility of deducting and reinvesting the annual amount contributed—such as into an IRA.

If our fantasy couple were able to contribute this money to an IRA or some other deductible retirement plan and reinvest the tax savings each year, the end result would be even more startling. The sum of money available for retirement at age sixty-five if the $2,000 per person, per year, savings were deductible would skyrocket to over *$588 million*. This is an increase of approximately 21,000 percent more with savvy tax planning!

Remember, nothing has changed here except the way the money was handled from a tax perspective. It was the same amount, the same rate of return, and the same frequency of investment. Now how's that for increasing your trading profits? I have just shown you how to improve your returns by 21,000 percent!

A Moral Obligation?

The next question I sometimes pose to my seminar attendees is to ask them if any of them think it is their civic duty or a moral obligation to pay high income taxes. Although few admit it, I have found that many people have this deep-seated belief.

I don't know where it came from—school, the church, toilet training at too young an age. It doesn't matter. It stands in the way of progress. You will never learn to implement any tax saving strategies if subconsciously you feel there is something wrong with what you are doing.

For those of you who might still be harboring this belief let me try to educate you. In case you haven't noticed, government is now big business—in fact, it is our country's biggest business. We used to be an agricultural country. In the eighteenth and early nineteenth century, more people were employed in agriculture than in any other sector of the economy. That changed with the Industrial Revolution. Throughout the late nineteenth and early twentieth century, manufacturing was this country's biggest industry.

In the mid twentieth century, Presidents Roosevelt, Kennedy, Johnson, and Reagan expanded the payrolls of the government to where the government itself became this nation's leading industry. There are more people working for government today than any other sector of the economy. (This started with Roosevelt trying to get over the Great Depression—come on, guys, it's been years!)

The government owes you over $4 trillion. For those of you not familiar with the term "Pork Barreling" let me introduce it to you. The government routinely spends billions every year just to fuel its own machine. Before reelection each year, our elected legislators routinely try to spend money on their districts to help them get votes. This way they can go home and say, "Look at all I've done for you—reelect me—please!"

Congress is somewhat of a good old boys (and girls) club, and each member is sensitive to this scheme and knows that he or she may have to get someone else's help to pass a special interest bill in the next few years. So it is somewhat of a "you scratch my back, I'll scratch yours" situation.

Pork barreling is the way in which one legislator will vote for another's (sometimes useless) project with the understanding that the favor will be returned. There have been some pretty stupid pieces of legislation passed as a result of this practice.

Investors Are Hit Particularly Hard

A prospective client was referred to me last year with a tax problem. He had heard that I was an expert in the field of investment taxation, and he wanted to confirm the fact that he had to pay the government almost $88,000 in taxes on what he considered to be a modest profit.

The facts of Mr. I. M. Screwed's circumstance were as follows:

1. He had recently started managing his own investment account.
2. In his first year of doing so, full time, he made a profit of over $300,000.
3. Unfortunately, he also had some expenses that consumed a great part of his profits.
4. He spent thousands on data-feed, computers, trading systems, office furniture, and so on.
5. His investment interest expense that year was considerable, since he did not have the capital necessary to do what he wanted with his own money.
6. He attended many investment seminars and had considerable expense in doing so.
7. He felt he had enough deductions to cover most of the income he made (a net profit of approximately $100,000), but for tax purposes, his prior accountant told him that many, if not most, of these deductions would be lost.

This is a situation I have found many investors to be in lately.

Here is a quick summary of Mr. Screwed's original 1999 federal and state tax liability. He owed approximately $66,500 in federal tax and another $23,000 in New York State and New York City income tax. This was almost his entire net profit, and obviously, the tax consequences of being considered an investor, rather than a trader, were dire!

Upon reexamination of the facts and circumstances and review of his trader questionnaire, I discovered that Mr. Screwed was, in fact, not screwed. He was really a trader in disguise. I found that he met most of the criteria for being considered a business and consequently was entitled to many tax benefits he had bypassed as an investor. Upon completion of the revised tax return, the difference in total tax liability, for federal and state, was significant. His taxes were reduced to under $24,500 federal and approximately $8,500 state and city—a reduction of almost two-thirds!!

The Hat Trick

In hockey, the scoring of three goals in one game is often referred to as "the hat trick." The next section illustrates how to score three tax reduction goals that will allow you to cut your current taxes by at least 50 percent (or even eliminate them entirely), build up substantial wealth for retirement, and ultimately create a multimillion dollar estate for your heirs—tax free. Having been in the financial services industry for the past twenty-eight years, and having practiced as a certified public accountant for most of them, these are the concerns that I most frequently must address. The solution to these challenges and the path to these goals can be found in a three-step plan of action that I call "The Hat Trick."

Goal Number One—Establish a Business

Most people don't realize that having a business is truly the last great tax reduction opportunity left in America today. There are really two tax systems in existence for U.S. citizens. One is for employees; the second is for the owners of businesses.

If you're an employee, you can deduct itemized deductions *below the line* such as mortgage interest, real estate taxes, charitable contributions, IRA contributions and other miscellaneous itemized deductions. However, if you are a business owner, you get all sorts of deductions in addition to the ones that employees get. These deductions are not only more numerous but also deducted in a different manner—*above the line* rather than below it. In other words, business owners get all the deductions of an employee plus a whole bunch of additional deductions not available to people without businesses. They not only get more deductions but also get to deduct them in a more advantageous manner.

Goal number one is to transform whatever you are doing into a legitimate business. Anyone already in business has the structure through which we can enact the second and third parts of my strategy. For those of you who have no business, let me offer you one—the business of trading.

The Trading Business

If you have read any of my other works (*The Serious Investor's Tax Survival Guide, The Trader's Tax Survival Guide,* or *The Trader's Solution*) you know that there is now a new breed of investor—the trader. In order to understand the exact nature of what a trader does and his or her advantages, you must understand the other types of participants in the market as a comparison.

The first is labeled a *broker-dealer/market maker*, and his or her function is defined within the law and is actually quite clear. Under Reg Section 1.471-5, the Tax Code defines a dealer in securities and delineates this participant as someone who engages in the purchase of securities for resale to customers with the intent of making a profit.

Keep in mind the distinction "resale to customers." The broker-dealer/market maker treats securities or commodities as inventory and, unlike other investors, these items that are held for sale to customers are treated as ordinary, not capital, assets. This results in the generation of ordinary income or loss, not capital income or loss. The difference is that the broker-dealer/market maker is not limited to a $3,000 per year capital loss to which other taxpayers are limited (including most traders). This is a major distinction. Also, any income generated from these assets will also be considered ordinary with regard to self-employment tax, retirement plan contributions, self-employed health deduction, and, as of 1993, he or she must mark-to-market his or her positions (Section 475). Broker-dealer/market makers must pay self-employment tax on their trading income.

An *investor*, on the other hand, is defined in the tax code under Section 263(a). This is a person who buys or sells securities for his or her own account. Investors are clearly defined as investing for *their own accounts* as opposed to dealers who buy and sell for *resale to customers*.

All expenses of the investing activity are considered to be investment expenses. They are treated as miscellaneous itemized deductions on Schedule A of an investor's tax return and are also subject to significant limitations and phase outs.

All income is considered to be capital gain income, not subject to self-employment tax, not eligible for retirement plan contributions and hence reported on Schedule D. Furthermore, an investor is always limited to a $3,000 per year net capital loss deduction, which can be carried forward (or even back, in the case of Section 1256 transactions).

The *trader*, on the other hand, is a hybrid category. There is no election on the tax return that one would make to indicate that he or she is a trader. There have been cases decided over the past sixty-five years in the Supreme Court and various district tax courts that have recognized this hybrid category. The decisions in these cases have recognized that traders are investors who engage in the purchase and sale of securities for their own accounts. However, they do so at such a high level of activity that it becomes a business to them.

There are no objective requirements in the Tax Code to qualify a person as a trader, and up until the Taxpayer Relief Act of 1997 the distinction was barely acknowledged in the Tax Code. It was agreed that the taxpayer must trade in stock, securities, futures contracts, or options on a relatively short-term basis; however, this classification was purely subjective. But now, in paragraph 341 of the new tax act, Congress has defined a trader as follows: "Traders are taxpayers who are in the business of actively buying, selling or exchanging securities or commodities in the market. On the other hand, dealers deal directly with customers when they regularly buy or sell securities in the course of their business."

What Congress basically has done is alluded to, but not strictly defined, the category of trader. The court cases throughout history have defined what really determines trader status. These cases still define the criteria that separate a trader from an investor:

- They are looking for someone who trades on a frequent, regular, and continuous basis.
- They're looking for someone who has a substantial number of trades.
- They're looking for someone who does short-term trading.
- They're looking for someone who spends a substantial amount of time trading.
- They're looking for someone who has the existence of a small percentage of income derived from dividends.
- They're looking for someone who takes these expenses on a Schedule C.
- They're looking for someone who has an office—either a home office or otherwise.

What they do *not* tell you is how regular and continuous the trading must be, although they do shed new light on what they consider it to be. They never tell you how many trades are "substantial." They never tell you what "short-term trading" must be in order to qualify you as a trader. They never tell you what "a substantial amount of time trading" means. They never tell you what amount of dividends they will allow you to earn before they disqualify you from being a trader.

They do tell you that trading expenses must be shown on a Schedule C. Although they do not discount a home office, they do require that an office be present. In fact, part of the provisions of the new tax act liberalized the deduction of a home office.

The Results

Here is a brief summary of the major advantages that a trader has over an investor:

- Expenses are not subject to a 2 percent to 3 percent floor on Schedule A that investment expenses are. They are deducted on Schedule C, dollar for dollar.
- Itemized deductions are not even necessary in order to deduct trading expenses. A trader can take a standard deduction and still deduct trading expenses in addition to this on Schedule C.
- Investment seminars, which were determined as nondeductible to investors in the 1986 Tax Act, are now considered trading seminars and are still deductible.
- Investment interest expense, which was severely limited under the 1986 Tax Act, is now considered to be trading interest (a normal business expense) and is 100 percent deductible. Section 179 depreciation, which was not allowed to investors, is now available to traders.
- The home office expense, which cannot be deducted by investors, now becomes deductible, and, in fact, becomes one of the criteria in establishing trader status.
- Traders can now elect to take their income and losses on their return as ordinary and deduct more than $3,000 loss in any year if the election is properly made.

Although most traders are still subject to a $3,000 per year net capital loss deduction for trading losses, they may deduct 100 percent of business expenses as ordinary. With the passage of the Taxpayers' Relief Act of 1997, this $3,000 limitation can be avoided if the trader elects to mark-to-market under Code Section 475. (Please consult with a professional tax advisor before taking this election—it must be done properly, and there is a great deal of money at stake.)

Goal Number Two—Forming the Proper Entity

The second component to my three-step approach is to put your business in an entity, which is most advantageous to you. The first step in my preferred structure of choice is the establishment of a corporation as general partner within a limited partnership. For those of you who have family members, a family-limited partnership is the ultimate vehicle.

A trader, trading as a business, can do so in one of several ways. He can initially set up on a Schedule C and file this as part of his individual income tax return (Form 1040). This is fine to start with; however, as one becomes more involved in the business of trading, it is clear that the formation of a separate business entity is the preferred way to go.

The creation of a corporation and family-limited partnership is ultimately the best way to add flexibility to your trading business as well as to insulate the assets from potential liability. A Schedule C trader, unless he or she elects Section 475—mark-to-market, reports all income on Schedule D and all expenses as ordinary on Schedule C. Although the expenses are ordinary, the income maintains the character of capital gain income. Because of this, it is not subject to self-employment tax, does not qualify for pension plan contributions, and does not allow the trader the opportunity to deduct self-employed health deductions.

A self-employed individual cannot accomplish this on a Schedule C. In order to do this, he or she must establish an entity such as a C-Corp, an S-Corp, a limited liability company (LLC), or a family-limited partnership. This will still not subject most traders to self-employment tax on trading income (unless the trading is done from the floor of an exchange).

A trader should consider forming a separate entity structure because it will make him or her a "small fish in a large pool" for audit purposes. I truly believe that corporations are less subject to audit than are individuals. This is especially true in light of the fact that a trader will generally trade a large number of transactions throughout the year and generate a large amount of gross proceeds. This huge gross proceeds figure, often in the millions, will be more susceptible to audit on an individual's tax return than in a corporation return.

A corporation, on the other hand, is in a pool with corporations such as Exxon, IBM, and Coca-Cola. For this reason, tax returns with gross proceeds in the multimillions will not even raise an eyebrow. Million dollar numbers on corporate tax returns are commonplace.

If you have read any of my prior books, you will recall that there is also a certain degree of comparison from year to year for audit selection. If one decides to be a trader this year and starts generating millions of dollars of gross sales from trades, this may be kicked out in a computer comparison between this year and last year. However, if one switches entity to a corporation, there will not be the discrepancy in the year-to-year figures on the individual's tax return (generated by multimillion dollar gross proceeds).

Furthermore, in electing Section 475, a trader has effectively made a one-time election for the entity he is trading in. If he decides next year or in subsequent years to go back to a non-475 election, he cannot do so in the same entity without first asking the IRS for permission. As an individual electing 475, this is a very difficult thing to do. However, as a corporate entity electing 475, it is much easier to terminate the corporation, along with the 475 election, and in subsequent years to decide whether or not to elect 475 in a new entity.

As a corporation, it is easy to deduct ordinary, normal, and reasonable business expenses associated with doing business in the corporation. There can be no question as to the nature of the business entity if it is set up and maintained properly (correct board of directors' meetings and minutes, contractual arrangements with you and others, proper placement of assets into the entity, timely filings of paperwork, and so on). Expenses such as these will now become dollar-for-dollar deductions:

- Voluntary Employee Benefit Association (VEBA) expenses for the key employee—you!
- Accounting fees
- Automobile expenses
- Books and audio/videotape courses on investing
- Trading seminars
- Brokerage account management fees
- Calculators, adding machines, cassette tape recorders, and typewriters
- Cost of managing investments for a minor
- Financial advice on audio and video tapes
- Tax advice (such as the cost of this book!)
- Home computers and software
- Data retrieval service
- Trading advice

- Business interest expense
- Legal fees
- Entertainment and meals during which business is conducted
- Safe deposit box rental and storage space for trading documents
- The salary of bookkeepers, accountants, or others who keep your trading records
- Subscriptions to trading publications
- Trips to look after your trading account, and conferences with trading advisors
- Audio tape recording used for education
- That portion of your home expense that qualifies as a home office deduction

If you decide to incorporate, you must choose a state of origin to be your home corporate headquarters. You may want to consider incorporating in a tax-free state. Most states charge an income tax all their own. There are several states, however, that do not charge corporate income tax. These states are: Florida, Texas, Nevada, Washington, Tennessee, Alaska, and New Hampshire. Nevada, for many reasons, is now our preferred state of choice. Each state has its own sets of rules on just how they handle local, nonlocal, resident, and nonresident taxpayers. You may contact the secretary of state yourself and go through the paperwork to set up a corporation. However, it is much safer to retain a professional to do this properly. It is my opinion that it will be well worth the cost of doing so. We have assisted taxpayers in incorporating their own trading businesses at a cost that is generally much less than an attorney's fees or a resident corporate office. It is well worth the initial expense to do so, and to make sure you have it done properly.

The Family Limited Partnership

Partnerships are on the cutting edge of income tax planning tools. Understanding the pros and cons of the partnership is essential for those who would like to have their wealth preserved and passed on to their heirs as well as providing many other significant current tax benefits.

There are a number of reasons why you need to have more than a cursory understanding of partnerships, as they are the centerpiece of tax planning for some of the wealthiest people in our country at this time.

Limited partnerships allow participation without taxation and can be used to significantly reduce federal and state taxes. Yet at the same time they allow us to maintain an impressive degree of control over our assets. Second, partnerships avoid estate death tax inclusion of life insurance contracts, just as they could in an irrevocable insurance trust. And third, a properly structured partnership can add a significant layer of creditor protection to our assets.

There are two types of partnerships: general and limited. In a general partnership, all partners have *unlimited liability* for partnership recourse debts and all partners are legally entitled to participate in the management of the partnership.

Now let's look at some of the attributes of limited partnerships. As the name implies in a limited partnership, at least one partner has *limited liability*. On the other hand, there must be at least one general partner in a limited partnership. Only the general partner assumes full liability for the partnership's recourse debts. In a limited partnership, the death of a limited partner will not terminate the partnership—only the death and withdrawal of all of the general partners.

Goal Number Three—The VEBA

The issues I started this chapter with were: how to put away money for retirement, use it as a tax deduction, allow it to grow on a tax-deferred basis, and eventually pass it on to your heirs, tax free. My answer to all of these questions is a solution that has been on the books since 1928 called the Voluntary Employee Benefit Association, or VEBA.

Section 501(c) (9) of the Internal Revenue Code describes the VEBA as a tax-exempt, ten or more multiple employer welfare benefit trust. It is further defined by Section 419(A)(f)(6), which was passed in 1984. Section 419(A)(f)(6) of the 419 and 419(A) rules were put in originally to curb abuses of VEBAs. If a program qualifies under this section, then it is exempted from the restrictions and prohibitions of Sections 419 and 419(a). In this manner, the greatest tax deferral and asset accumulation program allowed by federal law came into existence.

The problems that most people complain to me about are that tax rates are too high; retirement plans are too expensive; they don't benefit the employer as much as they do the employee; and most assets are going to be handed over to the government when they die anyway. The solution to all of these problems is the welfare benefit trust. If we had a wish list of advantages that could be attained in any investment vehicle, it would look something like this:

- To grow assets on a tax-deferred basis.
- To save money on a tax-deductible basis.
- To be available to any individual.
- To be completely approved by the IRS and U.S. Congress.
- To be fully protected.
- To be able to pass the investment to one's heirs, estate-tax free.
- To be flexible in the amount you can contribute.
- To have the principal guaranteed.
- To be affordable.
- To be versatile.

A question I'm often asked by other practitioners in the field and by people who should know about VEBAs but don't is, "Why doesn't anybody know about these things?" My reply to that is that VEBAs are the best-kept secret in the IRS Tax Code today, and the reason nobody knows about them is that up until recently no one needed them. In 1974 Congress instituted what could be looked back upon now as being one of the greatest "mass murder" schemes in corporate America. What did they murder? The qualified plan.

In 1974, through ERISA, Congress sounded the death knell for the small business qualified plan. They knew that the IRS had qualified plans in their sights and if the abuses were not curtailed in them, the IRS was going to kill them altogether.

Congress responded by trying to limit qualified plan abuse. However, in doing so, they limited the ability of corporate America to get the big tax deductions they got in the early 1970s. What they did later on, in 1982 and 1984, through the TEFRA Act and the DEFRA Act was to kill it further.

- They vested employees.
- They made nondiscriminatory rules.
- They killed the defined contribution pension plan.

What does corporate America do when they know they are losing something? They hire their team of high priced tax attorneys and CPAs to find something else. And what they discovered in the early 1980s was that these VEBAs had been around, on the books for well over fifty years. And that the unions, in fact, had been utilizing these plans since their inception. In my opinion, It took corporate America fifty years to discover the VEBA and about fifteen minutes to abuse it.

In 1928, VEBA became law, and there was no regulation of it at that time. Through the 1930s and up to the present, most labor unions adopted welfare benefit plans. There are billions of dollars in VEBAs, and most of them lie with big businesses and unions.

Most Fortune 500 companies have VEBAs. There used to be tremendous abuses within the VEBA system—yachts on the Mediterranean, villas in Switzerland—all of which were being deducted from corporate income. In this way, VEBAs became vehicles of extreme abuse when the deductions were virtually unlimited.

A large company could buy a corporate jet, a chalet in Switzerland, and a yacht and throw it all in a VEBA plan. They would then post a little notice on the bulletin board in the staff dining room saying that the company now owned these great assets for the benefit of the employees and that each employee had the right to use these perks whenever they wished. That's right, employees had one weekend a year when they could take the corporate jet, hire a pilot, fuel the jet up with expensive fuel, and fly to Switzerland for a week of skiing fun. Or they could charter the company boat. All they had to do was hire a captain and crew to staff it, and they could take it out for one week a year!

Now, how many salaried employees working in a large company would generally have access to the type of resources that they would need to utilize these employee benefits? But that's what happened—and then the IRS got wind of it. The story that I have heard goes something like this. The IRS commissioner was vacationing at a rather posh coastal resort. He was in his suite looking out over the boats when all of a sudden into the harbor pulled a huge yacht. The name of the yacht was *My VEBA*.

The IRS commissioner wrote this down, and all day it bothered him, because he had heard the term before, but he wasn't certain exactly what it was. Upon returning to his office at the IRS, he looked it up in the Tax Code and discovered that VEBAs had been around since 1928. He also quickly realized that, in fact, they were a good way for companies to abuse IRS breaks that were not meant to fund the purchase of yachts. The story then goes that he went to Congress, to the chairman of the House Ways and Means Committee, and said, "Kill it."

Congress, which normally obliges high-ranking IRS officials (for fear of not doing so would often lead to retaliatory actions against *them*), the chairman brought his committee together and tried to do just that—to kill the VEBA. What the chairman found out was that VEBAs had been in the Tax Code since 1928 and, in fact, most of the large unions had billions of dollars invested in VEBAs for employee benefit welfare programs. His congressional committee looked at him like he was crazy and said, "There's no way in hell we're going to kill the VEBA. That would be akin to committing political suicide."

And he agreed. To kill the VEBA program would, in fact, have been political suicide for any politician. Could you imagine going back to your district as a politician in—say—Oshkosh, Wisconsin, and telling the union officials there that you have just eliminated the employee benefit program that assisted the constituents of that district? There's no way that they could ever do that. So, in the 1980s, Congress and the IRS began limiting the abuses within the VEBA plans and added Sections 419 and 419(A) to the Tax Code, plus the discrimination rules (by adding Section 505). They hoped this would cut down on the abuse.

In 1984 Congress revised these laws and the VEBA restrictions. By the exceptions granted in Section 419(A)(f)(6), a tremendous potential has been unlocked for the welfare benefit programs. People like you and me can now take advantage of them, when prior to this only big businesses and unions could do so.

If a program qualifies under Section 419(A)(f)(6), it is not subject to the restrictions and prohibitions of 419 and 419(A). What has happened is that Congress has created a very versatile tool for accomplishing all of the objectives listed at the beginning of this section.

Under this program, contributions become 100 percent tax deductible. But more than that, the cash buildup inside a VEBA is 100 percent tax deferred, thus providing both a great investment vehicle as well as a tax-free death benefit. This may also be funded in addition to your current pension plan.

This is the greatest thing in the world for a company with an overfunded pension fund or a retain-earnings problem. The IRS states explicitly that you can have them both. You are not limited to one or the other. You can have a qualified plan as well as a nonqualified VEBA. This will also allow you to transfer retirement plans, income and estate-tax free, to your heirs.

You can even use variable, whole life, or even universal life insurance. This will allow you to participate in the greatest Bull Market in history, to have safety of principal, and to build up a huge nest egg for your future—and get the money out at very low tax rates.

Some of you skeptics are bound to believe that once again we have something that is "too good to be true." You will say either "it must be" or rather, as in this case, as I say, "it is another government program." I will, however, try to put your fears to rest. The VEBA is squarely in the black-and-white area of the code. It has been taken to court and tested time and time again.

The welfare benefit trust as structured properly has the approval of Congress, the IRS, and tax court. Every VEBA that we have assisted our clients to implement has been preapproved with a letter of determination. In addition, the trust is administered in a manner that fully complies with all regulations. There have been many court cases that have dealt with the welfare benefit trust, specifically as it applies to closely held businesses.

Now, this may indeed be the best part of the VEBA program. Although it is not meant to be set up as a retirement plan, it is, in fact, a wonderful vehicle for accumulating tax-deferred wealth. In addition to being a tax-deductible vehicle, if set up properly, it will allow the business owner to accumulate and compound wealth for many years and ultimately distribute it for his or her retirement.

The way this works is that the law provides that any business owner may, for reasonable cause, choose to terminate a VEBA program. This could mean that the business owner is going out of business, has an economic need not to continue VEBA program, or simply for any other reasonable cause (i.e., cannot afford to continue or maintain it). If and when this happens, the wealth built up inside the VEBA program will then revert back to the employees, including the owner/employee.

Keep in mind that in a qualified plan all employees are sooner or later vested. In a VEBA, on the other hand, employees never become vested.

The criterion that the business entity must have at least two employees aside from the owner, and the typical charge for setting up a VEBA program, make the program a bit more costly than the qualified plan, because there is a trustee fee involved. Keep in mind that a VEBA is run by a trustee. Also note the big difference in percentage of retained wealth to the owners.

One of the most attractive features of the VEBA is that it can be designed so that benefits paid from the trust *will never be exposed to estate taxes.* This is because the participants have no incidents of owner-ship in the assets, including the life insurance contracts held by the welfare benefit trust.

Other advantages are:

■ Contributions are tax deductible, growth can be tax free, and withdrawals can be nontaxable.
■ Assets are protected from all creditors.
■ A much larger percentage of contributions, often as much as 90 to 95 percent, are used to benefit the owners. Distributions can be taken from the plan before age fifty-nine and one-half or after age seventy and one-half with no penalties. This is a big difference from the qualified plan.
■ Assets accumulate and compound on a tax-deferred basis.
■ There is no $32,000 annual limit on contributions, and survivor benefits are income-tax free and can be free of estate and gift taxes.
■ Employees who terminate prematurely are never vested with respect to benefits.
■ This program can be installed to complement qualified plans such as 401Ks or profit-sharing plans, and they can be used to offset the tax on qualified plans upon distribution.
■ The benefits of the VEBA will be exempt from creditors of both the employer and the participants, since they do not possess title or ownership interest in the funds.
■ The employer can provide for life insurance needs of the partic-ipant, but the allocation of the distribution of these benefits can be structured to favor the business owners by providing larger death benefits and ultimately larger distributions upon termina-tion.
■ The investments of the VEBA are safe and held by major insur-ance companies that are highly rated.
■ Investments are managed by third-party independent trustees for greater safety (usually banks and trust companies).

In conclusion, recent case law has given us direction on how to structure one of the greatest tax reduction vehicles available today. With the VEBA you can now accomplish all of these objectives at once:

■ Avoid current tax through huge tax deductions.
■ Save an unlimited amount for retirement.

- Grow it tax free in addition to getting an up-front tax deduction.
- Pass the wealth down to your heirs, estate-tax free.
- Allow assets to accumulate on a tax-deferred basis forever.
- Have the full blessing of the IRS and Congress with a favorable letter of determination. In other words, this strategy is preapproved.
- Have no vesting for employees who terminate prematurely.
- Make contributions as flexible as you like in any amount.
- Allow large contributions in peak years.
- Allow early or late distributions without penalties for distributing prior to age fifty-nine and one-half or for contributing beyond age seventy and one-half.
- Provide favorable tax relief for business owners (traders).
- Provide full safety of investment.
- Provide the ability to grow funds in conjunction with market growth.
- Acquire tax-deductible life insurance.
- Provide funds to pay estate taxes.
- Protect funds from creditors.
- Is inexpensive to set up and administer.
- Access the funds after five years at significantly reduced tax rates.

One of the more favorable provisions of setting up a VEBA is that you can vary contributions from one year to the next. Although a VEBA is intended to be a permanent welfare benefit plan, there is no fixed obligation to make certain payments each year. This is a big plus.

This also sets up one of the best characteristics of the VEBA, which is that permanent cash buildup may be provided for the owners, whereas cheap term insurance may be provided for the employees without violating the nondiscriminatory characteristics of the VEBA. This is particularly significant when a VEBA is terminated and the amounts are distributed to all of the eligible participants. The owner/employee will be able to reap a greater amount of the seeds that have been sown.

The VEBA program, properly structured, is one of the most versatile and advantageous vehicles available for tax and financial planning today. The VEBA program should be an integral part of anyone's total estate, retirement, and overall financial plan.

PART FOUR

PROFESSIONALS— INTERVIEWS WITH TRADERS AND FIRM CEOS

CHAPTER

12

INTERVIEWS WITH TRADERS

One way to learn about day trading—its pitfalls and nuances, its tricks and traps—is to debrief experienced traders who have been in the trenches for many years. If a trader has survived—financially and psychologically—through his or her initial learning curve, has mastered the critical psychological factors, and has learned how to control risk and the size of each trade, then extracting knowledge from that person on how they accomplished this feat could be very useful to newbies (new traders).

In this chapter, we provide the insights of successful traders who trade either stocks, S&P futures, or other instruments for a living. The lessons learned about trading any of these items are applicable to day traders who just trade stocks. The interviewees provided their answers to specific questions that were posed to them via e-mail or telephone. Not only are you getting the benefit of each trader's experience, but also (in most cases) their experience in trading, watching, teaching, or speaking with hundreds of traders over the course of their careers. In essence, you are getting the input of over a thousand traders, not just the ten traders interviewed here. These interviews provide a slice of the real world of day trading—what mistakes the unsuccessful traders have made and what characteristics they exhibit that cause their downfall, as well as the other side of the coin with the winning day traders.

Each trader profiled has a varied background and uses different methods to determine when to buy and when to sell—but each shows a consistent profit. You should find their insights to be practical, enlightening, and useful to understand what individual characteristics and trading approaches can lead to success as a day trader—and conversely, what factors can lead to the downfall of a new day trader.

These traders have been in the trading battlefield, have taken hits, and have beaten the odds to survive. Their insights in many cases may seem obvious, but they were learned through painful trial-and-error coupled with the loss of capital (greatest pain causing element) and should be carefully studied. Each trader's experience is an education unto itself. While reading these interviews have a pen handy to underline key points that you will surely want to review again.

Areas of Agreement

Although each trader learned his or her craft in a different way, you should not be astonished to learn that the majority of these traders agree that trading success encompasses the following items:

- Having discipline.
- Mastering the mental aspects of trading (considered extremely important by *all* traders—and perhaps the most important factor of all in being successful).
- Preserving capital and cutting losses quickly.
- Treating trading as a business instead of a hobby and working full-time at it.
- Having a passion for the stock market and trading.
- Getting an education.
- Understanding as much as possible about the markets and all other aspects of trading before actually trading. (Not putting in the time to study the markets is a mistake.)
- Having no predetermined trading strategy can lead to disaster.
- Tracking trading results using a logbook or diary, as long as the losing trades were reviewed to learn from mistakes.
- Using a mentor to learn trading. (A good idea as long as the mentor is successfully trading now, has the skills to teach the subject, points out the trader's errors, and provides assistance in changing bad habits.)
- Using stop limit orders. (Generally an important practice to limit losses, but mental ones are sometimes better than physical ones, depending upon circumstances.)
- Reading trading and related books to provide more in-depth education.

Areas of Disagreement

Certain topics brought wide disagreement from the interviewees. These areas were:

Becoming a day trader. Most would encourage an individual to consider a day-trading career, while three traders strongly believed that most individuals should not consider it.

Minimum trading capital. The majority of traders felt $25,000 in "risk" capital was the minimum capital needed to day trade, but a few others felt you need $50,000, and others felt $100,000 was needed to make a living.

Trading at a firm versus at home. Traders were split on where a new trader should begin trading. Trading at home was suggested to provide no distractions, especially those of other inexperienced traders. Trading at a firm was suggested to provide an atmosphere of learning and to hear what other traders were doing. One trader thought it did not make any difference where a person traded as long as he or she was trained properly.

Paper trading versus real trading. Some traders felt that paper trading was a useful training tool, while others thought it was a waste of time, because real money was not on the table. One trader indicated that using small trades such as 100 or 200 share lots was superior to paper trading.

Using technical analysis. Using technical analysis tools was generally felt to be helpful in trading, but a few traders found them to be useless, while others used pattern analysis instead of other technical tools.

Interview with Teresa Lo

Teresa Lo is the co-founder and the conscience of IntelligentSpeculator (the Web site is: www.intelligentspeculator.com), an original noncommercial Web site focusing on technical trading, risk, and money management. It features extensive resources for those who would like to improve their trading performance. She was the subject of the cover story in the May 2000 issue of *Online Investor* magazine. Teresa can be reached at shesaid@ispeculator.com

Teresa Lo worked in the stock brokerage business for more than a decade prior to retirement from the industry in 1998. She is a technical trader and uses simple, classic techniques to analyze the market. She holds a B.A. in economics and psychology from the University of British Columbia.

IntelligentSpeculator Web Site

In an age where it has become fashionable to manage one's own investments, every investor needs to implement professional risk and money management strategies. Preservation of capital is the foundation of long-term success in today's volatile markets. Simple technical trading techniques can be applied to define risk, establish targets, and secure rewards to produce superior returns. IntelligentSpeculator aims to connect people, ideas and information in real time on issues related to improving trading and investment performance.

The Interview

How many years have you been involved in the markets?

About fifteen years. Previously, I was investing in mutual funds for five years as a teenager in mid-1980s.

In which markets do you trade?

I trade the S&P futures right now. In the past, I have traded gold and bond futures, index/equity options, junior and senior equities.

What makes you a successful trader?

For me, my motivation has always been a love of figuring out what makes the markets move, rather than a love of the money. I thought that it was very elegant how a buy and a sell ticket could be matched to produce profits. The main characteristic that has seen me through this whole thing is discipline. A lot of traders get attracted to the market because of the money they think they can make. In my opinion, this approach is wrong, and usually, they find out after they lose their money trying to make a quick buck.

Which technical analysis tools (such as MACD, RSI, etc.) do you find the most useful?

Basically, I use moving averages, Japanese candlesticks, Edwards and Magee patterns. I draw some trend lines and also mark out support and resistance zones. The important stuff from Edwards and Magee is available in the John Magee book entitled *Analyzing Bar Charts for Profit*. Basically, everything you want to know about classic patterns, pattern recognition, and reading charts are in that book. The book really shows you the essentials that every trader needs to focus on. Candlesticks are a good way to see what's going on right now in the market, but they obliterate patterns. If you are using candlesticks and a triangle begins to form on the chart, it is much harder to see it than with a bar chart.

Whenever I'm trading, I have one chart with candlesticks, and one chart with bars and volume. Whenever you deal with patterns you must use volume. There's no way out of it. Interestingly, I draw trend lines, but I never use them in my trading. My objective in using trend lines is to see where other people would be taking action and to see whether they will be trapped. In other words, I look for trend line breaches and pattern breaches. I don't trade patterns. For example, if I see a triangle, I stay out. If there's a wedge, I am not there. If a pattern of any type is forming, with the exception of flags and pennants, I stay out, because those are areas of prolonged consolidation. Therefore, things like triangles, wedges, and massive head and shoulders formations are just things to know and look at, but I do not want to get in there and be trapped.

What weaknesses have you overcome that have improved your trading?

Impatience. If you find yourself in the trend, then you have to ride it as far as it will go. Also, I have a saying that *if the market is not in motion, then there is no reason to trade.* Trading, by definition, is trying to take advantage of a move. If it's not moving, then why trade?

What minimum attributes (qualitative and quantitative) do you believe a person should possess before considering becoming an equities day trader?

I'd first like to define day trading. I think there are a couple of views of what trading really is. In my view, if you look at the direct-access firms, they talk a lot about Nasdaq Level II quotes, reading the bids and the offers, the patterns of the bids and offers, and trying to figure out who is trying to do what in the market. That's old-style tape reading. Now that's totally different than someone who is trading off of charts, even if it's a short-term chart. The people that are just scalping off of eye-balling Level II quotes are by definition not trying to make 3, 5, or 25 points per trade, but they are looking for in an eighth or a quarter of a point. From my standpoint, I'm involved in intraday trading using patterns and the other chart-based techniques that I mentioned.

These are the same charts that you can use on a long-term basis as well. Also, as an intraday trader working off five-minute charts, I close out my positions by the end of the business day. On the other hand if you are following trends on a larger time frame and using patterns on the fifteen-minute chart, then you might have to carry positions overnight if the pattern or the trend is still there.

To me trading is all the same, no matter what the time frame. The time frame you choose depends on your comfort level and how much capital you have. You just adjust your size accordingly to the time frame that you use. The technique is the same whether it's a one-minute chart or monthly chart. Time doesn't matter.

Getting back to the question on minimum attributes for trading, I believe that traders must have a certain type of personality. They have to be able to make decisions on a consistent and rational basis. Over the years, having watched clients and other traders, I consistently find that most people are unable to make x number of decisions per unit time. So as the unit of time shrinks, they just freeze or their decisions become very bad. If they never planned to make a certain trade, then they can't do it on the fly. That's one of the huge problems, but I am convinced that it goes back to not having enough knowledge about the market or about whatever it is about their trading in terms of technique and not really knowing themselves.

What minimum amount of "risk" capital is needed to begin trading stocks?
Trading for a living in my view requires $200,000 as a minimum. The average retail client should not be involved in day trading to begin with. If you go to my Web site, you will see that we write a lot about the "probability of ruin." We have devised a spreadsheet called "The Matrix." Basically, if a person has a very small trading account, then they have to take a risk—a bet size—relative to their account size in the time frame that they are looking at.

To make a living, assuming they need to make $250 a day in profit, an account size of $50,000 should do it. Also, they will be making proportionately smaller bets as well. If they're looking to go overnight, then their bets have to shrink even more. Trading is all about adjusting your time frame and your bet size so that you will always be within this matrix of different factors. For example, if you suddenly make a bet that's twice your normal bet size for a given time frame relative to your account size, or go from a smaller time frame to a much larger one, or go overnight on the same size bet, then your risk of ruin gets much higher. And therefore, a couple of bad trades can wipe you out. Whatever you do must be within the constraints of "The Matrix"—somewhere, somehow.

What knowledge or training does a potential day trader need at the minimum before beginning to trade?

I think they should first have a model of how the market works. Then they should trade this market model for at least six months on paper to work out their trading styles, habits, and techniques. After the six months the outcome has to be positive. Unless someone has actually successfully paper-traded, there is no reason to use real money. Keep in mind that trading is having two parties who disagree on the price of a security. And someone's got to be on the other side of the trade, otherwise there is no market. Another thing we also have to be keen about is to respect other people's opinions, because the market judges all, and it is not for us to judge what they think. Right in the market means that at the end of the month you've made money.

What are the odds that a part-time day trader (two or three full days a week) will be successful versus a full-time trader?

I think a person who trades part-time will probably be less successful. I think people who have real jobs tend to trade differently. For starters, if you talk to traders who have real jobs, if you ask them about what they trade and why, they typically say that they are trading with money that they can afford to lose. If I lose, it doesn't matter, they say. The hidden assumption is that they have a real job that pays the bills, and trading will not change their lives. Trading is a lottery ticket, or some form of entertainment or contest.

If you speak to a professional trader, he will tell you that his capital is his livelihood. I cannot afford to make dumb trades or lose money. And so, on one end you have the amateur trader who is only out to maximize gain. The professional trader, if he wipes himself out, has no more capital—he's cooked. So the professional trader's approach is always to minimize losses. These are polar opposite approaches to trading. The typical retail trader is much more likely to take undue risk than the professional trader. They will take risks that are unrelated to what the reward might be. And they're more likely to be blown out on the probability of ruin theory since they push the envelope with "The Matrix" every time they enter the market.

In my view, a professional trader is one who trades for a living and does not have an income from any other source. If you blow your capital you're done, regardless of whether you trade your own capital or that of a firm. Probably 90 percent of the people who claim to be professional traders out there are the so-called day traders with less than two years' experience. By their own admission, they have never actually worked inside the industry. I don't consider them professional traders in spirit. These people may be classified as retail traders who are very good at trading at the moment. They might be good traders now as the market goes up with lots of volume, and while they may be good for the next year or two, unless they've been through the grinder in a real brokerage firm and bad market conditions, they haven't fought in the trenches. I've watched the people in the business for a long time, and I'm only thirty-five. I've watched how traders blow themselves up and the signs and symptoms leading up to these catastrophic events. Clients blowout day after day at the office. You hear people moan and it's terrible.

Must the day trader view his or her trading as a "business" to be successful?

Absolutely. *A trader's capital is everything. Capital must be protected at all times and at all costs.*

Of the successful traders that you know, what characteristics or qualities make them successful?

Most of them love watching the market and are continually inspired by the challenge to analyze price action. Trading is also a process of self-discovery and self-improvement. It's actually a love of the market rather than a love of the money. They know themselves, they know the market, they can listen to the market, and they become "one" with it. And then when you're surfing with the market it becomes very easy to make money because you're in the groove. The market tells you what to do, and you really do not have to do much.

Of the unsuccessful traders that you know, what characteristics or qualities make them unsuccessful?

Their motivation for entering the business was the prospect of quick money. They were never students of the market. They couldn't care less. They just want to find some $3,000 cure—the magic bullet—that will make them profitable. The only person that can make them profitable is themselves. They come in with the wrong attitude and very little knowledge.

What are the most common mistakes made by the neophyte day trader?

Trying to pick tops and bottoms. Betting too big in relationship to their account size. Not cutting losses quickly. They don't ride a trend. They don't give their wins some rope. Listening to other people. Using other people's work that they really don't understand. I particularly have a dim view of indicators, because I think they do not work. People have been trained to think that indicators work, and when they don't work they think they can just change the periods of the different lines and somehow it will be magic and it will be fine. They don't question the indicators themselves and their construction. They assume that the indicators are good and that they just have to find the right way to apply to this particular thing that they are trading. *Price and volume never lie, and traders should concentrate more on looking at the bars themselves and understand what they mean in relation to each other.*

How critical are the mental aspects of trading?

It is everything. In order to understand the market, you really have to be tuned in to it. And you cannot be tuned in if you have all of these negative thoughts in your mind. You cannot be a perma-bull or a perma-bear. You cannot have an opinion. You need to just sit there and watch the market. Go with the market. If a trader is heavily opinionated, it is not going to work out.

Would you recommend that a beginning day trader trade at home or at a day-trading firm?

I think that they should probably observe at a firm. The reason why is that they can observe the behavior of all the traders. It's important to see the real human costs of trading. This typically occurs when the markets are plummeting, and the traders are going nuts. You see them all contorted—inside or outside—and that's a sign that they're not quite there yet. Those people are only like that because they have not adjusted the bet size to the size of their account, or they don't cut their losses. *In actuality trading is boring. It doesn't matter whether I just lost money or made $5,000. It is still very boring to me.*

I've seen so many people lose their homes, their families, and their wives. They go to Gamblers Anonymous. I've seen the real costs. This is the ugly downside that no one talks about. Of all the retail clients that I've met over the years, very few are left or have been successful in the long term, trading on a daily basis. I can tell you for sure that most of these clients could not trade if their life depended on it. They would invest their money in a buy and hold scenario and would do well when the market was up, but as far as trading per se, they could not do it with any type of consistency. I would be shocked if more than 5 percent of them were successful traders. I'm speaking out of personal experience.

I've seen hundreds and hundreds of clients and I believe that my percentage is pretty accurate. Also, I have a Web site where I talk with thousands of people a year. I get their e-mails. I don't get people saying good things too often about trading, especially in the past couple of weeks [March 2000]. People write to me, phone, and tell me how horrible their lives have become and what the market has done to them. The problem is that they have a lack of discipline and they don't follow "The Matrix" properly.

Trading should actually be a fun activity. It might be boring. But it should at least not be a negative experience. And it can only be fun if you apply the proper disciplines—how much you bet in relation to your account size.

Do you recommend that paper trading, simulated trading, or other training tools be used by a beginner before actually trading?

Absolutely. Before they go to paper trade, they need to read a few books and develop a plan as to the kinds of setups that they want to trade. They need to develop some sort of model in their mind of how the market works. If I see a chart it doesn't really matter if it's a stock, bond, or S&Ps. It is whatever instrument they are trading. Then they have to decide what areas of this model they want to get themselves into.

Some people might be into drawing trend lines. They might decide to buy or sell if a certain condition exists. Other people like to use patterns. They say to themselves, "If I see this pattern, then I'm going to do this." Or if people use indicators, they have to use indicators that are satisfactory to them. They should say to themselves, "If the indicators do this then I would do that." Basically, what they do then is to test out their theory on paper before they begin to trade. And if it doesn't provide a profit in life-like simulations, then it probably won't work in real life. Most people end up being discretionary traders where they make the decision on the fly in real time. They need to have the experience of punching in the orders in real time, and punching in the stop losses, and going through the process so that it becomes a natural process during the day. That's what they need to do.

A lot of people on my Web site did not even know how to punch in the orders or know what the orders are called. If I say to someone "stop limit," for example, they don't know what it is. So they don't even know the different order types. Inevitably if you start right away with real money something will go wrong with an order, and you will not know what to do. You will freeze. If the stock moves 5 points against you in five minutes the trader's confidence will be destroyed. Then the trader will be operating from fear. Once gripped by fear, the trader should call it a day, because it takes forever to restore confidence.

What steps should a new trader take to minimize his or her risk of losing capital?

Make sure that he or she is operating within "The Matrix." The text and explanations of "The Matrix" are at my Web site, free. Basically, you have to make sure that you bet according to your account size, and you have to pick a time frame where that bet will be able to hang in there for trend or take your losses quickly.

Typically, the neophyte concentrates on win/loss ratios, which is the last thing they should think about. But if you look at a lot of literature on day trading, people concentrate solely on win/loss ratios because they are way out of line with their bet size for their account. So they have to claim that their bets make money 70 percent of the time. But when you download the spreadsheet and plug-in some of these wins and losses that people typically have, they actually need a 70 percent winning average just to stay even or keep their head above water after commissions. Even Babe Ruth did not have a batting average like that.

What should a trader do to improve his or her skills and performance?

First, you need to write down all your trades. Indicate why you made each one, what the potential reward is by having a target somehow, and the amount you are going to risk. If it's a good trade, then indicate what you did right. If it is a bad trade, then indicate where you went wrong. Keep all of this information in a diary. I don't keep a diary anymore. I've been trading almost every day for thirteen years, but when I went to trade S&P futures it took me four or five months to get the hang of it. I did not make any money in the first six months. I used a diary to analyze what was going on just like everyone else should. When you change markets or you change stocks that you're tracking and trading, you should keep a diary.

How important is having a mentor or a person closely supervise the new day trader for the first few months?

In the best of all possible worlds it would be good. But the fact is that most people who pose as mentors are unsuccessful traders. So you have to find someone who has a record of success. Look at their monthly trading statements to see their actual performance. It doesn't matter if the person owns the firm and makes his money from commission or has written books or has made money on the lecture circuit. It must be someone who is in the trenches right now and who is pulling money out of the market. Otherwise, you are better off learning on your own using paper trading to learn what style is best for you. Even if you trade with someone that is really good, there is no guarantee that you can emulate his style. Your personality may not be suitable for that.

On my Web site, I post all my trades live, with commentary explaining my decisions. The odds of a novice trader picking the top or bottom of a move during the day are very low. I have a better shot at it since I've been trading the markets for many years. We have discussions about why the first thing a new trader should not do is make attempts to pick highs and lows in the market. The first thing you should do is to try to pick the safe entries. You should learn to trade retracements and failures first before trying to pick the extremes. I can pick the extremes, but I'm trying to show new traders that they need discipline. Beginning traders have to learn how to make the easy money before they can make the hard money.

Do you recommend that day traders use limit orders on the buy side and stop losses to prevent large losses?

Yes, and the orders should be used for everything.

Would you discourage or encourage a person who believes that day trading stocks is something he or she wants to try?

It's a very hard road to hoe. People say that I don't have to go to the office, that I can sit in front of this machine and the money will come flying out. Trading is an incredible process of self-discovery to learn about all of your own flaws. When people have to look in the mirror and see themselves without all of their psychological makeup on, it's very hard for almost all of them. It can be a very painful and terrible process. That's why sometimes we call it "truth in trading."

Are there any books you recommend that are a "must" for the beginning day trader?

My list of recommended books is on my Web site, as well as listed here:

1. Justin Mamis, *The Nature of Risk* and *When to Sell.*
2. Jack Schwager, *The New Market Wizards* and *Market Wizards: Interviews with Traders.*
3. Edwin Lefevre, *Reminiscences of a Stock Operator.*
4. Steve Nison, *Beyond Candlesticks.*
5. Greg Morris, *Candlestick Charting Explained.*
6. John Magee, *Analyzing Bar Charts for Profit.*
7. Charles LeBeau and David Lucas, *Technical Trader's Guide to Computer Analysis of the Futures Markets.*
8. Linda Bradford Raschke, *Street Smarts.*
9. Victor Sperandeo, *Trader Vic—Methods of a Wall Street Master.*

Interview with Alan Farley

Alan Farley is a professional trader and publisher of the Hard Right Edge Web site, a comprehensive on-line resource for trader education, technical analysis and short-term trading tactics. He is the author of the upcoming book, *The Master Swing Trader.* Alan has been part of the market scene for over fourteen years as a private investor, advisor, and author. He is a featured speaker and lecturer on "Pattern Cycles," his original strategies and tactics for modern traders, featured throughout his highly popular Web site.

In addition to writing and speaking, Alan has also been featured in *Barron's, Smart Money, Tech Week, Online Investor Active Trader,* MoneyCentral, and TheStreet.com. He has consulted with all the major news services on issues facing today's online traders and is a strong voice on the Internet revolution changing the face of our modern financial markets. Mr. Farley can be reached at www.hardrightedge.com.

His e-mail address is: trader@hardrightedge.com. His Web site is: http://www.hardrightedge.com

Hard Right Edge (HRE)

Founded in 1996, HRE offers traders and investors one of the most comprehensive financial resources on the Web. In addition to an excellent course on trading and market timing, the site also presents a wide variety of daily stock scans, original strategies, and practical tools. HRE features the Mastering the Trade online trading course and the free *Morning Trader* daily, which provides traders with comprehensive tools and techniques to locate outstanding short-term opportunities.

The Interview

How many years have you been involved in the markets?
About thirteen years.

What markets do you currently trade?
I trade the Nasdaq, as well as trading my 401(k) actively. I do have some NYSE positions.

What makes you a successful trader?
Years of knowledge. I'm not a momentum trader. I'm not interested in momentum trading. I like the edges of the market. I like the little quirks in the market and how little set-ups develop. I like to go my own way, and I tend to find opportunity fairly consistently. I'm definitely a pattern trader. I do a lot of writing on patterns. I believe that I have an advantage when it comes to that. I am able to see patterns develop and see the crowd interaction that shows up on price bars.

Which technical analysis tools do you use and find the most useful?
I use very few of them. I use different additional technical tools for specific purposes. I use fourteen-day relative strength index (RSI) on daily price charts to look at overbought and oversold conditions. During the trading day I'll use a five-period Stochastic to measure the intraday oscillations of buying and selling behaviors. I always use Bollinger Bands, and multiple ribbon moving averages. These are sets of three to five averages that "rainbow" from short-term to long-term on the same chart. The indicators that I use show me what I want to see.

What weaknesses have you overcome that have improved your trading?

It's emotional self-discipline. Usually the best trade is the one that makes you the most uncomfortable at the time.

What minimum attributes do you believe a person should possess before considering becoming an equities day trader?

Most individuals should not be considering becoming an equity stake trader to start. Most individuals need to pass it up. I think that *those individuals who have well-grounded personalities, have stable private lives, have found success in pursuits in their lives are the first ones who may be successful in equity day trading.* If you have individual quirks, or habits, or addictions, or you are not in touch with parts of your personality, then the markets will introduce you to your negative personality quirks very quickly if you day trade.

What minimum amount of "risk" capital is needed to begin day trading stocks?

About $50,000.

What knowledge or training does a potential day trader need at the minimum before beginning to trade?

I think that the training should focus on the technical side of it rather than on the software side of it. Short-term trading is very technically oriented, especially if you' re involved in futures trading. You need to have a sound understanding of technical analysis before you trade. I believe that that side is even more important than mastering the technology. I think eventually the technology will become very much a commodity—ECNs, Level II. And at a minimum, you're going to have to know how to use the technology. But what's going to separate you— between success and failure—will be your ability to use technical analysis to see how the crowd thinks, and then being able to operate to take the crowd's money.

What are the odds that a part-time day trader (two or three full days a week) will be successful versus a full-time trader?

I think the odds of success are probably less than one in ten. You take a hot momentum market like the one we have now, and everyone thinks they're a genius.

Must the day trader view his or her trading as a "business" to be successful?

Absolutely. Whenever you're managing that amount of money, you have to handle it as a professional or you can get into a tremendous amount of trouble. If you do not keep excellent records, if you do not know what your performance is, if you do not know what your profit and loss is during different points throughout the month and during the year, then you can get into a tremendous amount of trouble.

Of the successful traders that you know, what characteristics or qualities make them successful?

They are almost all type A personalities to start. I also think that women traders have an advantage over men traders because they are not as flamboyant in their need to display their success. I think that some of the most powerful traders are female traders because they are able to detach themselves from the crowd and the market a lot better. Another critical characteristic is being able to use your left and your right brain. Basically, you have to be able to deal with the mathematics side of your brain and artistic side of your brain. So much of it is a combination of intuition and logic. If you just use logic or just use intuition, you can get into tremendous amount of trouble. If you can apply the two together, I think that's a tremendous advantage. *If individuals do not have a knowledge of the markets, I think they're out of their minds to throw money at the market.*

Of the unsuccessful traders that you know, what characteristics or qualities make them unsuccessful?

The inability to learn from their mistakes. It is not a lack of knowledge. It is usually a lack of discipline. You have to cut your losses very quickly and learn from your mistakes. At the same time, you can fail from a slow bleed just as you can from a couple of big losses.

What are the most common mistakes made by the neophyte day trader?

Chasing momentum is the most common mistake.

How critical are the mental aspects of day trading?

90 percent of it.

Would you recommend that a beginning day trader trade at home or at a day-trading firm, and why?

If you' re between twenty and forty (remember that there are a lot of neophytes in their forties) and you don't have a lot of experience at a day-trading office environment, then the environment may be helpful, because you're surrounded by older traders and you may have good role modeling. When you get older and have already spent time in an office environment, then your motivation is probably much different, and you want to be out of the office.

Do you recommend that paper trading, simulated trading, or other training tools be used by a beginner before actually trading?

If you do, it's just to learn the work flows. I personally think paper trading is a waste of time. You need to know how you react with your money. You're better off throwing away a few bucks actually trading, since you'll learn a lot faster.

What steps should a new trader take to minimize his or her risk of losing capital?

First, you need to get out of the training mode. Then you need to start small. Typically you may want to start with 100 shares and build up the number of shares as your performance gets better.

What should a trader do to improve his or her skills and performance?

They need to find experienced people or sit at a guru's feet. They must find someone who knows more than they do. They should ask this person to tell them what their bad habits are. There is only so much you can get out of books and the software. It is so important to get someone who knows what he or she is doing.

How important is having a mentor or a person closely supervise the new day trader for the first few months?

Most new traders do not want mentors, because they do not want them to participate in their errors. Mentoring programs are very popular thing. This is being pushed by many on the education side. The individual traders do not access it well, because they do not want people to see their errors. They'd rather commit their errors in private and have private pain than with a mentor. The new traders do not want someone smarter than them seeing them fail. *This is a big mistake for the traders—not having a mentor right in the beginning.*

Do you recommend that a diary be kept by the trader of all transactions with notes on all trades?

Yes, for a period of time, not the rest of their lives. It makes a really good tool for as long as they need it. It may be needed for a couple of months or maybe a couple of years. At some point they're going to know what they do right and what they do wrong. Until that point comes, and they've imprinted that in their deeper memories, I think it's a good tool.

Do you recommend that day traders use limit orders on the buy side and stop loss orders to prevent large losses?

If your trading direct access, everything is a limit order and you have no choice. On the loss side of it, I personally don't believe in physical stop loss orders. But, I believe in mental stops since it builds better discipline. I don't believe in the crutch of physical stop losses because the point at which you're proven wrong changes after execution. It may be at a different price. So the price you put in at the time of execution may not accurately reflect what your risk is on that trade.

Would you discourage or encourage a person who believes that day trading stocks is something that he or she wants to try?

I would discourage them, unless they have a lot of skill doing other things. For example, being a good position trader, knowing how to invest, and understanding the markets would be a good beginning.

Are there any books that you would recommend that are a "must" for the beginning day trader?

Yes. *Trading for a Living* by Alexander Elder. I do not know if you have to read any electronic trading books anymore, since there is so much information on the Internet. I tell people to read books on technical analysis such as John Murphy's book on intermarkets and Edwards and Magee, *Technical Analysis of Stock Trends*. I also recommend the two books on market wizards that were written by Jack Schwager.

Interview with Larry Pesavento

Larry Pesavento, a forty-year veteran trader, managed Drexel Burnham Lambert's commodity department and is a former member of the Chicago Mercantile Exchange (CME), where he was a local in the S&P 500 pit. An author of seven books on trading, he currently is a private trader for a large hedge fund. Larry uses a system of pattern recognition in his trading. This approach eliminates the random nature of market action. Since 1995, his focus has been weighed heavily on Nasdaq stocks with special emphasis on Internet stocks. He has one of the most extensive trading libraries in the world, which he utilized in his personal training of over three hundred traders in the past thirteen years.

TradingTutor

Larry's firm, TradingTutor, offers one-on-one personal training, and each student progresses at his or her own pace to achieve maximum goals. Larry can be reached at (520) 529-0469. His e-mail address is: larry@tradingtutor.com. The website is www.tradingtutor.com.

The Interview

How many years have you been involved in the markets?
Forty years.

In which markets do you trade?
Currently, I trade the S&P 500 futures, treasury bonds, Japanese yen, and the sixty most active stocks on the Nasdaq and New York Stock Exchange.

What makes you a successful trader?
Basically past experience, and I have a methodology—pattern recognition—that consistently works. It works on probabilities and it works over and over again. It doesn't work all the time, but the odds are heavily stacked in your favor. And over a period of 100 trades you're going to win.

Which technical analysis tools do you find the most useful?
I do not use any technical tools at all. I don't believe in any oscillators or moving averages. I've tried these tools. I've found that most of them don't work. I just look at the patterns that stocks are forming, and I know what those patterns are, I know what the ratios and proportions of those patterns are, and when those line up, that gives me a trading opportunity. That's when I put my trade on.

What weaknesses have you overcome in order to improve your trading?
Lack of patience, lack of discipline, and lack of preparation.

When you first started trading what mistakes did you make?
Greed. I did not use stops, and I did not have a real methodology on how to trade.

What minimum attributes do you believe a person should possess before considering becoming an equities day trader?
The minimum attribute is that they want to have an intense interest to do it. It should be the focal point of what they want to do. When

they get up in the morning, that should be the first thing that they think about. And when they go to bed at night, it should be the last thing that they think about. The amount of intelligence to trade is very small. So the very best traders are mediocre on the bell-shaped curve as far as IQs are concerned. The people with the higher IQs usually have much greater difficulty because their egos get in their away. Trading is a journey not a destination. Patience and discipline have to be worked on.

What minimum amount of "risk" capital is needed to begin trading stocks?

To begin day trading, a trader should have around $20,000, but to make a living, about $100,000 is required.

What knowledge or training does a potential day trader need at the minimum before beginning to trade?

I would think a minimum of three months of study and practice day trading before they put on their first trade. Paper trading is also a good thing to do. They should use a service like Audit Track (www.audittrack.com) where you have to pick up the order and put in the order, and stuff like that.

What are the odds that a part-time day trader (two or three full days a week) will be successful versus a full-time trader?

My guess would be that 10 to 15 percent would be successful, but everyone is different. Some of the people that prepare themselves for trading can be very successful. Most people that start day trading quit and go on to do something else. People that start and keep losing for two years can learn what mistakes they've made and are then able to focus on what they're supposed to do. So they can probably make a living after that. But many people drop out before the two years is over.

Must the day trader view his or her trading as a "business" to be successful?

Yes, it is a business. If you don't treat it as a business you'll end up at McDonald's as a fry cook.

Of the successful traders that you know, what characteristics or qualities make them successful?

I've trained over three hundred people in the past thirteen years. They all have the same traits: they do their homework; they're disciplined; and they're able be patient waiting for the setups.

Of the unsuccessful traders that you know, what characteristics or qualities make them unsuccessful?

The unsuccessful traders come in with no game plan. They see what CNBC is promoting. They move emotionally. They work under fear and greed. It's just a question as to how soon they are going to give their money up. Ninety-nine percent of the individuals who want to day trade have these characteristics. "Let's light this candle," according to Stuart in the Ameritrade commercial, is typical of the average person's approach to trading. In this business only 10 percent of us are successful, while the rest are just feeding us.

What are the most common mistakes made by the neophyte day trader?

Lack of a trading plan. Lack of money management.

How critical are the mental aspects of trading?

Ninety percent.

Would you recommend that a beginning day trader trade at home or at a day trading firm?

I would not recommend that anyone trade at a day-trading firm, since they are commission merchants who extract commissions from the traders and don't care if they win or lose. That's why 95 percent of them lose. And they just rotate the cattle coming through.

Do you recommend that paper trading, simulated trading, or other training tools be used by a beginner before actually trading?

Yes.

What steps should a new trader take to minimize his or her risk of losing capital?

Find a mentor who will teach him from day one and follow him through until he is ready to trade. It doesn't matter if the mentor is onsite as long as he's watching what the trader is doing. Be skeptical of everything. Check as many references of everybody that you can with live people, hopefully within the same city that you are in. Run away from anybody that claims that they are at 96 percent profitable or 80 percent profitable, and anybody that says that they are making 200 percent or more per year. That's all baloney. If they were that good, then Goldman Sachs would hire them for $10 million, if they could consistently do that.

What should a trader do to improve his or her skills and performance?
Read everything that is available on the psychology of trading.

How important is having a mentor or a person closely supervise the new day trader for the first few months?
Ninety-five percent. Where else are you going to learn it? There are no schools to learn the stuff. Most of the schools out there are not doing the job. My approach to trading is different than others. First of all, I stay with the person from the very beginning. I'm able to teach them the very basics of what they are supposed to know, and I follow them through to the very end. And I give a 100 percent guarantee that if they are not happy, they get their money back. And I've never had anybody ask for his or her money back. The problem with the other training programs out there is that they are using the wrong methodology. They're using oscillators, moving averages, and point and figure charts that characteristically do not work. And they did not use money management along with that.

Do you recommend that day traders use limit orders on the buy side and stop losses to prevent large losses?
Anyone that doesn't use stops will not be in business very long. On the buy side, I go to the market with everything, and I do not use limit orders.

Would you discourage or encourage a person who believes that day trading stocks is something he or she wants to try?
I would encourage them very much. I believe that if the person really wants to do it, he or she can take the time to learn to do it right. It took me five or six years to figure out what I was doing.

Are there any books you recommend that are a "must" for the beginning day trader?

> *Profitable Patterns for Stock Trading,* by Larry Pesavento.
> *The Disciplined Trader,* by Mark Douglas.
> *Trading in the Zone,* by Mark Douglas.
> *Market Wizards* and *The New Market Wizards,* by Jack Schwager.
> *Reminiscences of a Stock Operator,* by Edwin Lefevre. This is a classic and should be read by people that are not day traders. This is probably one of the finest books ever written.

Interview with Ken Johnson

Ken Johnson is CEO of sixthmarket.com™. He started trading in 1995, founded an independent broker-dealer in 1996, and became president of Cornerstone Securities in 1998. At Cornerstone, he directed the expansion to nineteen trading offices across the country and helped to position Cornerstone as one of the leading trading firms in the country.

From the beginning, Ken has been a leader in the development of highly effective training programs for new traders. His innovative training efforts at Cornerstone helped to solidify its reputation as the "home" of the very best electronic traders in the country.

Ken is a proven entrepreneur. He has an MBA from Harvard and has started, owned, or operated companies in real estate development, hotels, water purification, mortgage lending, software development, recreational boating, long distance communications, and educational services.

sixthmarket.com™

sixthmarket.com™ is a leading provider of educational services to the online trader, offering a comprehensive trading curriculum built around The Six Steps™, "Trading Fitness for Life," which are:

1. Think Discipline.
2. Learn Market Fundamentals.
3. Understand Charting.
4. Use Reliable Trading Setups.
5. Master Your Trading Plan.
6. Commit to Your Education.

The company teaches this curriculum in two-day seminars and in online classes delivered over the Internet. Ken can be reached at ken@sixthmarket.com and at (512) 391–4976.

The Interview

How many years have you been involved in the markets?

I began trading equities in 1995, with no prior preparation. I quickly decided that I needed to become a student of trading if I expected to enjoy trading success. Before the end of 1996, I had begun teaching others how to trade. I don't believe the way I started is a good way for others to follow, because I had no one to help me. First, two personal traits helped: (1) I am lucky to be a very fast learner, and (2) I never seemed to allow my "ego" to get in my way. The market and price movements never seemed difficult to me. I studied chart patterns on the stocks I traded until I thought I understood how they moved. I kept records of my trading victories as a way to try to replicate successes. *Mostly,* I was determined to succeed. I felt that if others could master trading, then I could as well.

What makes you a successful trader?

Knowledge. From study and experience, I have learned to trade high-probability chart patterns. My confidence in the ultimate profitability of these setups gives me the focus and discipline to follow my trading plan without exception.

Which technical analysis tools do you find the most useful?

I use Omega Research's TradeStation to develop and test new setups, and I use it to scan the market each night for possible trading opportunities.

I use candlestick charts (intraday and daily charts) with simple moving averages (5, 40 and 200 period) to track my high-probability opportunities.

What weaknesses have you overcome that have improved your trading?

I was hampered by cockiness and impatience when I first started. I'm not sure that I did anything to overcome these flaws—the market knocked them out of me!

When you first started trading stocks, how long did it take you to begin making a consistent profit?

I started as an active daytrader (fifty plus trades per day) just two hours after I first saw a Level II screen. In fact, many times I do more than fifty trades a day. Within six weeks I had taught myself enough to become consistently profitable as a scalper.

What minimum attributes do you believe a person should possess before considering becoming a full-time equities day trader?

Qualitative: The willingness to take the time to learn the skills necessary to succeed and the mental openness to make the psychological changes necessary to deal with uncertainty, lack of control, and losses.

Quantitative: At least $100,000 that they can lose without any change in their lifestyle.

What knowledge or training does a potential day trader need at the minimum before beginning to trade?

The Six Steps™—without this complete immersion, any trader is at a disadvantage against the professionals in the market. This is a very brief summary of the program:

- Identification of a compelling motivation to succeed as a trader.
- A clear understanding of what you want to get out of trading (your goals).
- The choice of a suitable trading style.
- Recognition of the characteristics of winning traders and thoughts on how to emulate them.
- Knowledge of trading fundamentals and rules.
- Knowledge of charting and charting studies.
- Knowledge of specific proven high-probability setups.
- Skills in money management.
- Recognition of the risk and reward in every potential trade.
- How to construct a winning trading plan.
- How to develop the discipline to stay with your plan.

Simply put, we believe that success in trading comes from a comfortable, working knowledge of these things. More precisely, we have seen that this Knowledge leads to Confidence, which leads to Focus, which leads to Discipline, which leads to Great Results, which leads back to increased Confidence, and on and on. As president of Cornerstone, I was fortunate to work with many of the best traders in the entire world. I have seen their strengths and weaknesses. I have seen their different trading styles. They have almost nothing in common except an intense desire to succeed—and the determination to keep learning and keep improving.

What are the odds that a part-time day trader will be successful versus a full-time trader?

I don't believe the amount of time trading each week makes a difference—the difference is in the commitment to quality education. Everything depends on the training they receive. At most day-trading firms, I believe that the odds of success are only about one in ten. At Cornerstone, however, we had developed a thorough and effective twelve-week regimen that increased those odds to above seven in ten!

Must the day trader view his or her trading as a "business" to be successful?

I think so. Successful trading is not a game and it is not gambling. It is based on skills.

Of the unsuccessful traders that you know, what characteristics or qualities make them unsuccessful?

They cannot learn or execute a trading plan, which is knowing the entry point, exit point, and stop loss before they get into the trade. There are many reasons the loser can't execute his plan—lack of knowledge about the markets, lack of knowledge about high-probability trades, inability to deal with uncertainty, inability to deal with losses, and the inability to stop trying to outguess the market, etc.

What are the most common mistakes made by the neophyte day trader?

Trying to go too far too fast—not committing to education first.

How critical are the mental aspects of trading?

It is impossible to overstress this area. Let me give just one example. Many people start trading to "make a lot of money." Although it may not be obvious, this dooms them from the beginning. The desire to make money is not strong enough to sustain them. When they suffer a big loss—and they will—they conclude that "trading is not for me" and they quit as a loser. Every trader needs a stronger motivation—for example, the determination to master the challenge of the market—that will keep them going when times get tough.

Would you recommend that a beginning day trader trade at home or at a day-trading firm? Why?

Immaterial. The important point is to start by selecting a reputable, effective training firm. Knowledge, not location, is the key to success.

Do you recommend that paper trading, simulated trading, or other training tools be used by a beginner before actually trading?

I am probably in the minority, but I don't think there is much value in "paper" trading. The real challenge in trading is the "battle within yourself"—and you can't simulate that. I believe that you learn trading by doing it.

What steps should a new trader take to minimize his or her risk of losing capital?

Learn the trading software. Start slowly, one position at a time, using proven setups—100 shares maximum.

What should a trader do to improve his or her skills and performance?

Take the sixthmarket.com™ OnLine Courses to learn a comprehensive set of trading skills. If I sound like a "broken record" it's just because I have seen this work.

How important is having a mentor or a person closely supervise the new day trader for the first few months?

This is of unquestioned importance—if such a person is available. However, many times they are not. Much of the value of a "mentor" can be gained by taking comprehensive training.

Do you recommend that a diary be kept by the trader of all transactions with notes on all trades?

I have not used this method, so I can't comment. Instead, I have always kept a diary of "lessons learned," the mistakes and/or victories that helped me change and grow my trading skills over time.

Do you recommend that day traders use limit orders on the buy side and stop losses to prevent large losses?

Yes!

Would you discourage or encourage a person who believes that day trading stocks is something he or she wants to try?

Encourage, without question. Let me be blunt. Trading is not hard—the concepts for success are pretty easy to learn. If a person really has the desire to succeed—and a motivation beyond simply making money and access to good education—I am convinced that success will come.

Are there any books you recommend that are a "must" for the beginning day trader?

The Intuitive Trader and *The Inner Game of Trading* by Howard Abell and Bob Koppel, Van Tharp on money management, books by Mark Douglas, and my new book, *The Sixth Market:* The Electronic Trading Revolution.

Interview with David Alexander

David Alexander is a professional trader based in Shorewood, Minnesota. He was a former executive vice president of VirtualFund.com, Inc. (Nasdaq: VFND). David can be reached at dave@transactual.com

The Interview

How long have you been day trading?
I started in the Fall of 1999.

Do you day trade full- or part-time?
I trade full-time, five days a week, at a home office.

Are you a day trader or swing trader?
Both. Swings work well in trending markets. But I also play break-outs intraday.

Are you connected to your broker via Internet, DSL, or cable modem?
DSL with 56Kbps modem backup.

How much are you paying in commissions for each buy and sell?
$14.95 per ticket, but $5 per ticket for the first sixty days while learning (this is an MB Trading special for new accounts and it was very helpful).

Why did you get involved in day trading?
I left my executive level position because I was spending too much time at work and on the road. I was considering a small business, such as a franchise or retail operation, but I realized that the time commitment would be as much or more than my executive position. I had been trading my investment accounts and did quite well. I started to investigate day trading and found that it presented exactly what I was looking for—a small business that I could run from my home with the exact level of time commitment set by myself.

What was your starting capital?
I put $50,000 into the day-trading account.

What is your trading philosophy?
I trade trending stocks and I buy pullbacks for one-to-three-day swing trades. For intraday breakouts, I buy consolidating stocks basing at their highs as they break to a new high on the day. I use technical analysis trend lines, simple moving averages, and candlestick charting techniques.

What markets and type of stocks do you trade?
Nasdaq and listed. All types of trades.

Do you have a specific profit and loss target for each trade?
I use strict stop losses and will only risk 2 percent of my account on any one trade, and usually only 0.5 percent to 1 percent.

How many trades a day do you make?
Between ten and forty.

How have you gained knowledge about the markets?
I have read twenty-five day-trading books and studied everything available on the Internet.

Did you take a day-trading training course before beginning to trade?
No, but shortly after I started, I attended the Online Trading Expo in New York City.

What are your strengths as a trader?
Discipline and cutting losses immediately.

What are your weaknesses as a trader?
I don't let my winners run long enough. Sometimes I chase a stock as I try to get in and pay too much.

How are you trying to overcome your weaknesses?
Learning better execution so I don't chase and trying to let my winners run by strictly adhering to my stop losses and not letting the profits influence me to "take the money and run."

Do you place stop orders to limit your losses?
Mental stops. I have a direct-access broker. There is no broker to place stops for me. I execute my trades directly.

Do you place limit orders when you buy?
Always.

Do you treat day trading as a business or a hobby?
A business.

What mistakes did you make when you first started trading?
Jumping in without having a better handle on order execution.

What advice would you give to someone who wants to get into day trading?

Read. There are now probably 150 to 200 books out there about trading and day trading. Also, go to Silicon Investor and Day-TradingStocks.com on the Internet. There is enough information there for you to figure out if this is what you really want to do.

Paper trade to start. You will get unreasonably fast fills, but you
will learn the game.

Get a good broker. You can't do it with E*Trade, Ameritrade, or
Datek. You must have a direct-access broker (I use MB Trading
and have found that 80 percent of the day traders I deal with
use MB Trading or Cyber Corp.)

Join a reputable group. Having someone to walk you through things
when you start is invaluable. I joined Swingtrader.net. It is great
to have the camaraderie of other traders (even if it's only an
Internet chatroom) when you are home alone in your office.

*What do you plan to do, if anything, to improve your trading skills and
learn more about the markets?*

Read more. Study my past trades to learn what I could have done
better. Learn more about some technical analysis techniques such as
Fibonacci retracements.

How do you determine which stocks to trade?

Technical analysis.

How do you determine when to buy and when to sell?

Trade trending stocks, buy pullbacks for one-to-three-day swing
trades. For intraday breakouts, buy consolidating stocks basing at their
highs as they break to a new high on the day. I use technical analysis
trend lines, simple moving averages, and candlestick charting techniques.

What tools and indicators do you use to determine buy and sell points?

Besides what I mentioned, I watch the Dow, Nasdaq Composite,
Nasdaq 100, TICK, TRIN, and S&P futures.

What is the most important lesson you have learned so far in your trading?

Cut your losers immediately. Hope will not bring them back.

*What have you learned about the market makers and how they "manipu-
late" the price to shake out the weak traders?*

I use Level II to figure out where to buy and sell (i.e., which route
to take) and to watch the depth of the bids and asks. I don't worry
about market marker manipulation, and I think it's just an excuse for a
bad trade. If you are scalping sixteenths, maybe it affects you. If you
are going for several points, it's not an issue.

*What minimum attributes (qualitative and quantitative) do you believe a
person should possess before considering becoming an equities day trader?*

Adequate capitalization ($30,000 to $50,000), money to live on while you learn, and a supportive family. Scared or emotional money cannot trade well.

What knowledge or training does a potential day trader need at the minimum before beginning to trade?

Must know the markets and order execution routes.

How critical are the mental aspects of trading?

Trading is *all* mental. You must excise all emotion or you will lose. Trust your technical analysis and if you are wrong, cut your loss and move on. There are always more stocks setting up.

How important is having a mentor?

Fairly important, but that person doesn't need to be with you in person. An Internet chatroom buddy or group works well, too.

Do you recommend that a diary be kept of all transactions and comments about each trade?

Absolutely. If you have a losing streak, you can go back to where it started and see what hit you.

Do you recommend that traders use limit orders on buys and stop losses on sells?

I think market orders are only used by people who are going to end up giving their money to me or to others.

Would you encourage or discourage someone who believes that day trading stocks is something he or she wants to do?

I would encourage them to study and learn and decide for themselves. I would discourage them if they are not adequately capitalized.

What books would you recommend that a neophyte day trader read?

In order:

The Complete Idiot's Guide to Day Trading Like a Pro, by Jennifer Basye Sander, et al.
Stock Trading Wizard, by Tony Oz.
Electronic Day Trading to Win, by Baird and McBurney.
Trading for a Living, by Alexander Elder.

Interview with Michael P. McMahon

Michael McMahon is an instructor and subject matter expert at the Online Trading Academy. While he has been in the equities markets since 1968, he was not a professional trader until 1983. In the intervening years, Mike owned and operated two scuba shops in Southern California, where he taught basic and advanced diving for about ten years. He was in the U.S. Army with the Eighty-second Airborne, and he did a tour (temporary duty assignment) at Fort Polk as an assistant drill instructor, where he taught battlefield first aid and a little demolition. Additionally, he worked in the chemical field (urethanes) for a number of years interspersed with trading. Since 1993, he has made a living off the market by trading equities and some options. Mike has a B.A. in political science from UCLA and a Series 3 commodities futures license. Mike can be reached at mike@tradingacademy.com or at (949) 759-3809.

Online Trading Academy

Online Trading Academy.com (OTA) is one of the leading educators in direct-access trading fundamentals and electronic executions. OTA's mission is solely education for the serious investor and active trader. The firm teaches basic theory through advanced studies and provides additional classes in options, taxation, and (soon) futures. OTA is constantly developing new content to satisfy the public's "need to know" in the financial arena, delivered either in person or virtually over the Internet. OTA teaches nationally and internationally. The company can be reached at www.tradingacademy.com.

The Interview

How many years have you been involved in the markets?

About thirty years over all and highly concentrated work for approximately eighteen years.

What markets do you trade?

Currently, I trade only the U.S. equities and with the advent of direct-access trading, I have concentrated on the Nasdaq in the last two-and-a-half years. I have positions on the NYSE, use limited options, and have traded commodity futures in the 1980s.

What makes you a successful trader?

Belief in myself is my best trait. Over the years I have developed a discipline that works. I follow it religiously. This gives me the confidence to do the right thing in virtually every situation. That confidence allows me to be more decisive. And the better decision making affords me a very nice return. I guess you might wish to distill that into a simple comment of "discipline is my success secret." I return a couple of hundred percent typically on my risk capital. 1999 was a very good year for me with a 600 percent return. I trade with about 20 to 25 percent of my financial assets, the rest being in long-term portfolios. I am strong in equity right now, but I change my portfolio to match the market character.

Which technical analysis tools do you find the most useful?

I use quite a variety in my trading. First, understand that I employ momentum, swing, and position trading in my arsenal. Needless to say, the advent and proper interpretation of Level II is my main source for decision making in momentum trading. Your question leads me to swing trading, which by definition is based on technical analysis. I use a standard RSI in conjunction with a very simple approach to support and resistance lines. I analyze generally with 15 minute charts and watch with 1 minute charts. Market indicators help with decision support for entry and exits. I keep a close eye on S&P futures, the TICK, the TRIN, and the market index that I am trading in, typically Nasdaq composite.

One of my better tricks is looking back ninety days for high/lows approach on Nasdaq stocks. These tend to breakout (up or down) more frequently than Big Board stuff. By using a simple consolidation lines/channels, I look for confirmed breaks through support or resistance and act accordingly. I am currently studying Fibonacci analysis (Fib Nodes, confluence, 3x3 displacement) which is fascinating and appears fruitful, but I am by no means an expert in this field. To re-answer your previous question—another winning trait is that I fully realize that I am in a learning mode. There is never a day that goes by that the market does not present me with a new challenge or a different thought. You need to be flexible and open-minded to achieve.

What weaknesses have you overcome that have improved your trading?

The single biggest weakness I had was in not allowing my positions to fully develop. I was taking money off the table too quickly, while there was a still potential profit. This led to the next problem of ego. After getting out early, I would convince myself I was right and not get back in immediately, again forgoing profits that eventually were there. In order to overcome this problem, I set myself the task of loosening my trailing stops (in swings and positions). This was quite a change and took a couple of years to get used to. I now will allow a profitable position to erode a bit to confirm it has finished its run. While I am not maximizing my profits, the ability to allow the trade to develop to its fullest has more than paid off, even if I am leaving a little on the table. Needless to say, this is not the strategy I employ in momentum trading. There, my stops are very rarely over ¼ point and generally as tight as a teenie.

What minimum attributes do you believe a person should possess before considering becoming an equities day trader?

Qualitative: Decisive, disciplined, nonegocentric yet individualistic (tough combo), bold (not foolhardy), and enjoys the trade (You have to like this, you have to have a passion for it).

Quantitative: Several years of market study (to be successful, not to start), minimum of $25,000 risk capital (with little emotional attachment to it), ability to devote time to a rather harsh mistress (no less than sixteen hours a week in research and study—does not include actual trading time).

What minimum amount of "risk" capital is needed to begin trading stocks?

$25,000 absolute minimum. A person just starting is going to pay tuition to the market, whether they get formal training or not. Formal training merely cuts down the time span of the learning curve. During the first few months (all of this depending on ability, savvy, and perseverance), the novice tends to lose dollar after dollar. If you start with $25,000 and lose $12,000 in the first months, this becomes psychologically damaging ("My God, I am down over 50 percent of my hard-earned money; I will never get this right!"). Whereas, if the novice with $50,000 still loses the $12,000, he does not react with the same depressed attitude. Beginners never learn that it simply takes time. By the time they do learn, guess what, they are no longer beginners.

What knowledge or training does a potential day trader need at the minimum before beginning to trade?

There are three ways to learn. The first way is the school of hard knocks—trial and error (expensive error!). The second way is the self-study method of reading every book and listening to every guru and then placing money at risk. And, the third way [is] getting a formal education, which must include discipline, risk management, and capital preservation. Some may think those are the same thing, but they are very different when inspected. Of course, you must learn about the market, the influences of the political arena, indicators, sentiment, world financial influences, and human psychology. Certainly, there must be training in the new tools available, Level II reading and interpretation, technical analysis, understanding that there is manipulation in the markets (it is not just supply and demand), and so on.

There are other topics that need to be understood. For the beginner, you do not have to "master" them all, but you must be familiar with them. As you progress, their importance becomes more clear, and you then start to use them more effectively. Of them all, my personal beliefs and strategy tend to place more import on the psychological aspects. The market works on perception—right or wrong—perception of danger, perception of profits, perception that someone else perceives differently. Having a working understanding of these aspects allows me to anticipate where the herd is going.

Ultimately, the best education is the experience of being in the market. Formal education simply gives you some protections and a few tools to get started with. Longevity is the real need. Those without training squander money, get caught up in trying to get even, doubling up on the next trade, etc., and, lo and behold, just about the time they "get it," they no longer have any risk capital to work with. They become "wannabe" traders that almost made it—they just didn't last long enough. Formal education informs them of the risks, sets a true framework of discipline to work with and develop, and teaches them how *not* to lose money as fast, thus, allowing time and experience to do their job.

What are the odds that a part-time day trader will be successful versus a full-time trader?

My belief is simple. If it does not add, it must subtract—there are no neutrals. This distills into the philosophy that you must be aggressive in your efforts. Anything that does not enhance your abilities must be a distraction at best. Therefore, while there are successful part-time traders, I would have to say that the full-time professional would have an advantage (all things being equal—capitalization, talent, etc.). I believe that you can trade part-time as a business, I believe you can trade full-time as a business—I do not believe you can profitably trade as a hobby. Eventually, the market will dissipate any luck the hobbyist had and start to take back the money. I cannot explain why, but I have seen it countless times before.

Must the day trader view his or her trading as a "business" to be successful?

Absolutely. This is true on many different levels. Psychologically, if it is not a business, then it must be "play." Play is wonderful, however, you tend to do foolish things during "play." You can pretend, you can be someone you are not, you can afford to be emotional, both exuberance and depression. None of these things are winning traits in trading. It must be a business. You must realize that there will be business losses, business profits, business taxes, business expenses. If you are not organized, punctual, determined, and aggressive, your business will fail—trading, selling ice cream, or writing software. Because of my psychological makeup, I need to trade on a floor. I need to "go to work." While this is not necessary for all, and in fact many successful traders do trade remotely, shielded from the "noise," I have learned, however, that for "Mike" to work well, I need this little discipline (heck, it is actually a big discipline).

Of the successful traders that you know, what characteristics or qualities make them successful?

Pretty much the ideas and traits I have already mentioned. Decisive, bold, ambitious, nonemotional (or at least trying), disciplined, and (did I mention it?) disciplined. Most of the traders that I know who are returning handsome profits all have developed a discipline and style over time. All have a "plan," a strategy, yet to a person, they are all flexible to stay with an everchanging market. By the way, most are very tight-lipped on exactly what their strategy is. Both trading strategy and discipline can be very personal.

Of the unsuccessful traders that you know, what characteristics or qualities make them unsuccessful?

Simply take the reverse of the last question and the question on minimum attributes. I think fear is the mind killer. As I noted, beginners lose, some lose big, some small, but all lose. It is getting over that emotional pitfall, "I am a loser," and simply realizing that nothing good comes without work and setbacks. Fear also works on decision making. Too often a trader sits and watches a price move up the ladder, all the while saying, "This is going up, I should buy—maybe I will let it confirm—yeah, it is going up, on the next dip I am a buyer." Needless to say, this person eventually bought it at the top, only to see the position turn over on them, reinforcing the defeat by the fear that disallowed the decision in the first place. There is no straight road to success—even Mr. Gates had his ups and downs. Undercapitalization is another big killer, as I already mentioned. Surprisingly, over the last year or so, I have seen less of the "get rich quick" attitudes in our classes, so either we are getting more serious students or the media has had a salutary effect on "day trading."

What are the most common mistakes made by the neophyte day trader?

Wow, alphabetically or numerically? Sorry, the novice and apprentice are faced with countless challenges that must be overcome one by one. I can break it down into two groups—analytical risk and execution risk. I may be oversimplifying but let's start there. Again, most see a price going up and they buy. They need to see that a price "will" go up but buy it as there are still sellers, that is, as it is about to find support and turn around. This is very difficult psychologically. I have just demonstrated another problem with bias—for the second time I have used a "buy situation." Most neophytes do not see anything but up trends. They are biased to the long side. Again, analysis has failed them because they do not "believe" that the market can go down and that they can make money at the same time.

Execution has become a major issue. The public is waking up to the fact that they are not necessarily getting the best fills in a timely fashion from their brokers. Thus the hue and cry for more self-directed trading that online brokers offer. Many do not understand the simple differences of limit versus market orders, what the spread (and therefore the load) is, and so on. Additionally, with the advent of the direct-access trading platforms, simple keystroke or mouse-clicks get many into trouble.

I tell a story on myself from last year: I was short 1,000 shares of CSCO before it split. I was bucking the market and thought I had a retracement I could take advantage of (needless to say, this was a momentum trade). The momentum turned on me and I quickly closed the position—sold that sucker fast—oops, now I was short 2,000 in a up market. I did not panic, I changed my share size to 2,000 and sold it off. I stared in disbelief. I had done it again! (Yeah, Joe Professional, huh?) I finally changed it over to 4,000, took my left finger in my right hand and pushed the *buy* button and finally got out with about a $700 loser—all due to a lapse of concentration and poor execution.

This was a classic beginner's mistake, not buying to cover a short position. Beginners often buy the wrong stock—they have a chart they are looking at but the wrong symbol in their execution box. The bad news is that most will freak out and close the position. Often, the mistaken position will move in the desired direction because the entire market was moving, it was in the same sector, etc. When that kind of mistake is made, don't be too hasty, look it over and decide. Panic and rash decisions can be devastating. In teaching scuba diving, one of our tenets is "Think and then act"—it cuts down on panic.

A major mistake that beginners make is in overtrading. It is fun and exciting. However, even with little losers and few moderate winners, commissions and fees add up. They do not take the time to analyze what they have done (why the trade was good or bad) and end up with a large cost for the day without learning anything. Not learning is the biggest mistake.

How critical are the mental aspects of trading?

Incredibly crucial. Again, for me, psychology is a major aspect. Therefore, understanding yourself first is vital. How do you react in times of stress? Are you decisive—both ways, in and out? Are you happy to be doing this? (it is amazing how some are drawn to trading but eat antacids all day—what's the point, you should like what you are doing). Can you be mentally tough enough to let losers go or do you fret over them? Again, the mental aspects are there or they are not. You can learn to read charts, you can train to "see" momentum, but if you are not mentally fit, you will lose.

Would you recommend that a beginning day trader trade at home or at a day-trading firm?

As I mentioned earlier, it is important for me to trade on a floor. I have developed enough mental discipline to ignore the noise and distractions of the hubbub of trading. However, I do feel that most will gravitate to remote systems. It is easier to focus on a trade, more comfortable in familiar surroundings (you can put your feet on the desk if you like)—but there are pitfalls. It is a business and you should start work early to see that your platform and systems are all functioning properly, not to mention a check to see if you are functioning properly (awake, alert, informed). You need to have an isolated area.

If trading noise is a distraction, what then of children screaming, phones ringing, or the demands of your Significant Other. I think, if possible, the newbie should start on a floor to be around trading, to be able to ask questions, to see how it is done. After a time, I am sure that their natural comfort level will guide them to the right spot. How long? I would suspect that two to three months would be enough to base a decision on—remote or floor.

Do you recommend that paper trading, simulated trading, or other training tools be used by a beginner before actually trading?

Absolutely, but as everything else in trading is double-edged, so too is simulation. Simulated trading allows the novice to see the workings of the market, if they pay attention. Seeing price action and the movements of the market participants (market makers and ECNs) is invaluable. Simulation also helps establish execution skills—picking the right trade route, the right buttons or clicks to complete the trade, and so on. The two bad things about simulation is that it is not *live*. I said two—the simulators I have worked with all fill the orders easily or with great difficulty. This is not how the real world works. Unfortunately, the bias is to "easy fills." This gives a very false impression to the novice. They simply do not know any better.

The other half to the *live* problem is that there is no money at risk. Again, psychology comes into play. It is amazing to me that many have risked large sums of money in business or in investments with little emotional response; yet, the aspect of trading with real money will cause sweaty palms and heart palpitations. Simulation, paper trading, or "play-dough" is very necessary but needs guidance and insight from an experienced trader or trainer to avoid these pitfalls.

What steps should a new trader take to minimize his or her risk of losing capital?

Everyone he can. Seriously, there are some simple steps to minimize risk that all should employ, especially the beginner:

1. Keep share size small until you are sure—novice or experienced—test the waters, add to winners. Increase share size slowly with experience and comfort.
2. Don't take home overnight positions until you have the risk capital to withstand large losses. The beginner usually does not have unlimited risk capital and certainly no way to know what will happen by tomorrow. Never take home a loser.
3. Decide, and if it doesn't perform as expected, decide to get out. Simply put, "When in doubt, get out!"

4. Set stop limits both on the individual trade and for the day. I already mentioned my "in trade" stops, but how about this as a daily quit point: "1 percent of risk capital down, quit for the day." This tells the beginner that if he has $50,000 buy power he should quit if he loses $500, whether it be in the first few minutes or near the end of the day. Stop losing! Find out *why*.
5. Leave Internet stocks, IPO's, and volatile stocks to the pros. Yes, an Internet stock may soar twenty points, but it can fall that easily too. I have seen too many accounts melted down because of a mistake in judgment. When these guys move, they really move quick, and the novice tends to focus on the problem, not the solution.

There are plenty more methods. Avoid trading during major announcements, don't add to losers, be patient, learn the characteristics of one or two stocks and don't stock hop, to mention a few.

What should a trader do to improve his or her skills and performance?

Learn every day. Make a plan and stick to it until the plan does not work. Then modify the plan and work it again. Write down every trade with "why you took the trade" as the most important aspect. Then review and analyze why it worked or didn't. Write down a list of disciplines, review it every week, and rewrite it. Writing is important. You tend to fool yourself with mind games, but if it is right in front of you, in print, it is hard to lie to yourself.

Start simple and develop your disciplines over the course of your trading career. I have found some strange disciplines in my life—I stop trading for one week when I have had thirty days of wins (I tend to lose focus and think too much of myself). I do not trade the opening (clearing). The old adage holds true for me: "Amateurs open the market, pros close it." I do one week (minimum) of study and research before I will take a trade if I have been away from the market for more than two weeks (like a vacation). Ultimately, discipline will be the most benefit to the trader—new or old.

How important is having a mentor or a person closely supervise the new day trader for the first few months?

Invaluable, however, the old joke is that if I were to help you with golf, do you really want to shoot a round in the low 130s? The mentor needs to be seasoned and successful. It is tough enough for the neophyte, but bad leadership or poor habits will only contaminate them. They are new, fresh. Old pros have habits suited to their particular personality. I believe mentoring is wonderful, but it should be done by a "teacher" who understands the needs of the student. The Strategic Trading Center offers this kind of service, and it has been getting rave reviews. The STC is part of Online Trading Academy's overall education service.

Do you recommend that a log book be kept by the trader of all transactions, with notes on all trades?

As noted above (no pun intended), log your trades and *look* at them. It does no good to write them down if you do not go back and review and analyze. If you think it is too much writing, then I offer that you are overtrading. As experience and skill develop, you will find alternate methods for reviewing trades.

Do you recommend that day traders use limit orders on the buy side and stop losses to prevent large losses?

This is a tough question in that it is too broad. There are many times in a running market that a market order is preferable to a limit order. This is also modified by the method of trading—online through a broker or with direct-access trading (DAT). DAT affords you greater transparency and control. However, once dealing directly, market orders are almost unheard of as the use of ECNs requires limit orders only. Again, most experienced traders would never limit themselves to one execution route.

As for stop losses, absolutely, they need to be used. Again, different methods arise. Some will actually set mechanical stops with conditional orders, while I almost exclusively use mental points. I also don't tend to fool myself anymore—kind of like cheating at solitaire. Novices need to use both right away. They are the beginning of the self-discipline. They are also the most often breached.

Would you discourage or encourage a person who believes that day trading stocks is something he or she wants to try?

People are curious. Many things attract them to trading. The mystique of being a market mogul. The appeal of fast action and high risk. The deep hidden hope that they will strike it rich. All of these, and host of reasons more, lead people to the Online Trading Academy. We are happy to answer their questions and, we hope, they honestly answer ours. We constantly strive to warn, disclose, and educate these inquisitive people about the risks of this market and its suitability (or not) as a profession. Some immediately see the hard work involved and leave, with their hopes of quick profits destroyed; others want to press on. These few we try to serve to the best of our abilities. Finding a teaching, active trader is difficult. The cadre we have all enjoy teaching for teaching's sake. Sounds awfully noble, but there are real rewards other than dollars and cents. To answer simply, yes, I encourage people to find out if this arena is for them, but I also stress that it is not for all.

Are there any books you recommend that are a "must" for the beginning day trader?

I have provided a short list of books that I have read and found valuable. There are many other fine publications, articles, and what-not that I would have the beginner read. Many of the higher level books are just that—too advanced conceptually without the basic foundation of the trading world.

> *Reminiscences of a Stock Operator,* by Edwin LeFevre
> *Secrets of the SOES Bandit,* by Harvey Houtkin
> *The New Market Wizards,* by Jack Schwagger
> *The Disciplined Trader,* by Mark Douglas
> *The Art of War,* by Sun Tsu
> *Strategies for the Online Day Trader,* by Fernando Gonzales and William Rhee
> *How to Get Started in Electronic Daytrading,* by David Nassar
> *Computerized Trading: Maximizing Day Trading and Overnight Profits,* by Mark Jurik
> *Secrets of the Electronic Day Trader,* by Mark Freidfertig
> *Japanese Candlestick,* by Steve Nisan
> *Technical Analysis Explained,* by Martin Pring

I also recommend the following: *Investor's Business Daily, The Wall Street Journal, Barron's, Financial Times, BusinessWeek, Forbes,* and *Inc. Magazine.*

Interview with Tim Cho

Tim Cho is president and CEO of Tim Cho Investment Corporation (DBA TCI CORP). He began his trading career as a broker at Merrill

Lynch. Tim became one of the top brokers in the Western United States Region. He left to become a vice president at Smith Barney. Throughout the years, he developed and refined many trading systems. In 1992, he left Smith Barney to trade for his own account. Many of Tim's previous clients called him to trade their accounts again, since their trading accounts were not performing to the level of his management. Tim helped them to set up a trading system and taught them how to use his systems to trade. They experienced great success using these systems. More and more people contacted Tim wanting to take his classes. So, it's really by accident that he got into the training business in 1993. Since then, TCI has grown to eleven offices across the United States and the company has become one of the world leaders in the investment education industry.

TCI Corporation

TCI Corporation is one of the premier trading systems' training and development companies in the financial industry. TCI's main business is to teach individuals how to become professional traders. Its main focus is on the psychology of trading and the TCI trading systems. Students are taught systems for day trading, swing trading, and longer term trading. TCI specializes in the futures market and the stock market. Tim can be reached at TCITIM@19200.NET or (949) 622-5505. The company's Web site is: www.tcicorp.net

The Interview

How many years have you been involved in the markets, and what markets do you trade?

Fifteen years; futures and stocks.

What makes you a successful trader?

I have the commitment and burning desire to succeed, always be positive, thrive on pressure, and have high level of discipline—follow my trading rules. I also set demanding goals for myself, know my limitations, have patience, and am ferociously persistent.

Which technical analysis tools do you find the most useful?

I use candlestick charts, other charts, and the combination of %D, %DS, MACO moving average convergence divergence momentum, acceleration, on-balance volume, volume, trend line, support line, resistance line, and channel lines.

What weaknesses have you overcome that have improved your trading?
    Discipline.

When you first started trading stocks, how long did it take you to begin making a consistent profit?
    One year.

What minimum attributes do you believe a person should possess before considering becoming a full-time equities day trader?

> Get the proper education on trading from a professional.
> Have a high level of self-control.
> Be financially stable.
> Know your limitations.
> Be self-motivated, driven, and have a burning desire to succeed.
> Set demanding goals.
> Control your emotions.
> Be patient.
> Have high self-esteem.
> Thrive on pressure.
> Be ferociously persistent.
> Learn from adversity.
> Be meticulous, detail oriented.
> Always be positive.
> Be a decision maker—have the aptitude and the ability to make sound decisions.
> Be a leader.
> Have commitment.
> Have a high level of discipline—follow the trading rules.
> Cut losses.
> Let profits run.
> Keep trading capital small.
> Follow all the system rules without question.

What minimum amount of "risk" capital do you believe is needed to begin trading stocks?
    $25,000.

What knowledge or training does a potential day trader need at the minimum before beginning to trade?
    Individuals need to learn the knowledge and education on trading—from a day-trading company or school that specializes in teaching

day trading. They must have a successful track record. For example, if you want to learn how to fly a 747, then you need to go to flying school and put in the hours. Or if you want to be a lawyer, then you need to go to law school. You can't learn it by just reading books.

What are the odds that a part-time day trader will be successful versus a full-time trader?

The odds that a part-time day trader (two or three full days a week) will be successful are better than a full-time trader. The trader doesn't have the pressure to succeed now.

Must the day trader view his or her trading as a "business" to be successful?

No. How you view trading has no effect on your trading results.

Of the unsuccessful traders that you know, what characteristics or qualities make them unsuccessful?

Lack of discipline—guarantees you will fail.
Lack of self-control.
Lack of commitment.
Low self-esteem.
No goals.
No plans.
Afraid to make decisions.
Undercapitalized.
Out of control type or overly aggressive individual.
Highly and easily stressed individual.
Negative thinker—negative outlook on life and always expecting the worst, likes to blame others when things go wrong.
Disorganized.
Impatience.
Crowd follower—this is a sure way to lose money.
Compulsive gambler.

What are the most common mistakes made by the neophyte day trader?

Lacking knowledge and education on trading—individual needs to learn from a day-trading school that specializes in day-trading or a day-trading professional with a successful track record.
Trading more capital than they should—lack of discipline and patience.

Lacking or having no risk management skills.

Lacking or having no money management skills.

Increasing position size after losses to try and make it back.

Trading with negative emotions.

Basing trading success on winning trades versus losing trades. For example: "I will get out when I am even."

Basing success on money (should be based on doing the right thing).

Trading without a proven system or methodology.

Taking small profits and letting losses run: the primary rule to successful trading should be cutting your losses short and let your profits run.

Failing to follow your system.

How critical are the mental aspects of trading?

Trading is 90 percent psychological and 10 percent mechanical. That's why if you teach a hundred people how to trade a system, they all will get different trading results.

Would you recommend that a beginning day trader trade at home or at a day-trading firm?

You should trade at home so you can focus better. You don't have to listen to all the negative comments from other traders.

Do you recommend that paper trading, simulated trading, or other training tools be used by a beginner before actually trading?

This is a must.

What steps should a new trader take to minimize his or her risk of losing capital?

Get the proper education on trading from a professional. New traders should use paper trading or simulated trading until successful before trading real capital. Also, the trader should trade small amounts—no more than 5 percent of the risk capital at first.

What should a trader do to improve his or her skills and performance?

Repetition builds confidence. Take training classes from a professional or high-quality training firm.

How important is having a mentor or a person closely supervise the new day trader for the first few months?

Very important.

Do you recommend that a diary be kept by the trader of all transactions with notes on all trades?

Yes. Write down your goal and your plans first. Keep track of the mistakes. Make a conscious effort not to make those mistakes again.

Do you recommend that day traders use limit orders on the buy side and stop losses to prevent large losses?

Day traders use limit orders on the buy side—depends on the systems you are trading. Stop losses to prevent large losses—it is a must.

Would you discourage or encourage a person who believes that day trading stocks is something he or she wants to try?

If you have the characteristics and the mental makeup of a successful day trader, then I would encourage the person. If you don't have the characteristics of a successful day trader, then I would discourage the person.

Are there any books you recommend that are a "must" for the beginning day trader?

Market Wizards: Interviews with Top Traders, by Jack D. Schwager.

Interview with Donald R. Bright and Robert A. Bright

Donald R. Bright and Robert A. Bright, both of Bright Trading, Inc. a professional day-trading firm, are interviewed in chapter 13. "Interviews with Firm CEOs." Their complete biographies, firm description, and contact information is provided in that chapter. Since they are both day traders, each with over twenty years of experience, they are included in this chapter as well.

The Interview

How many years have you been involved in the markets?

Robert started in 1978, and I [Don] started in 1979.

What markets do you trade?

Over the years, we have traded stocks, options, and futures. We currently stick with stocks.

Which technical analysis tools, if any, do you find the most useful?

None. "At the bottom of the ocean, next to every shipwreck, you find a chart . . . it knew where it was coming from, but obviously had no clue where it was headed." The market can only be predicted with a 70 percent accuracy out six minutes. The rest is a "random walk." This is not merely my theory, but one proven by a market wizard who has made over a half billion dollars in the market. Instead of technical analysis tools, we focus on tape reading. Tape reading is both an art and a science that is far more useful to the professional trader than technical analysis tools. Being able to identify a large "short seller" or an institutional buyer is primary to success. We try our best to teach new traders this skill. Those who have a knack for it do very well. Those who either resist or don't understand the significance of tape reading have problems.

What weaknesses have you overcome that have improved your trading?
Many!

What minimum amount of "risk" capital is needed to begin trading stocks?
Risk capital is simply that. If you trade with a professional firm, you use the firm's capital to trade with. Your "risk capital" is simply another tool that allows you to enter the market: $25,000 to $50,000.

What are the odds that a part-time day trader will be successful versus a full-time trader?
Zero. You must have continuity.

Must the day trader view his or her trading as a "business" to be successful?
Absolutely!

What are the most common mistakes made by the neophyte day trader?
Listening to "analysts" on the TV, "market gurus," or any of a number of other charlatans. That, and trying to pick stocks. You should only trade a small handful of stocks, day in and day out.

How critical are the mental aspects of trading?
Very critical!

Would you recommend that a beginning retail day trader trade at home or at a day-trading firm?
Never at home. You need to be within a group of successful people to have a chance in this business.

Why is being with successful traders so important?
Being in a room of other traders, you have a better "feel" or understanding of what is happening in the market at any given time. You are sharing information (not "touting" your own positions—which is not

allowed!). It makes a big difference having ten or twenty sets of eyes and ears to help you monitor the market.

Do you recommend that paper trading, simulated trading, or other training tools be used by a beginner before actually trading?

Absolutely not! That is the most bogus of tools to suck in the neophyte and let them think they are actually doing well. The truth is you do not get all those trades that you go after. If simulations worked, we would all simply program our computers to trade for us.

What steps should a new trader take to minimize his or her risk of losing capital?

Get training, trade small, and know your costs. Develop a winning game before adding to your share size. We suggest that new traders start off with small order size (500 shares or less), and adjust upwardly as their skills improve. If they are struggling, then we may have them cut back to 100 share lots for a while. It's like throwing a baseball. You must trade over and over until you get the feel for it. I would rather that a person make 100 trades of 100 shares than 10 trades of 1,000 shares at first.

How important is having a mentor or a person closely supervise the new day trader for the first few months?

Very helpful, if you can find the right person. Most cannot afford to pay a successful trader enough to cover their time. Some good traders will take on a student, but not to the detriment of their own trading.

Do you recommend that a diary be kept by the trader of all transactions with notes on all trades?

Yes, so that their mentor can analyze the trades after the market closes. And the mentors had better be trading themselves, or don't use them!

Do you recommend that day traders use limit orders on the buy side and stop losses to prevent large losses?

Use "mental stops" based on other market conditions rather than stop orders. Why alert others of your threshold of pain?

Would you discourage or encourage a person who believes that day trading stocks is something he or she wants to try?

I would explain the facts, and probably discourage more than I encourage.

Are there any books you recommend that are a "must" for the beginning day trader?

Not really. Most are either vanity pieces or marketing tools.

Interview with Thomas L. Busby

Thomas L. Busby, founder of the Day Trading Institute, has been a professional securities trader, broker, and registered investment adviser for more than twenty years. He began his trading career with Merrill Lynch, and before founding the institute in 1996, he was vice president of Salomon Smith Barney.

Tom has a bachelor's degree in business administration from the University of Georgia, and a juris doctor degree from the Oklahoma City University School of Law. He was a distinguished graduate of the U.S. Air Force Budget Officer School, and served seven years as an officer of U.S. Air Force prior to becoming a professional securities broker and trader.

Tom's unique trading approach incorporates lessons learned from over twenty years of actual trading rather than based on untested theories. The method is accessible and understandable and is based upon straightforward principles of money management combined with technical indicator analysis. Since Tom was trained as a lawyer, his methodology emphasizes the importance of careful risk management in trading.

At the heart of his teaching, Tom has created the *Roadmap to the Market* that he shares with his students as an easy-to-use guide to applying his method of trading the market. It is a powerful tool to understanding and putting to use the interplay he teaches between critical time zones, key numbers, and significant market directional indicators. Tom has appeared on business and investing programs on national television and radio, and his opinions are often featured in newspapers throughout the country. Tom can be contacted at: tbuz@daytrading school.com. His phone number is: (800) 970-9791

Day Trading Institute

The Day Trading Institute, located in Mobile, Alabama, is a school that provides training to day traders in a methodology for trading the S&P 500 futures market and its applicability to trading other markets including, but not limited to, stocks, commodities, futures, and options. The institute is unique not only in its methodology but also because it is committed to the success of the students through a process of continuing education, an ongoing relationship of support, and an applied learning hands-on instructional approach. Website: www.daytrading school.com.

The Interview

How many years have you been involved in the markets?
Approximately twenty years.

Which markets do you trade?
I actually trade all the markets, but I specialize in the S&P futures market.

What makes you a successful trader?
You have to take the mistakes that you make and eliminate them from your trading. It is just like a professional golfer. What makes him different than the amateur is that he starts eliminating mistakes. The key to being successful is being able to last long enough to figure out what it is going to take. The majority of people that open a trading account are gone within thirty days.

Which technical analysis tools do you find the most useful?
I've found that I use a lot of indicators. I like to watch the tape. In the old days, the traders used to watch the tape. I do the same thing with computers. And we've developed our own software to do that. What we're doing is capturing certain information off the tape and making decisions based on that information. What we're trying to do is to integrate three different elements. One of the keys is support and resistance. Next is deciding what the trend is. And lastly, I look for certain time patterns that I trade during the day. I basically have three trade zones: The first lasts from 10:30 A.M. EST to 11:15 A.M. EST; the second is from 1:30 P.M. EST to 2:15 P.M. EST; and the last is from 3:15 P.M. EST to 3:45 P.M. EST.

What weaknesses have you overcome that have improved your trading?
My own personality.

What minimum attributes do you believe a person should possess before considering becoming an equities day trader?

I think the trader has to have an ability to learn. He has to have to the ability to change. And he has to have the ability to execute.

What minimum amount of "risk" capital is needed to begin trading stocks?

The minimum amount set by the exchange is around $2,000. But I believe someone needs at least $10,000 to start. I would encourage people, even if they have a lot of money, to start out trading small numbers of shares and dollars.

What knowledge or training does a potential day trader need at the minimum before beginning to trade?

Prior to trading his first stock, a trader must learn how to read the S&P futures. The S&P futures drive the direction of the majority of stocks. It will teach the trader how to look at his individual stocks in the big picture. And that gives him the big picture of the market. There is a direct correlation between the Nasdaq and the S&P futures. If you look at a pyramid, for example, the S&P futures is at the top of the pyramid, followed by the Nasdaq futures. The futures market is a core ingredient that most stock traders are missing from their stock trades. The reason to use the futures is that the futures lead stocks and other indexes and indicate where the market is going. If you can follow and understand the S&P futures, then you'll know when to be long and when to be short in your individual equities.

I'm not focusing on S&P futures as a chart pattern, but rather looking at the movement of the stock in question as well as some fundamental issues with that stock. I'm looking at support and resistance with the futures, as well as looking at whether or not you should be long or short or out of the market.

What are the odds that a part-time day trader will be successful versus a full-time trader?

Even if you only trade two or three days a week, I believe that you should study the market every day. If you're able to study the market every day, then your odds of success will go up. It's good to review what happened each day at the close of business for about five minutes. We don't do any preparation other than that for the next day's market. I think it's a mistake studying and preparing for hours for the next day's market. By doing this you create a bias. You have to approach each day as a new day. That's an attitude you must have as a day trader. Bias cannot enter into the picture as a day trader. You have to look at the market and each stock without prejudice and with complete objectivity.

Must the day trader view his or her trading as a "business" to be successful?
Most definitely.

Of the successful traders that you know, what characteristics or qualities make them successful?
There are three critical things:

1. That they are willing to deal with their losses—and that means persevere.
2. That they are able to evolve with the market—the market changes. They must change with the market.
3. That they worry about risks of the trade—the rewards will take care of themselves.

Of the unsuccessful traders that you know, what characteristics or qualities make them unsuccessful?
They are too greedy—they're always trying to hit a home run. Or they may be too fearful—unable to pull the trigger.

What are the most common mistakes made by the neophyte day trader?
Not understanding the mechanics of how to trade—entering orders, protecting themselves, having a certain portfolio exposure.

How critical are the mental aspects of trading?
Very critical. You can take a great method and take a great person, but if he can't control himself, he will be not to be able to control his account.

Would you recommend that a beginning day trader trade at home or at a day-trading firm?
I would think that it would be better for him to trade at home and establish some fundamental rules for himself. And then, I think, if he wanted to go to a trading firm, that it would be okay. But he needs not to be entirely influenced by a bunch of neophytes.

Do you recommend that paper trading, simulated trading, or other training tools be used by a beginner before actually trading?
No. I think what you should do is just trade a lot smaller. Use scale. You've got to know how you're going to react yourself to situations that you are faced with. Paper trading is sort of like playing golf.

You can make great shots off the driving range, but once you're on the course, you don't get the opportunity to redo the shot.

What steps should a new trader take to minimize his or her risk of losing capital?

The very first step should be to seek out a place that he can go to get training from someone who has been trading. He should have a mentor or someone to go to that will help him eliminate a lot of the mistakes that most new traders make. This mentoring stage is different for each individual. For some people it doesn't last very long, and with other people it lasts for a few years.

What should a trader do to improve his or her skills and performance?

After a trader trades, he should review his trades to look at the outcome and try to keep eliminating mistakes from his execution of whatever methods he is using. As we teach down here, after every ten trades you need to review things and make changes to the way you are putting trades in.

The first thing that we cover in our training course is to learn the language of the markets. As in any field, you have certain words that mean certain things. We spend a lot of time going over the different terms—for example, what a trend is, what a tick is, and what is an opening.

The second thing we do is to discuss how you're going to get the information you need to trade. That means that you need a data provider to do that. We discuss the different data providers and their capabilities.

The third thing we do is to review the type of software you need to analyze the data so that you can make your interpretations.

Then we discuss how the market works, how the market responds to different news events, and how it responds on typical days. We try to go through the entire spectrum of what a trader would be exposed to all the way down to order entry. In addition, we cover money management, risk management, and the psychology of trading.

How important is having a mentor or a person closely supervise the new day trader for the first few months?

I think that it is very important, because it is good to have someone you can trust and who you can bounce your ideas off. The person will tell you the way it is. And of course you want someone that's going to teach you in the reality of the market and not give you a dream world.

Do you recommend that a diary be kept to track all trades?

Yes.

Do you recommend that day traders use limit orders on the buy side and stop losses to prevent large losses?

First, I believe that a trader should use any type of order that's available to him to do the execution. At the minimum, whether a trader is a short-term or long-term trader, he should always use a stop. It should be a physical not a mental stop. The problem is that a trader can get caught up in the hypnotics of the market and not execute his mental stop, if that was his plan. That is why a physical stop is critical. Even if you do get stopped out, you can always get back in the market.

Would you discourage or encourage a person who believes that day trading stocks is something he or she wants to try?

I would encourage them.

What is the most important lesson that you've learned about trading in your career?

Don't give up.

Are there any books you recommend as a "must" for the beginning day trader?

Yes. The best and the first book I ever read was Edwin Lefevre's *Reminiscences of a Stock Operator*.

Interview with Chris Manning

Chris Manning is an internationally renowned trader. He is president and founder of Manning Advanced Trading Seminars, one of the highest rated investment workshops in the world today. He is a frequent guest on the television program *The Money Channel*. He has been quoted in *Financial Times*, *Shares Magazine*, *Investors Chronicle*, *Online Investor*, and *Dividends Magazine*. Mr. Manning has taught thousands of investors the most proven and profitable systems for using technical analysis (charting). He is a master of trading systems and indicators that produce massive profits in trading stocks and options.

As an acknowledged expert of highly successful strategies, Mr. Manning is frequently invited to be a keynote speaker at investment seminars in the United States, Australia, and Europe. He is currently the number one financial speaker in England.

Manning Advanced Trading Seminars

Manning Advanced Trading Seminars provide one of the highest rated investment workshops in the world today. It is currently the number one stock selection seminar in the United States, and the number one financial seminar of any kind in Europe. The three-day advanced course consists of:

Day 1: Successful Investing—How to Get Started
Day 2: Mastering Chart Reading and Trading
Day 3: Advanced Trading Strategies and Live Workshop

The course teaches the most proven and profitable systems for using technical analysis (charting). The investment strategies covered have been tested for thousands of hours and have produced incredible results. The company can be contacted at (800) 684-7100 or via e-mail at: seminars@manningtrading.com

The Interview

What is your background?

For six years I worked at Arthur Anderson in San Francisco as a strategic consultant. Then, in 1996, I attended a nationally known trading seminar. I got excited and quit my job to became a full-time trader and got crushed. At that point I decided to become systematic about this game. I began to list every major pattern in the market, whether based on news, fundamentals, or charts. Then for three years I systematically tested each pattern to identify which truly worked and which were coin flips.

I ended up very quickly identifying certain combinations of technical analysis patterns that were the most profitable. After being asked to keynote quite a few seminars and conferences in the United States, Europe, and Australia, I decided in mid-1999 to create Manning Advanced Trading Seminars. The focus was to teach the results of that three-year study and to take beginning traders and turn them into advanced traders in a three day period. Currently, I am teaching in the evenings and on weekends and generally trading during market hours.

How long have you been day trading?

I began full-time trading in 1996.

Do you day trade full- or part-time? If part-time, about how many days a week?

I traded full-time for three years, and I currently trade part-time about four hours a day, five days a week. This includes about two hours of setup in the evenings and one hour near the open and one hour near the close. Most of my entries occur near the close.

Where do you trade from?

I trade using my laptop and a phone line from wherever I happen to be that day. I work hard to never fly during trading hours. I am forced to trade using my laptop from hotel rooms often, since I teach seminars in different locations. When teaching a live trading seminar I use the hotel phone line and my laptop in front of the class (day three of the seminar).

Are you a day trader or swing trader? Why did you choose that route?

I am mainly a position trader or swing trader, meaning that I typically hold a position a few days to a few weeks. I'd say that only about 25 percent of my speculative trades are put on for a day or less. I chose position trading as a result of an incredibly stupid trick I tried a few years back. At the time I was mainly day trading. I went to Hawaii for a conference and decided to just let everything ride and let the chips fall where they may. I didn't even put in stops. The result of this incredibly stupid experiment was that when I came back, I had accomplished my best two-week gain ever.

At that point I analyzed the market and determined that the largest swings in the market took a few days to a few weeks to occur, rather than a few hours. Those are the swings that I focus on, but having the same passion and obsession as many other day traders, I found that I also love to be in the game. Thus, purely for variety and excitement, I also do shorter-term trades using five-minute charts.

Are you connected to your broker via Internet, DSL, or cable modem?

I am connected to my broker via the Internet since I invest using my laptop from hotel rooms in various cities. At home I have DSL, and at one time I had cable modem. I find my current modem and the speed of the Internet more than adequate.

How much are you paying in commissions for each buy and sell?

I pay approximately $15 per trade in commissions. The most recent study I performed on brokers with $5 commissions indicated unacceptable levels of slippage. Since I trade higher dollar amounts, the execution is far more important. Tomorrow the landscape may change, however.

Why did you get involved in day trading?

Trading has been a passion and an obsession ever since the first seminar I attended. I remember having a difficult time sleeping for about a week after that first workshop. Trading for me represents, above all, freedom to do what I love.

What was your starting capital?

I started with approximately $10,000.

What is your trading philosophy?

My trading philosophy is best summarized as probability stacking. That is:

1. List all the patterns in the market that you are aware of.
2. Test each pattern one-by-one and in combination.
3. Rank all the patterns and combinations of systems based on the actual track records of each.
4. Focus your incredibly scarce time as a trader on those patterns and systems that have the highest net profitability within your acceptable level of risk.

What markets and type of stocks do you trade?

I trade mainly the U.S. equities and options markets. I focus mainly on technology stocks.

Do you have a specific profit and loss target for each trade?

I do not use an arbitrary profit or loss target; rather, I hold on as long as the trend continues. My initial target for the trade is usually a recent major peak or resistance level, unless I am buying near new highs—then the sky is the limit. As long as the trend continues, I will ride it. If that is for a 10 percent ride, that's fine. If the stock goes up 100 percent, that's even better. If you utilize a specific target, you automatically eliminate those few trades that make an insane amount of profit and that end up paying for a large number of previous losses.

How many trades a day do you make?

I make anywhere from zero to five or six trades a day.

How have you gained knowledge about the markets?

I acquired nearly all of my trading skill through the process of methodically and systematically testing pattern after pattern after pattern to find out what the true track record of a pattern or system was. When I first began trading I read nearly everything published I could get my hands on, and attended every major trading seminar in the United States, Europe, and Australia. However, books and seminars generally teach you the glossary terms of trading, and, in some isolated instances, even teach specific patterns or criteria to select stocks.

However, the missing component is usually the track record of the patterns that you are learning or which combinations of patterns work the best in a complete trading system. It is rare to find an author or a seminar leader who actually trades successfully himself. My most profitable and innovative systems have been conceived in the shower, in the middle of the night waking from sleep, or from other full-time traders (you have never heard of) who keep their systems to themselves or within their circle of trading buddies.

Did you take a day-trading training course before beginning to trade?

The very first trading course I attended was given by Wade Cook. Since then, I've been to every major seminar, as previously mentioned. However, none of the courses I attended left me feeling I had the certainty to trade—including all facets of the trading system. For example, it is extremely rare for a trading course to give you all of the necessary criteria to actually implement the system; rather, there is usually a certain amount of discretion required in any trading system that is taught in the seminar.

It is even more rare that a course will give you the actual track record of the system they are teaching. That leaves individual traders with homework that they must complete before using anything that they have learned in the seminar. That is, they must test their interpretation of the system they have learned to understand the true track record in an up, down, and sideways market and over a minimum of thirty trades to be statistically valid.

What are your strengths as a trader?

My number one strength as a trader is my willingness to sit in cash and be completely at peace as long as the market is dropping. When I began trading, I felt I always needed to be in the market and placing trades even if the market was weak. Most professional traders learn very quickly that what determines whether they are still standing long term is the size of their largest losses. Most of the largest losses result from an inability to obey one's trading system and to exit when the system indicates a sell. Eventually, traders with an inability to cut losses quickly get weeded out of the market. Any trader still standing when the dust settles must, by definition, acquire this skill.

What are your weaknesses as a trader?

My obsession with the markets and my thirst for knowledge are a major hindrance in my trading. The reason it took me three years of solid testing to get a handle on the markets was that I wanted to know every major pattern and strategy that existed and the track record of each. This was a daunting task. The great part about being that obsessive is that I now have a very solid handle on what works and what doesn't. The difficulty with that weakness is that it only really takes one pattern to become a winning trader. I probably could have avoided carpel tunnel and a few eyeglass prescriptions by settling on one system quite a long time ago. I still would have been fine.

How are you trying to overcome your weaknesses?

The answer is to document and systematize your strategy in the form of either a computerized trading method or a spreadsheet checklist. This is an excellent way to overcome a lack of focus.

Do you place stop orders to limit your losses?

I place stop orders on every trade just below a support level, which represents the point at which the stock has broken below its normal random range.

Do you place limit orders when you buy?

I use buy stops to enter trades, and I do not use limit orders. If the stock gaps up through my buy stop, then I may not have the greatest entry in the world, but then again breakaway gaps out of a trading range tend to follow through anyway. So the buy stops work quite well.

Do you treat day trading as a business or a hobby?

For me trading is both a business, as it was my sole source of income for a number of years, and a hobby, in that if I could do anything in the world, I would be sitting in front of the fire with a big fat technical analysis book and reading and testing pattern after pattern. What a geek, huh? So it is both what I do for a living and my love.

What mistakes did you make when you first started trading?

My initial mistake was simply not having a system in the first place. My second mistake was not testing my system to find the actual track record. Once I had a proven system, my next mistake was not obeying that system with discipline. The solution I found was to further test the system. Eventually, one of two things will happen. Either you will acquire total certainty that your system will work over time, or you will learn that your system does not work well enough.

What advice would you give to someone who wants to get into day trading?

This will be difficult in two sentences or less. I have a three-day trading course where I talk as quickly as I can to answer this question. Here's my advice:

1. First, identify a complete written trading system by modeling a successful trader.
2. Next, identify the track record of that system with a minimum of thirty trades in up, down, and sideways market conditions.
3. Focus on one pattern or system to learn the details of that system. Especially valuable will be learning what a false signal looks like in that system (and which nuances help you avoid it).
4. Implement that pattern with discipline.
5. Limit your losses with proper asset allocation, and place your stops below the normal random range of the stock.
6. Track and refine your system so you are not repeating the same mistakes.
7. Last and most important, as soon as one trade makes more than you are used to making in a year, buy your dream car and put the play on the license plate. In Silicon Valley, you see number plates with something like QCOM FEB 4!

Of course, the most efficient way to learn trading that I can humanly imagine is by attending the Manning Advanced Trading Seminars three-day workshop. By the way, I am not kidding.

What do you plan to do, if anything, to improve your trading skills and learn more about the markets?

The markets and the traders who trade them are continually evolving. Therefore, you must consistently test the markets to ensure that the patterns you are using are still the most consistent available. Thus, I plan to test, test, test.

How do you determine which stocks to trade?

First, I screen the universe of trades using fundamental combinations that consistently beat the market year after year. Those fundamental strategies include a component of quality of earnings and a second component of valuation—how cheap the stock is. That reduces the universe of possible trades down to a much smaller listing of stocks, which are ready to explode even before I look at the charts.

Then I use technical analysis. Within technical analysis, I combine chart patterns with indicators based on price and volume using combinations that during my three years of testing the patterns proved to be the most consistent. I spent three years testing trading systems to determine which patterns in the market work and which do not. The most efficient method a trader can use to improve their skills is testing. The technical patterns that I utilize include a component of price, volume, momentum divergences, and Fibonacci levels. My outcome in trading is to find a stock ready to explode, buy it when there is a high probability that the breakout will hold or that the reversal will reverse, then hold on during the majority of the trend until high probability indicators determine that the stock has moved out of its normal random range and thus broken the trend.

How do you determine when to buy and when to sell?

Before buying a share you want the planets to align. That means you must have a number of different variables that all measure different things to all line up. For example volume, price, chart patterns, indicators, different time frames, the market, the sector, and sentiment.

My setups are usually a combination of chart patterns and indicators, which had high probabilities of winning in the past on this share on this time frame. My actual entry comes down to price following through. I do not want to step in front of a freight train. I want to wait until the freight train is heading in my direction, and then I jump on it.

I sell when the stock breaks out of the normal random range of the current trend. For that you can use bottoms (e.g., pivots and fractals), trend lines, a break of the low of the day. My setups to sell may also be a combination of indicators that have proven in the past to be highly predictive on this stock on this time frame in the past. There are a number of extremely profitable systems and indicators to assist a trader in selling, such as volatility breakouts, blow-off volume, and momentum divergences.

What tools and indicators (e.g., technical analysis, tape reading, Nasdaq Level II, candlesticks, S&P futures, tick, and so on) do you use to determine buy and sell points? Explain what you use and how you use them

I use fundamental analysis for my initial screening and then technical analysis for my buy and sell points. This includes chart patterns that predicate high probability breakouts or reversals and indicators on price and volume, including moving averages, time segmented volume, proprietary settings on RSI, Fibonacci retracements, ADX, and momentum divergences, among others. Day three of my advanced trading course includes nine complete trading systems. It takes a few hours to teach the best combinations of indicators that resulted from the three year study I mentioned earlier. I use the price as my actual entry and exit techniques and use indicators and combination of indicators as my setups.

What is the most important lesson you learned so far in your trading?

The most important lesson is to focus on one system and learn all the details of that system, including what a false system looks like and including which indicators are the best for confirmation and which of the possible sell techniques worked best on this share on this time frame in the past. Of course, that one system must consistently and systematically reduce losses.

What have you learned about the market makers and how they "manipulate" the price to shake out the weak traders?

A false signal occurs when a stock makes a peak, breaks above that peak by a little, then reverses. Or vice versa, when a stock makes a bottom, barely breaks that bottom and then shoots upward. The amount of those false signals is due to both market makers manipulating the market and the investors having second thoughts. Some stocks have virtually no manipulation occurring and, as a result, no false signals. Other stocks have a consistent pattern of false signals.

About three years ago, I began adding "fluff" to my buy stops and sell stops. Fluff is the amount by which you were faked out by a false signal in the past. First, I quantify the amount of each false signal on this stock on this time frame. I then add that amount of fluff to my buy stops and sell stops to ensure that I don't fall for the same fake outs that have happened in the past.

What books would you recommend that a neophyte day trader read?

For a beginning level trader to learn the fundamentals, I would buy *How to Make Money in Stocks* by William O'Neil. To learn the basics of technical analysis, I would recommend *The Technical Analysis Course,* by Thomas Meyers, or *The Visual Investor,* by John Murphy, and for more advanced technical analysis I would read *The Computer Analysis of the Futures Markets,* by Lebeau and Lucas. I also love *Street Smarts,* by Linda Bradford Raschke and Lawrence Connors.

What minimum attributes (qualitative and quantitative) do you believe a person should possess before considering becoming an equities day trader?

First, the person must have a passion for technical analysis. Second, he or she must be fully associated to a big enough "Why" for investing in the first place, otherwise discipline will not occur. Next, the person must have the ability to focus on one system and to eliminate any distractions that minimize their attention to that system. A trader must have the discipline to test a system before using it, and then to trade only that proven system and not a series of other untested systems. A trader must also have the discipline to exit when the system says to exit. Good trading should have very little emotion and in fact should be quite boring. A good trader finds one system or pattern and repeats that pattern over and over again.

What knowledge or training does a potential day trader need at the minimum before beginning to trade?

First, the trader must have knowledge about charting or technicals, specifically how to use software, any software. Learn which price patterns have the highest probability of winning. Test to determine which indicators in combination are the most robust. Next, a trader must obtain an understanding of trading vehicles that he plans to use, be it stocks, stocks on margin, calls, puts, covered calls, bull call spreads, call ratio writes, and so on. And, of course, the speed at which a trader becomes skilled is directly proportional to the amount of time that is spent testing trading systems or the markets. You learn very slowly by screening stocks during the day to find a good play. You learn very quickly by testing during that day.

How critical are the mental aspects of trading?

Psychology in trading comes down to two things. First, are you in the market at all? And second, are you trading a proven trading system with discipline?

To obtain the mental desire to be in the market at all, you must become fully associated with it and feel what it would be like to have total financial freedom.

Lack of discipline in nearly all cases is simply the trader's brain telling him that he does not believe the system he is trading works. The way to solve that is to test the system even further. Once you find a system that works, wild horses cannot stop you from trading it.

How important is having a mentor?

A mentor is important only from the perspective that the fastest way to learn proven successful patterns or systems is by modeling. This is the process of finding out another trader's strategy so specifically that you can replicate that system.

I highly recommend having an inner circle of traders that you correspond with regularly. There is a massive amount of synergy that can happen when a number of people who trade the same system share the time required to research it. For example, you could get a group of five people who are all at the same trading level to each test a different system. Cumulatively, you can obtain five times the knowledge.

Do you recommend that a diary be kept of all transactions and comments about each trade?

In order to improve anything in life, you must measure it more often. Larry Williams noted that losing traders do not seem to understand why it is necessary to track their total equity, while winning traders track it almost daily.

Traders must keep a diary of their trades to document their mistakes and to then change their system of monitoring it to ensure that they do not repeat the same mistake over and over again. Every trading diary should have three components. First, it should indicate why you entered the trade. Second, it should indicate why you exited the trade. Third, about thirty periods (e.g., price bars) later, it should indicate the lessons that you learned. It will not be apparent what you did wrong immediately. If you knew what you did wrong, you would not have done it at the time. Usually about thirty bars later, it is quite apparent what your mistake was.

Do you recommend that traders use limit orders on buys and stop losses on sells?

I recommend that traders use buy stops to enter and stop losses to exit.

Would you encourage or discourage someone who believes that day trading stocks is something he or she wants to do?

I would highly encourage anyone to follow his passion. If trading is a passion, go for it. If it is a hobby, be careful. Winning traders focus fiercely on one system, test that system, and then implement that system with discipline. That is a difficult thing to do if you dabbling in the trading game as a hobby. For traders starting out, I suggest you keep your day job. Once you have proven to yourself that your system is consistently profitable in all market conditions, then you may slowly increase your trading time. It is far easier to have the correct psychology if you are not dependant on your trading results for your lunch money. Personally, I cannot imagine a more enjoyable or rewarding career.

13

INTERVIEWS WITH FIRM CEOs

To obtain a perspective on the day-trading industry, I interviewed CEOs of five large trading firms and one discount broker. The questions related to their firm's growth, the future of day trading, and their views on the success and failure factors for potential day traders. All these individuals have years of investment market experience. Their insights are interesting and informative. Even though these CEOs may not agree with each other on a number of points, they provide a unique perspective on the industry.

The CEOs interviewed were:

Gary Mednick, president and CEO, On-Site Trading, Inc.
Joe Wald, CEO and co-founder, EDGETRADE.com
Kyle Zasky, president and co-founder, EDGETRADE.com
Robert A. Bright, CEO, Bright Trading, Inc.
Donald R. Bright, trader and director of education, Bright Trading, Inc.
David Nassar, CEO, Marketwise Securities, Inc.
Steven P. Goldman, CEO, Yamner & Co.
Ronald Shear, CEO, Carlin Equities Corp.

When I contacted Yamner & Co. to participate in the interview process, I was under the impression that they were a day-trading firm. I was mistaken. They are a traditional discount broker, and they have some day traders that use the firm's services. Steven Goldman, the CEO, had such a strong viewpoint on day trading that I felt it would add value to this chapter. Therefore, I've included his interview as well

Interview with Gary Mednick

Gary Mednick is president and CEO of On-Site Trading, Inc. Prior to forming the company in 1994, Mr. Mednick was the executive vice president of the Professional Trading Division of Redstone Securities, which he founded 1991. Previously, he was executive vice president at Schonfeld Securities, where he was in charge of recruiting and training proprietary and agency traders, from 1989 to 1991. Mr. Mednick has a B.A. in psychology and business from Hofstra University.

Company Description

On-Site Trading, Inc., is an electronic brokerage firm catering to professional traders. Gary has spearheaded the growth of On-Site to its current level of twenty-three national offices servicing 1,300 traders, including 650 traders using its direct-access trading systems remotely.

The Interview

How long has your firm been providing day-trading services?

We have provided services for active traders for almost six years. On-Site Trading was founded in 1994, and its first clients were professional traders. Most of our traders are not technically day traders. That is, they do not enter and close out every position during each trading day. Most use other, longer term strategies, such as swing trading and holding positions over several days or even weeks.

How many individuals trade at your firm's office versus remotely?

We have twenty-three offices in seven states, where about 750 traders work the trading stations. We have another 500 or so traders who trade remotely, usually from offices in their homes.

How has your firm changed (for example, number of clients, technological infrastructure, order execution method, and execution time) in the past two years.

Most obviously, we've grown substantially, adding traders and offices to accommodate them, most recently adding more offices in New Jersey, Florida, Chicago, and Denver. And we've even gone international with the new millenium, with an office in Jerusalem that has just opened and tie-in with a bank in Spain that will let us begin operations there soon.

We're also offering more services, both technical and advisory. And this is essentially an outgrowth of our origins. We began as a proprietary company, but because we were all professional traders, we understood what active traders need, and perhaps equally important, what they don't need. So we began to offer our services to active traders and it's been a bit of "If you build it, they will come." Now we cater mostly to active traders, and I'm delighted because that is where the growth is going to be.

Has the Mark Barton incident in Atlanta had any impact on the way you run your business (for example, more careful screening of clients)?

I have a lot more sympathy with the Postal Service now, because this horrifying incident has unfairly tarred "day trading" with the "going postal" brush. Prior to the killings at the trading offices, this man apparently killed his wife and children. I don't think these killings had much more to do with trading than the shootings in post offices had to do with the mail or the shootings at insurance companies with insurance. It is all too easy for people with serious psychological problem to get guns, and if you closed every stock market in the country, you would still have this problem.

Having said that, I think this made every small business in the country a bit more conscious of security. We don't have the elaborate system of badges and passes you see in large corporations, but on other hand people can't just walk in. However, that's a basic precaution against theft as opposed to a random attack.

We have probably taken a closer look at people who have not traded well, and we are also more interested in the backgrounds of new traders, as I will discuss later.

What responsibility should your firm have, if any, to determine the suitability of a potential client for day trading?

We take our responsibility very seriously. We started as a proprietary trading operation, and our traders were former brokers with Series 7's or other licenses. So they knew what they were doing, and they knew the risks. As we've added traders from outside the industry, we have taken care to see that they have the resources and the knowledge.

We were the first in the industry to introduce a qualifying exam, which is posted on our Web site. Everyone who wishes to trade with us must take and pass that exam. The only exception is people with Series 7 licenses, who have already proven their knowledge.

We have other minimal standards. We require a minimum of $25,000 for opening an account and advise people to have more. We have set a minimum annual income of $50,000 and a net worth of at least $150,000. We also ask prospective new clients if they have ever had a gambling problem. And to be sure that we do not overpromise prospective traders, our advertising is cleared with the NASD.

Did you expect that day trading would become as popular as it is today?

Again, I would prefer that we call it active trading, but in fact I did anticipate a growing demand for the kinds of services active traders need. I developed a business plan in 1991 that was predicated on the assumption that there would be an explosion in electronic trading, brought on in part by the reaction to the 1987 stock market crash and the availability of electronic trading systems like SOES, SelectNet, and DOT.

As a result of the crash, there were scores of thousands of layoffs at the brokerage houses, and even though many people were able to land on their feet, in the back of their minds was the realization that it could happen again. They also knew they had the skills to trade for themselves. After all, they'd been trading for others successfully. And thousands had amassed sufficient capital to absorb the losses inherent in operating a new business. When employment at the brokerages became shaky, people would want to trade on their own. Then, as people saw it was possible to make a living trading, other people who had accumulated capital in their careers would want to have a go at it.

Did I anticipate it would become *this* popular? I'm not psychic, so I can't say that. But I knew that veterans of the industry were looking to strike out on their own, and others would follow. And that is just what happened.

In selecting a day-trading firm, what should a day trader look for?

You want the same essentials as any active trader. But above every other consideration is quality of execution. One of our advertisements explains how that $9.95 trade can cost you plenty, and SEC Commissioner Arthur Levitt recently made the same point: "If your order is executed at one increment away from the best price—$1/16$—that's $62.50 out of your pocket on a 1,000 share order. That's more than four times the commission that many online brokers advertise today."

Professional traders are always seeking the best price, and the only way to get that is instant execution on the ECN or market maker of your choice, executing your orders yourself. For that, direct access is the only way to go. You know you are going to get the best price. In fact, On-Site Trading's execution software automatically routes your order to the ECN offering the best price.

Web brokers pose another problem for active traders. Many sell your orders to a third party who actually executes them. Two things can go wrong here. First, as Arthur Levitt suggests, you lose time. Anyone who follows today's markets knows how quickly that $\frac{1}{16}$ movement can occur. Delay your order three minutes and it's gone. Second, someone else is getting a piece of your order, since the broker placing the sale will take his cut. And his cut is coming out of your hide.

It's important to make the distinction between professional traders and people who are trading for retirement and other longer term purposes. Nobody likes to give up that $62.50, but if you are buying to hold for months or years, it's ridiculous to sweat sixteenths of a point. Lower cost coupled with slower speed execution can be acceptable. Someone who is trading for a living is making far more trades, and that $62.50 on even some trades may represent the difference between a profitable trader and a loser.

But speed isn't everything. You also want to be working with people who take their business seriously and are responsible corporate citizens. Again, Arthur Levitt recently offered ways for consumers to tell that brokerages are acting responsibly. One criterion was the best execution rules I've already discussed. Another is practicing what they preach. That is, advising people of the risks involved and monitoring the suitability to their trading strategies and behavior. Brokerages should speak plainly and disclose all key information about costs and risks.

Finally, they should advertise responsibly. If you see an ad for a trading firm that looks more like an ad for "the road to El Dorado," beware. You can make a good living trading, but it requires study, experience, and hard work. If a firm's advertising suggests that it doesn't, take your business somewhere else.

Beyond speed and ethics, you need information. Your firm should offer multisource, real-time Market Intelligence. On-Site, for example, offers the Dow Jones news wire, Reuters, Bloomberg, First Call, and Wall Street Source. And, of course, a constant up-to-date flow of real-time quotes, charts, and analytics. On-Site offers Track Data, e-Signal, A.T. Financial, and NAQ.

What characteristics distinguish your firm from the other large firms in the industry?

Most importantly, we are traders ourselves. We know what traders need and how to serve them. We have selected a technology set that meets our needs, as opposed to picking software programs because they are "cool apps."

Everyone emphasizes service, of course, but we have kept it as personal as possible. For every thirty traders we have one person assigned to answer any technical questions they may have and/or untangle any technical problems. When traders encounter a glitch, they want to be able to talk to a human being immediately, not leave a voice mail message that may not be answered for hours or even at all.

We are the first online brokerage to require remote traders to pass a qualifying test, which people can take by visiting our Web site.

If you offer a training program to new customers, how long have you been offering it, what is its length and cost, and how many customers have taken it?

Because most of our traders have come to us from other brokerage houses, they already know the ropes—or most of them. As the great interest in trading for a living has grown, we're seeing more and more people coming into the business from other sectors of the economy. To meet their needs, we are creating a course that covers all kinds of investing, from planning for retirement or a kid's college education to day trading. It should be available by early this fall (2000).

What personal characteristics and attributes does a person need to become a successful day trader?

Knowledge *plus* preparation *plus* discipline are the keys to success. And the truth is you can have all of these and still fail. The only meaningful test is the trading floor—or computerized trading station—itself. You see people with an excellent education and knowledge who do not do well, and guys who seemed like they struggled through high school do brilliantly. They say that Marine Corps fighter ace Joe Foss was nothing special as a pilot in peacetime, but he found his calling in the skies over Guadalcanal. It can be like that in trading. You find if you're good by doing it.

You have to know enough to absorb the mechanics of the market and read the trends behind the numbers in the same way sailors read the sky and waves. The time taken to acquire that knowledge is all part of your preparation. The other part is developing a trading strategy and sticking to it. That is where discipline comes in.

Napoleon liked his generals to be lucky, and that helps too. But as Branch Rickey liked to say, "Luck is the residue of design." People get lucky in the stock market and other areas of life because they have prepared themselves to recognize the opportunity, no matter how fleeting. And in professional trading, opportunities are indeed fleeting. Which brings me to the last essential, the ability to adjust quickly.

I know some of these traits seem to contradict themselves, but that is why trading is such a difficult profession. You must have discipline to stay with your plan, while also having the ability to adjust quickly and appropriately to changing situations. In other words, you must be able to resist changes while also being able to make changes quickly. Those who can master these paradoxes will do well.

What personal weaknesses can lead to a trader's downfall?

The weaknesses are the converse of the strengths. You need to bring a strong work ethic to the trading station, because trading is inherently hard work, made even harder when you're trading with your own money. You are up against very tough and very smart competitors who have access to the same information you do.

You need to concentrate on your work. The trading station is no place for daydreaming. Opportunities are fleeting, and seizing them requires a high level of alertness. And you have to see them, because missing a market move can cost you money.

Traders who are successful do not get emotional while trading. The ability to make objective decisions in the face of fire is a must. Getting too emotional leads to bad decisions. At the same time you need the patience of a fisherman waiting for the trout to strike. Get bored or try to rush things, and you start making useless or wrong moves.

Do you expect to see a consolidation among ECNs within the next two years? What impact will this have on the ability of traders to obtain rapid and competitive price execution?

Yes, I expect to see a consolidation. The nature of ECNs is such that only one is really necessary to post the information, but to keep execution costs under control, we also need competition. I just think it will be competition among fewer players. Already three or four ECNs are dominant anyway.

Do you believe the regulatory authorities are misguided in their attack on the day-trading firms for their aggressive advertising campaigns and their playing down of the dangers of day trading to the general public?

Yes and no, but mostly no. They are right to closely scrutinize the industry, especially at a time when technology is bringing the general public into it in an unprecedented manner. This is a regulated industry, and people are entitled to no less protection than passengers boarding an airliner. In this case, what the public expects is a level playing field and open dealings. Misleading advertising promising easy money shatters that confidence. And I'm not talking about the use of humor in advertising—we believe in that ourselves.

Brokers have certain responsibilities, and an important one is monitoring the suitability of the client and investment. Obviously, people seeking to trade professionally must have a certain amount of leeway to pursue their strategies. But brokers should insist upon minimal standards of know-how, income, net worth, and account sizes. At On-Site Trading, we have already essentially adopted the standards recently proposed by the NASD and SEC. We require a minimum account size of $25,000, net worth of at least $150,000, and annual income of at least $50,000. We also require all prospective traders to pass our online exam.

Where regulators—and to a greater degree the press—have gone wrong is in lumping all brokers into the same mold. Most brokers want a long-term relationship with their traders because that's the best way to make money. This is like any other business. Finding new customers is hard. The old adage about fools and their money remains true, but almost by definition, few fools have a lot of money to begin with. And when they do, they have plenty of other ways to squander it.

So the cost of recruiting people who quickly deplete their resources through inept trading is high. It gets harder for firms to find the next round of traders after the current one is wiped out. In the long run there aren't that many people with scores of thousands of dollars ready to take a plunge into active trading. And as others get wiped out, word spreads that this isn't a bright idea.

But basic misunderstandings have colored the discussion, for example, the frequently cited statistic that 70 percent of day traders lose money. Active trading has to be compared to a business start-up, not investing for retirement, but the press has persistently refused to do that. The fact is that about three-quarters of all business start-ups fail, whether they involve opening a restaurant, a video store, an advertising agency, or a law office. Active trading is also a business or a profession. There is no reason to expect radically different results. Active trading without knowledge or a reasonable amount of capital makes about as much sense as opening a restaurant with no ideas for a menu and without knowing how to cook, and enough capital to fund your operation for a period of time.

If you were to list the decision criteria that a person needs to evaluate to determine if day trading is suitable for him- or herself, then what would they be?

The key traits I've already mentioned. But first of all, you have to decide that you are ready to go into business for yourself, because that is what day trading is. Not everyone is able to do this, and I do not say that to be derogatory. If you have serious doubts—and I don't mean the usual uneasiness we all have when trying something new—then it almost certainly is not for you.

How well do you understand the lingo and mechanics of stock trading? If you have to pause to remember the meaning of a term for even a second, you are probably not ready. How well do you know the market sectors? Successful traders do not trade at random; the market is too big. They pick an area of interest to concentrate on, but doing that requires enough knowledge to know what to eliminate.

How good is your concentration? If your mind wanders during a baseball game and you have to keep checking the balls and strikes, remember that monitoring the market demands essentially the same skill, for longer hours and with a lot more at stake.

Do you tend to pause and rethink your decisions before making a final choice, say in selecting a restaurant order? Remember that active trading requires making split-second decisions in a constantly changing environment. Pause to think about it for thirty seconds and that sixteenth of a point is gone.

How easily do you brush off failures? In the early stages you are going to make a lot of mistakes—in fact, you are going to make a lot of mistakes no matter how experienced you are. One of the things experience teaches you is to move on and not brood over the wrong calls.

How emotionally committed are you to your decisions? Successful trading means listening to the market, not your heart. People who have done well with a strategy or a stock tend to stay with it after it has ceased to perform to expectations. Cutting losses is always difficult, but it has to be done.

If you were to list the steps that a person needs to take to become a successful day trader, what would they be?

If you believe you have the requisite character traits, you then have to organize your activities. The first step is developing a long-term trading strategy. What sector do you want to concentrate in? How do you plan to allot your resources? Do you want to day trade at all—that is, close out all your positions at the end of every day—or pursue some other strategy? Think hard about this strategy, because the next step is going to be sticking with it long enough to give it a chance to work. And here we are talking about months, not days. And when you start out, you can be sure these will be rocky months. It will be easy to get discouraged. You have to get past that.

Beyond strategy, there are the tactics—your daily approach. You must have a plan for every day. Your day begins at least an hour before the market opens. Check the previous day's profit and loss positions. Review news and earnings on your positions and those you are thinking about buying or selling short. Do some fact-finding. Look for hot stocks, preannouncements or takeovers, significant industry events. Then set your strategy for the day: develop a target list.

As the market opens, assess the situation and place trades accordingly, always remembering that market openings are unreliable indicators of day's performance. Watch for overbought and oversold conditions, but stick to your exit strategies. Stay disciplined. As the day progresses, keep watch on news, rumors, volumes, charts, and Level II.

As market closing approaches, it's time for a new set of decisions. What will you hold overnight? Do you want to close out your other positions? Do you want to add other positions to hold overnight? Am I hedged against market risk? Remember, you are running low on time, and decisions have to be made quickly. Once the market closes, of course, trading can still go on. The new extended trading hours means watching the news (CNBC, Dow Jones, Reuters) to evaluate entering or exiting positions postmarket.

Finally, the time comes to assess your day. Did you stick to your pre-open game plan? What went right—or wrong? Review your money management. Did you let winners ride? Did you cut your losses? What will you do differently tomorrow? Now is the time to identify and correct recurring faux pas.

Last, but by no means least: *Call it quits.* Leave the PC, relax, and enjoy your family and friends. This is an intense business. Without down time, you will burn out quickly.

What would your definition of a "professional" day trader be?

All active traders should consider themselves professionals. This is a full-time business. Anyone making a career out of trading may be called a "professional." The term "day trader" is limited to people who mainly close and open their trades in the same day. Professional people are in it to make their daily bread, not to save up for retirement—indeed, part of their retirement income will come from their trading earnings. If you don't approach day trading or any other form of active trading in that spirit, you are making a mistake.

Based on your knowledge, what are the odds that a part-time day trader can be successful (make money each year)?

Very poor. This isn't something you can dabble in, like stamp collecting and antiquing. Trading takes place during business hours, and opportunities are continuous and fleeting. You have to be there all the time to take advantage of them—or avoid being clobbered. So if you're working another job, you're fighting with at least one hand tied behind your back and probably both. Moreover, a good trader will have no more than 5 percent of his or her assets in a single position, which means that at least twenty positions have to be monitored constantly, not only to avoid taking heavy losses but also to assess new opportunities.

What advice would you give a twenty-five-year-old and a fifty-year-old who want to day trade full-time for a living?

No matter what your age, you need to educate yourself. Prepare for a two-year learning process, so have enough cash on hand to live on as you learn the ropes. Don't trade with it.

Secondly, day trading is a bit like combat or professional sports—it's a young person's game. You need the reflexes, endurance, ability to snap back from disappointment, and, frankly, the lack of experience of youth to pursue day trading on a full-time basis. It takes too much energy for the middle-aged, and even the "kids" start burning out after a while.

There is no reason why persons of any age can't make a living trading, but they have to adjust their strategies to their capabilities.

Most seasoned traders use short-term techniques not strictly day trading. Just like if the Mets want to keep getting Mike Piazza to hit forty homers a year, they're going to have to move him to first base.

And to reiterate, treat this as a business start-up.

How critical to the success of a day trader is the use and understanding of Nasdaq Level II?

I'm in the minority here, I think. It is critical, because active traders should simply know these things to take advantage of the full spectrum of opportunities that arise. But it is not a necessity to trade successfully. The New York Stock Exchange offers an ample playing field, and I actually prefer to trade on the NYSE.

Do you believe that day trading is preferable to "swing trading" (three-to-five day holding period)? Please explain your answer.

Actually, I, and most of the traders at On-Site Trading, prefer short-term trading strategies like swing trading to day trading. It's easier to master, requires less attention, and can be just as lucrative. There is no real reason to liquidate every position daily. Most of the news that may affect a stock's price also occurs during business hours.

It's true that posttrading announcements occur that can affect stock prices—a recent example is the Microsoft antitrust decision that was announced an hour after the market closed. But these things rarely come as bolts out of the blue. They are almost invariably telegraphed. The Microsoft decision was expected, and the big sell-off began during trading hours in anticipation of it. Announcements of a lesser scale are also usually indicated during trading hours. If you see that a company you hold a position in or are interested in has scheduled an announcement for after the close of trading, you usually have time to make your move during trading hours.

In short, if you are paying attention, you are not going to get completely blindsided and will almost always have time to make a move. It may not be the right move, but you do have the time.

Two years from now what major changes do you expect to see in the day-trading arena?

I think the biggest change will be a consolidation in the industry as the bigger players either buy up the active trading specialists or build their own capability. Since you get the traders along with the firm when you buy an active trading company, that will probably be the route taken. It's easier to retain customers you already have than to find new ones. Most of the big firms will probably buy, not build.

One reason for the interest is the larger trend toward online trading generally, with customers doing their own research and making their own trades without consulting their broker, or indeed using any brokerage service other than order execution. Firms that aspire to full-service will want to have an active trading component. Schwab, I think, has been a leader here. Others will follow, and sooner rather than later.

I also expect to see more regulatory intervention over the next two years. The SEC and NASD are going to demand that firms adhere to higher standards for levels of investment capital, overall capital, and income levels for aspiring active traders. They are also going to require that brokers monitor suitability more rigorously.

Yet another change that will probably arrive in the next two years is the expansion of the scope of trading beyond the domestic stock markets into commodities, bonds, mutual funds, and probably into the overseas exchanges as well. We have opened an office in Israel and are about to open another in Spain, where traders in those countries will be able to trade in the American markets. This will spread world-wide—in both directions. Americans will be trading in European, South American, African, and Asian markets and Europeans, South Americans, Africans, and Asians will be trading on our markets. Of course, this will mean traders will be putting in astronomers' hours, but the technology is here now, and hundreds of thousands of people already work nights. I also believe that new markets for trading will develop. Some of the business to business e-commerce players are setting up new markets, although they aren't being called that yet. For instance, is it possible that auto parts and computer components may be tradeable in the next few years?

What will the day-trading industry look like in five years?

My own theory has been that there is a potential market for about 400,000 active traders—people making their living through stock trading—and that it has still not been fully tapped. In five years, that potential will have been realized. Assuming the American economy continues to grow, and all the signs for that are positive, people are accumulating sufficient capital, usually in the form of stocks or mutual fund holdings, to start thinking about trading for themselves. As the active trading universe consolidates into fewer, but larger players, it will create a momentum of its own. Firms with national reputations, backed by national advertising campaigns (not necessarily promoting active trading), will offer active trading services, and the very fact that they are will encourage people to take them up on it. Active trading will be well out of its "Wild West" phase.

Within five years we will see trading beginning to extend well beyond stocks, bonds, commodities, mutual funds, and overseas stocks. I think trading will become the model for the next stage of capitalism itself, with markets evolving to accommodate trading in goods like auto parts, airliners, and heavy equipment of all kinds, and perhaps even for service contracts. You are seeing the earliest manifestations of this on the consumer level on sites like eBay and Priceline.com, but I think trading is the future of business-to-business transactions as well.

How many of today's day-trading firms will still be in existence in the next three years?

"Fewer" is about the best answer I can give. I think the best active trading firms will be absorbed in mergers, either with the larger, established brokers or among each other. The era of the start-up in this business is largely past, not so much because of the costs of installing the technology, which aren't that great and will probably continue to fall on a unit basis, but because of the high costs of attracting traders. The market niches are just about all occupied with established firms—as much as any firm can be considered established in such a new industry—and there is a finite number of traders. Secondly, stiffer regulatory oversight, which I believe is inevitable, is going to make starting up more complicated. Aside from weeding out the cowboy element that the press is so fond of complaining about, stricter oversight will also cause the more raffish elements to look elsewhere for opportunity.

Interview with Joe Wald and Kyle Zasky

Joe Wald is the CEO and co-founder of EDGETRADE.com. He founded and funded the company with Kyle Zasky. They were both successful SOES traders and then momentum day traders. After college, Joe became a broker, then a money manager for some active investors. By dealing with these active investors, Joe saw the need for them to be able to execute their own trades, rather than having to bring tickets to an order desk. Joe has been a pioneer of this new industry as it has grown and developed. He has been the prime motivator in the development of EDGETRADE.com's training course, and has passed on his trading techniques to class after class of "would-be" traders. As a trader and the CEO, Joe ensures that the technology, training, and support of EDGE-TRADE.com is of the utmost quality and that all of the firm's customers trade with the best tools available.

Kyle Zasky is the president and co-founder of EDGETRADE.com, which was formed in 1996. Kyle has been a pioneer of this new industry as it has grown and developed. Originally a bond broker and later a SOES trader in 1994, he brings quick thinking and a proactive management style to the EDGETRADE.com team. Kyle has appeared on *48 HOURS, Nightline,* and CNBC *Power Lunch,* discussing EDGETRADE. com and the future of the industry. Kyle believes that the firm has been very successful in bringing direct-access and day-trading tools to a wide audience.

Company Description

EDGETRADE.com, Inc., established in 1996, is the premiere provider of direct-access trading and educational services. The firm's products and services are delivered through state-of-the-art technology and offered both online and at the corporate offices located in the heart of the Wall Street community. The firm adheres to a simple philosophy, which is the basis of its success: What is in the best interest of customers is in the best interest of the company. The company's mission is to empower customers through technology, education, and service.

The Interview

How long has your firm been providing day-trading services?

We have been providing direct-access services since 1996. That is, we formed the company 1996, and we started doing business in 1997.

How many individuals trade at your firm's office versus remotely?

At our office there are approximately fifty to sixty traders, and another three hundred fifty traders who trade remotely.

How has your firm changed in the past two years?

The biggest difference for our firm has been the technological advancements, allowing us to grow via the Internet. Our infrastructure has exploded. The number of employees has expanded from six or seven to approximately fifty at this point.

Has the Mark Barton incident in Atlanta had any impact on the way you run your business?

It was definitely a very unfortunate incident. But it has not impacted the way we operate at all.

What responsibility should your firm have, if any, to determine the suitability of a potential client for day trading?

We have the same responsibility as any firm would in terms of their clients. Our responsibility hasn't really changed since day one at our firm. We make sure that the customer is suitable for this type of activity. We have always made our customers aware of the risks inherent in day trading. And we always make sure that they understand how difficult it really is, as well as how important it is to have the capital behind them to be able to afford the type of activity or business venture that they're trying to engage in. All of our customers sign an agreement regarding the risks of day trading.

Did you expect that day trading would become as popular as it has today?

Yes. And not only that. We believe that it's only the tip of the iceberg at this point. We believe that direct-access trading is going to democratize the capital markets and the way in which people are going to execute their equity transactions. In the next few years trading will only be through direct access and not through any method where there is a hidden middleman who is taking money away from the customer.

In selecting a day-trading firm, what should a day trader look for?

Educational services. Services that help a customer understand exactly how to use the powerful technology that the day-trading firms provide. You can't just sit down in the cockpit of an F-15 fighter and expect to know how to fly. So we make sure the customers are prepared to use the technology that we have.

In addition to education, the paramount quality that people should be looking for is the ability to control their own execution without any vested interest in directing their order flow. They should have the ability to use any system that's available—SOES, SelectNet, all of the ECNs, and any other system that will allow the customer to control how his own order flow is directed and how they will get their execution.

What characteristics distinguish your firm from the other large firms in the industry?

Our educational services distinguish us from our competitors. We have a variety of services depending upon what your level is as a customer. If you are a neophyte and you have never used direct-access before, then we have very intensive basic training to help you use the software and basic trading techniques and market psychology. We have advanced courses for people who have been trading online for a long time. We have even more sophisticated courses for people who are currently day traders who want to have supervised trading and learn from the experts. We are a full-service online direct-access firm. And this is really a new definition of full service. Our idea of full service is to make sure that you have all the technology and all the educational services that you need to take control of your investment decisions and executions.

If you offer a training program to new customers, how long have you been offering it, what is its length and cost, and how many customers have taken it?

We have been offering our training program for about a year and a half. However, Kyle and I have been informally training our customers since we founded the firm. Currently, we have an in-house course that lasts for three weeks, which is geared to the person who wants to become a professional day trader. And we have online courses of varying lengths. Most of them are night courses that last three hours—beginner, intermediate, and advanced courses. We also offer a course that has supervised trading.

The three-week in-house course is $3,500. The introductory basic course online is $399. The fee for the training is independent of trading costs, and we do not rebate the training fee if a potential customer decides to trade with our firm.

What personal characteristics and attributes does a person need to become a successful day trader?

The first one that is most important is discipline. The second one is tied to discipline. It is being level headed. Regardless of whether the person is making money or losing money, from our experience, the composed trader is the one that has the most opportunity to really maximize his gains and cut his losses.

What personal weaknesses can lead to a trader's downfall?

Someone that always has to be right. Another weaknesses is carelessness. Another is not treating trading as a business.

Do you expect to see a consolidation among ECNs within the next two years? What impact will this have on the ability of traders to obtain rapid and competitive price execution?

We do expect a consolidation. At this point, the consolidation will probably benefit the customers, because there are a lot of ECNs that do not have enough liquidity. And if they combine their forces, it would increase their liquidity. Rather than having five places to go with each having thin liquidity, you can go to three places with more liquidity. Too much consolidation might, in the long term, be a detriment, if there is only one ECN. Right now the situation is too fragmented from our perspective.

Do you believe that the regulatory authorities are misguided in their attack on the day-trading firms for their aggressive advertising campaigns and their playing down of the dangers of day trading to the general public?

We applaud their efforts to protect the public and the integrity of our industry.

If you were to list the decision criteria that a person needs to evaluate to determine if day trading is suitable for him- or herself, then what would they be?

Whether or not they wanted to do this full-time as a career—that is the first step. Secondly, whether they have the capital resources to invest in their learning curve—that can be anywhere from six months to eighteen months. They should have enough capital to pay for living expenses during this time frame. They should not expect to take a paycheck right away. If anyone is going to treat this in a different way than going into an entrepreneurial venture with the same associated risks, then they are misleading themselves.

If you were to list the steps that a person needs to take to become a successful day trader, what would they be?

The first would be to do their due diligence, to start evaluating the types of educational services that are available so that they can learn about the career they are going to embark on. You wouldn't want to become a doctor without going to medical school, and you wouldn't want to become an attorney without going to law school. So that is the first step—to make sure that you gauge your level of expertise. And then put that aside and see what types of services are available to increase your chances for success.

Secondly, you have to take a gauge of your financial situation to make sure. A lot of people call and want to do this, but they do not have the financial resources. And fair or not fair, this is not really a good career choice if you do not have the capital to make it work.

So those are the two decisions. Decide whether you want it. Then start doing the due diligence of the firms that are out there and the services that are available. Make sure that you have the capital. And lastly, find a firm that you feel comfortable doing business with.

What is your definition of a "professional" day trader?

Our definition of a professional day trader is someone who treats this as a full-time career, who wakes up every day at 8:00 A.M. and is prepared to look through the newspapers, go to the financial Web sites, and listen to CNBC. He or she should be ready and prepared to sit in front of the computer from 9:00 A.M. until 4:30 P.M. whether or not any trades are executed each day. The trader has to be in touch and have his or her finger on the pulse of the market.

What advice would you give a twenty-five-year-old and a fifty-year-old who want to day trade full-time for a living?

The first piece of advice for twenty-five-year-olds is that if they have the capital or if they have the backing to attempt day trading as a career, then they are well positioned. In general, younger individuals tend to be more computer proficient and familiar with technology. So what the younger client needs to be aware of is the capital restraints that are involved.

What the older clients tend to need—they tend to have the capital but are not computer savvy—is a comfort level with the computer or the willingness to learn the technology and have an interest in honing their skills with the software, keyboard, and execution.

How critical to the success of a day trader is the use and understanding of Nasdaq Level II?

Essential.

Do you believe that day trading is preferable to "swing trading" (three-to-five-day holding period)?

Yes, definitely. You have more control as a day trader. Overnight you are exposed to overnight risk, since the market doesn't necessarily open where it closed. Intraday you have far more control over your entry and exit prices.

Two years from now what major changes do you expect to see in the day-trading arena?

Two years from now we expect that the term "day trading" will be phased out. We expect the term "direct-access trading" to take its place. Out of the 10 million online accounts right now, less than 15,000 have direct access. We believe that the majority of online accounts, several years from today, will have direct access, regardless of whether you're day trading or investing. There won't be day traders—there will be professional traders, and there will be active investors, and there will be long-term investors. And they should all have the right to have the best technology available.

What will the day-trading industry look like in five years?

We believe that what we have just said in the previous question will hold true for the next two to five years. More people will be trading on the Internet. The customer base will continue to be more educated. Americans demand transparency, liquidity, speed of execution, and control over their lives. If you want to have an investment adviser, in five years you certainly can. But if you want to make your own buy-and-sell decisions, the tools and the technology are only going to increase as long as you and your brokerage are complying with applicable laws and regulations. You should be able to do whatever you want, wherever you are, at any time and not have anyone stand in your away.

How many of today's day-trading firms will still be in existence in the next three years?

Less than five.

Interview with Robert A. Bright and Donald R. Bright

Robert A. Bright is CEO of Bright Trading, Inc. After receiving his bachelor of science degree in accounting, Robert Bright spent several years as an executive for Johns-Manville Corporation. In 1978 he joined the Pacific Stock Exchange and began trading computer modeled option strategies, many of which he designed himself. In the mid-1980s he joined the Chicago Mercantile Exchange and the Chicago Board Options Exchange to trade sophisticated arbitrage strategies using derivatives and equities.

Seeing more opportunities in equities trading in 1992, Robert formed Bright Trading, Inc. Since then Bright Trading has become one of the largest professional trading firms in the United States with several hundred traders in thirty-two locations. Bright Trading, Inc., traded approximately 2.5 billion shares in 1999, over 1 percent of the entire NYSE volume.

Donald R. Bright is a trader and director of education at Bright Trading, Inc. After receiving his dual bachelor of science degree in accounting and business administration from the California College of Commerce in 1971, Don spent his next few years in public accounting. By 1975 he tired of "counting other peoples money" and went into business for himself. In 1979 he became a member of the Pacific Stock Exchange (options market maker). In 1981, he, with his brother Robert, started Bright Equities, a fulfillment equity brokerage for exchange members. Within a few months the business was flourishing, primarily due to the lower costs and quick executions offered by the firm. In the early years the Bright brothers were told that they could not compete with the entrenched interests on the equities floor and were discouraged from doing so. This only added to their motivation to provide better and more inexpensive services. In the mid-eighties the firm was passed on to others to run the daily operations, and Don returned to making markets on the options floor.

In 1995, Don again joined with his brother and Edward Franco to assist in the growth of Bright Trading, Inc. He started Bright Marketing and Management to focus on recruiting and retention of qualified day traders. In the years that followed, Don literally answered hundreds of questions about trading in general, equity trading in detail, option, and index relationships to the overall marketplace. Don also added the Internet site stocktrading.com to further assist current and future traders. It was then that Don decided to host seminars that could reach more people with an interest in securities trading. During 1996, he helped Bright Trading by setting up and speaking at several of their conferences.

In 1997, after seeing the gap between the "get rich quick" type of presentations, and the costly (up to $5,000 per week) training courses, he decided to start Investor Awareness, Inc. (the education branch of

Bright Trading). With the current interest in the market growing rapidly, and the decades of experience and network of professional friends, it is the intention of Investor Awareness to fill that informational gap. Don can be reached at (800) 249-7488 or bright@wizard.com.

Company Description

Bright Trading, Inc., is a professional, proprietary stock trading firm with hundreds of independent traders who trade from thirty-two nationwide locations. The firm provides professional traders with an opportunity to enhance their trading results through the use of high-speed, high-quality execution systems, use of the firm's capital, and extremely low transaction costs—with no ticket charges.

Bright Trading, Inc., is a growing enterprise. The firm is always on the lookout for active, professional traders (and those who would like to become professional traders), who would like to experience the Bright opportunity. The firm also offers a five-day comprehensive trading course for new traders. Information on the firm can be obtained from the Web site www.stocktrading.com.

The Interview

I believe your firm has been in business since 1992. Can you explain what type of services it offers day traders?

We provide low-cost market access and trading stations along with the use of the firm's capital. All of our traders actually use the firm's capital to trade with. They do put up a $25,000 performance deposit that is kept separate from our trading capital.

What is your definition of a "professional" trader? Is this different than a "retail" day trader?

A true professional trader is licensed (at minimum, a Series 7), registered (with the SEC), and has experience on either a stock exchange trading floor or with a professional firm, not simply a "retail" customer who happens to be making money currently.

How does your firm differ from the other day-trading firms?

These people are all retail firms, and the bulk of their traders are simply customers. They are restricted as to margin, and so on.

How many traders trade at your firm, and what percentage are successful?

We have approximately three hundred traders. Those with us for one year or longer have a 70 percent success ratio; two years or longer—80 percent successful.

What percent of new traders that start with your firm do not last the year?

A little over half of those who start quit before they make it through the first year. Many quit after they realize that this is a true profession that requires dedication and discipline.

What are your firm's minimum requirements for hiring a trader?

U-4 application (SEC), fingerprint card, background check, Series 7, and either ready to be trained or having a year or more experience.

Do all your traders have to pass regulatory exams before they begin trading your firm's money?

Yes.

Do you train new traders or do you expect them to already be "ready" to go the day they start, or take a training course?

Either or both, in the case of floor trading experience.

Are the traders' positions monitored by someone at your firm real-time, and is any action taken if positions are going against them?

Absolutely, we monitor "tick-by-tick" [trade-by-trade] in both our headquarters office and our Chicago location all traders profit and loss and positions. We call the individual office managers, verify that our risk numbers are correct, and adjust the open positions accordingly. If a problem persists, we modify share volume and limit activity. And, again, continued schooling is advised.

What do you do when you find a problem with a trader during your monitoring?

We monitor the risk of each trader, both in Chicago and at our corporate headquarters, on a tick-by-tick basis. We identify a problem, then adjust share volume, or close trades as the situation indicates.

Are all your traders required to take your five-day training program?

They are not required to take the course, if they qualify with enough experience.

What are the major components of your $1,000 training program?

Our education is based on floor trading experience—market fundamentals (order flow, specialist system, market maker system, ECNs, listed versus OTC). And many more proprietary techniques and tactics. Traders can take the course as many times as necessary without any additional charge.

Can you describe your firm's office environment for traders?

Each office is set up with between sixteen and thirty workstations. The traders have four monitors for data feeds and one for executing trades. So there are actually two computers to monitor news, prices, dedicated ticker tape, futures activity, historical data, and so on. We are also connected directly to floor of the Chicago Mercantile Exchange (so we can save a couple of seconds in receiving S&P future pricing).

What type of people do you hire to manage your offices?

Generally, we look for good, profitable traders. We refuse to have a manager if he or she is not willing to "lead the troops into battle" by example. Many firms have people who just "manage" and do not trade. This makes no sense to us at all.

Are you planning to offer "remote" day trading from the day trader's home?

No, because it is virtually impossible to make money trading from home. We call it "hermit trading" and explain the pitfalls in our course. At-home "investing" can be fine, but it just doesn't work for full-time trading.

The "at home, pajama trader" is a pipe dream, a fantasy perpetuated by retail brokers and software peddlers. We have some of the top traders in the country, and we allow some of them to trade from home—and most come back to the office, because they find it more difficult to make money from home. These are people with trading floor experience. If they cannot do it, how could an untrained outsider do it? The Bull Market has made experts out of a lot of people who aren't. When the market gyrates, it shakes out all of the amateur traders.

If a person wanted to become a "professional" day trader, as you have defined it, then how should he or she go about entering the field?

Travel to a stock exchange city, get a clerk position for a year or two, move up to a broker position, then on to a trading or market making position. Buy a seat on an exchange and trade for him- or herself. The alternative is to work your way up through a firm like ours.

Do you believe "retail" full-time day traders can be successful?

No, not as traders. Anyone can be a successful "investor" if they "buy and hold" (especially in the Bull Market).

If a person wanted to day trade at one of the other firms, what are the odds against them making money on a consistent basis?

The true numbers are somewhere around 5 percent of retail day traders ever make decent money.

What attributes or characteristics are needed to be a successful day trader?

As described earlier, plus large helpings of discipline, flexibility, money management skills, and enough of a mathematical understanding to "visualize" risk-reward scenarios (and to analyze costs).

What weaknesses cause a day trader's downfall?

Stubborn behavior, adding to losing trades, thinking they can actually predict anything based on charts and graphs and all the fancy charting systems that are being sold like snake oil to the uninitiated. Whenever a trader gets opinionated, he starts to lose money.

If a twenty-five-year-old college graduate and a sixty-two-year-old retiree want your advice on whether they should consider day trading at home for their own account, what would your advice be?

The twenty-five-year-old should have the opportunity to choose trading as a career path (we actually have fully accredited internship programs at UCLA and UNLV [University of Las Vegas, Nevada]). The 62-year-old would be advised to take whatever money he has and enjoy it. Why start a new career at this time of someone's life? It takes years to become proficient at trading.

Do you believe that the regulatory authorities are misguided in their attack on day-trading firms for their aggressive advertising campaigns and their playing down of the dangers of day trading to the general public?

No. I do think that they need to focus more on the big retail firms (E*Trade, Schwab, etc.) who let anyone with money trade with no education or training. And why are they not going after the NYSE specialists (the biggest day traders in the world) or the Nasdaq market makers? (Probably because the big firms are the ones benefiting from restricting the growth of other trading firms. *Please realize that we execute around 1.5 percent of all the NYSE volume on a daily basis.* That is a big number, considering that there are thousands of retail brokerage firms. Where are the regulators when each state is starting a new lottery scam to tax the poor and unknowing? Talk about odds—boy!!

Do you believe that day trading is less risky than "swing" or "position" trading?

Yes. Both of those terms are misunderstood by most people. If you buy something, and it goes against you, then you keep it until it goes back up. They call that position trading—I call it holding on to a loser. We tell our people that winners take home winning positions, and losers take home losers. When the market turns, a good day trader can get out of a position and get back into at better prices.

Projecting out two to three years, where do you see the amateur day-trading boom continuing?

It will probably continue in more refined levels. Additionally, you will see less trading on regional stock exchanges and more trading from professional offices.

Are there any other comments you'd like to make on the subject of day trading?

Professional stock trading should be viewed like any other career or profession. Any business endeavor is risky (how about restaurants?). If we try to restrict good, honest entrepreneurs from participating in American business, are we not limiting our growth as a nation? Must everyone be pigeon holed in a "standard" career where they have an unlimited downside (firing, layoff, failure of a business), and limited upside (salary caps, etc.)?

Interview with David S. Nassar

David S. Nassar is founder, president, and CEO of Market Wise Securities, Inc. Market Wise Securities is an online broker/dealer providing online and electronic direct-access execution and specializing in initial and continuing trader and investor education. Mr. Nassar recently published *How to Get Started in Electronic Day Trading,* a home study course (Spring 2000) and *How to Get Started in Electronic Day Trading* (1998), which hit the best-seller list of the *New York Times, Wall Street Journal,* and *Newsweek.* It also reached the number one spot on the Amazon.com best-seller list. Mr. Nassar has finished another book, *The Rules of Trade,* which is due out in January 2001.

Company Description

Market Wise Securities, Inc., is an online broker/dealer specializing in investor and trader education. Today's technology has given many individuals better and quicker access to trade the market. The firm offers access to this online trading technology and the educational services that are essential not only to survive the market, but also to thrive in today's market. The firm can be contacted at (303) 430-4040; (877) 658-9473, or www.marketwise.com.

The Interview

How long has your firm been providing day-trading services?
Four years.

How many individuals trade at your firm's office versus remotely?
We have approximately a thousand remote traders, and about twenty in-house proprietary traders, and growing. Our niche now includes in-house training and trader. We have seven offices around the country, but our main focus is on trader education, training facilities, and marketing.

How has your firm changed in the past two years?
Our firm has changed dramatically in that we are not just a day-trading firm. We are really in the business of providing electronic execution whether the person wants to be a day trader, a swing trader, a momentum trader, or a trend trader. All those different styles of trading we know and teach. And not only do we trade in those styles using a multidimensional approach, but we also support those trading efforts. So we go far beyond a strict day-trading shop.

Has the Mark Barton incident in Atlanta had any impact on the way you run your business (for example, more careful screening of clients)?
No. It really hasn't. It was an anomaly. I think it is completely irrelevant to day trading.

What responsibility should your firm have, if any, to determine the suitability of a potential client for day trading?
I think we have to have a lot of responsibility. I think it's a dual responsibility for the customer as well as the sell-side brokerage firm to look after the customer's best interest. Ultimately, the suitability falls to both parties. So I think there is dual responsibility there.

We are way beyond the minimum criteria for allowing individuals to day trade. Our account applications have very rigid suitability questions and it is very in-depth. Risk management from the perspective of a brokerage firm means selecting clients very carefully. So we think that our risk management begins with suitability of the client. We do turn away clients if need be.

Did you expect that day trading would become as popular as it is today?

I have to admit that I am still surprised by the growth in some ways. What has surprised me the most is that so many people have tried to get into trading that really shouldn't be involved in trading. It surprises me that there is not enough fear and respect for the market. It seems that people think it is easy. I think a lot of that has been exacerbated by a strong Bull Market that we have seen up until March 24 of this year [2000]. This is the beginning of the bear cycle that we have seen. I think we hit the bottom on May 24, but I'm still surprised that people are not shaken and more respectful of the market even given that major correction.

Another thing that surprises me is the level of technology and rule changes that allow access to the market through various mediums. Five years ago, most seasoned professionals would never have predicted this growth. On the other hand, the technology that has been created didn't surprise me because I pay so much attention to the technology side of the business. It is the rules that allow the technology to be used that fascinate me the most.

In selecting a day-trading firm, what should a day trader look for?

First and foremost they have to look for continuing support. I think that if commissions are the paradigm and you are just looking for the best commission, then you're making a mistake. Things that are important are a strong network that's behind the technology—that you don't see. A trader learns very quickly through "down time" how important a vibrant network is. Trade support must be available for those systems when they do fail, and they will from time to time no matter how good the network is. When systems failures occur, such as slowdowns, you need to call and talk to a trader right away—not by voice mail and not by e-mail—you need to get right to the trade desk. Companies that don't provide those services are providing their customers with a disservice. A trader that doesn't look for that service when he is doing his due diligence is making a big mistake.

What characteristics distinguish your firm from the other large firms in the industry?

Well, some of the things I just mentioned. We are traders, and we are born from a trading heritage. There are very few firms that can say that. We are different because we are traders. We put our capital at risk every day trading stocks and options. There is no better teacher than the market itself. It blows my mind how other firms can claim they can teach you to trade when the owners of the firm and others at the firm do not trade themselves. I think it's hypocritical, frankly.

How long has your firm been offering training programs, what are their length and cost, and how many customers have taken them?

Since the inception of our company, we have been offering training programs. The cost ranges anywhere from $1,500 for a one-day course to $3,000 for our full week course. Not only that, but we offer our customers continuing education at no additional charge, because we do not think that any course will deliver what a trader needs in just a few days. It has to evolve over many months and time. We are there for that journey with our customers.

What personal characteristics and attributes does a person need to become a successful day trader?

Aggressive, competitive, humble, intelligent, and passionate.

What personal weaknesses can lead to a trader's downfall?

Greed, laziness, exuberance, and shortsightedness. You have to be patient. Those that want to get into the market for fast cash get just the opposite of the what they are looking for—they get fast losses. And they are out quick. These types of individuals will be quickly filtered out through the markets self-cleansing mechanism, which has existed since its inception.

I don't think that an individual should get into the market initially in anticipation of making money or quitting his job. Those are all nemeses to your success. You have to come in with the mindset that you are going to lose money as tuition towards the learning process. The learning curve is not that long if you go in with the right attitude and if you're willing to accept it. The rest of your life is yours to have that knowledge and enjoy the market. I think it takes about a thousand trades for the average person to even get a feel for the market in general during the initial learning process.

Do you expect to see a consolidation among ECNs within the next two years? What impact will this have on the ability of traders to obtain rapid and competitive price execution?

I do see a consolidation. I also see that if it doesn't come about in the traditional form of consolidation, which is M&A (merger and acquisitions), that you will see it through third party systems that aggregate all ECN liquidity into an algorithm that matches order flow similar to the way the ITS and CQS for the listed markets aggregate quotes and prints. I think you'll see technologies like OptiMark, as an example, that have the ability to aggregate order flow from various ECNs and exchanges become more prevalent. That aggregation process has to include market makers as well.

And the reason I think it is more the latter rather than the former is because you're not going to see M&A consolidation with market making firms as you would with ECNs. This is because the market making firms have a much richer heritage, a much stronger asset base, compared with ECNs, which are relatively new. The exception to this rule would be large ECNs like Instinet—which was developed in 1971, the Island ECN, Archipelago, and so on. But the smaller ECNs will struggle and consolidate, in my opinion. So I think a third market system that can aggregate liquidity from market makers and the ECNs is the real answer.

Do you believe the regulatory authorities are misguided in their attack on the day-trading firms for their aggressive advertising campaigns and their playing down of the dangers of day trading to the general public?

I couldn't give you an absolute answer. I think there have been abuses and hype associated with day trading that some firms have put out. I also think that the regulators must recognize what day trading is. It is not a new phenomenon. It has been around since you've had traders on the floor. Day trading is really defined as more of a daily awareness of the market than it is how many trades a person would make in a day. If you are hyping day trading as a firm and promoting overtrading and self-churning of one's account, then regulators should step in.

On the other side, the regulators must understand that there are quality firms out there trying to promote the industry in a favorable way through education. They should recognize that as well. Overall, I think it is a learning process that is common in any new industry or segment of an industry, as day trading is. The real winners in the end are the responsible customers who trade with discipline and responsibility, and I think day trading has ushered this process much better than the traditional brokerage business has.

If you were to list the decision criteria that a person needs to evaluate to determine if day trading is suitable for him- or herself, then what would they be?

Evaluate yourself first—understand yourself. If you do not understand yourself right now, then you are never going to understand trading until you do. I think that people that aren't steady in their occupation and are not steady in their personal lives are really people that do not know themselves. Trading stocks is one of the purest things that you'll ever do. It is very nonpolitical—there is no politics. If you cannot get a grasp on who you are as a person, then you're going to have a real hard time trading stocks. So that has to be the first evaluation.

The second thing that must be reconciled is if you feel you have the personal attributes and personal psychology for trading—and that begins by being honest with yourself. Just because a person likes the idea of trading does not mean he or she is suited to trade. To help discover this, we have developed a quiz (using a psychologist that is also a trader) to help a person in this discovery process. While no quiz is going to predict outcome 100 percent, it is a great start, and it also forces people to ask themselves some hard questions they would not otherwise have asked themselves in most cases.

In my new book, I expressed that there is a literal fork in the road that traders face. One leg of the fork is the mechanical cognitive learning process—understanding the market mechanics and how the market works, systems, technical analysis, and so forth. On the other side is the psychological fork in the road. I think it's when those two roads converge that success is found. Too many people focus on just one road—mainly the mechanical side—and they cling to trading systems and electronic software programs believing that they are going to be the "holy grail" to their trading needs. And that is a mistake as well. You've got to evaluate those systems, certainly, but psychology and the convergence of these two roads is where success will be found. One without the other, success will be difficult.

If you were to list the steps that a person needs to take to become a successful day trader, then what would they be?

First and foremost, you have to have the capital. If you do not have the capital, then you shouldn't engage the market—scared money never wins in the market. You have to have freedom from that money and break the emotional ties. If you are emotionally tied to the money, then it's a problem. It's a roadblock.

Second, once you've got that, you have to have the time to dedicate toward obtaining the mechanical knowledge of the market, while having the passion to do the work.

Third, again, knowing yourself is so important. That is critical. Too many traders do not understand themselves and what motivates them. I have seen traders with an incredible propensity to trade who have destroyed themselves because somehow, subconsciously, low self-esteem issues, self-sabotage, or some other mechanism makes them believe they don't deserve the success. It's an incredible thing to watch. I've also seen traders with no confidence whatsoever who have little conviction to stay with their trades. These traders are always looking over their shoulder trying to figure out what to do or looking to others for answers that only they can provide. Chatrooms and subscription services tend to be where they spend their time, instead of educating themselves. The point is, you must know yourself well to trade well. Confidence and conviction come from hard work and education. Those that ignore these commandments lose. Those that obey them, learn to lose but take their losses fast and in the end learn to succeed.

Do you believe that simulated or paper trading helps or hinders a person learning the ropes?

It really depends on how you approach it. I think that if you are going after a simulator for mechanical training and motor skills training, it is a good tool. If you're going after it to give yourself some kind of false sense of security or confidence that you can beat the market, then is a very bad tool. You're better off not even touching the thing. Before using a simulation or paper trading, you have to ask yourself why you are doing it and what you are going to gain from it. In the end, my answer is to use it for mechanical and motor skills training and nothing more. Remember that you can never simulate emotions or psychology.

What is your definition of a "professional" day trader?

The person who trades full-time that makes a living at trading. It would be an individual who is engaged in no other financial endeavor but trading—not real estate, nothing else. This is the only thing that they want to do. I think that is mainly it. I think if those attributes exist, assuming they have the personal psychology, motor skills, and a mechanical understanding of the market, like an invisible hand, the results will come.

Based on your knowledge, what are the odds that a part-time day trader can be successful (make money each year)?

I think that the odds are definitely there as well—again, assuming that they adapt a trading strategy and time horizon consistent with their lifestyle, time commitments, risk tolerances, and personality. I know a lot of people who make great money trading stocks part-time. It is not about time, it is about mindset and commitment. For example, swing-trading strategies are a very good approach that many of our clients employ while they have vibrant careers. Swing trading in fact can be a good way to start trading. At some point it will be very clear if you want to make that crossover to full-time trading or not. That will be up to the individual, but it is definitely possible. I've seen it happen many times.

What advice would you give a twenty-five-year-old and a fifty-year-old who want to day trade full-time for a living?

Well, you're talking to a guy who puts no relevance on time or age. I know professionals who have been in the market for a year or two. And I know amateurs that have been in the market for thirty years—with one year of experience thirty years in a row. I think that age is irrelevant. I think it is all about mindset. Of course, I voted for Nolan Ryan and Cal Ripken to go to the All Star games as well during their careers.

How critical to the success of a day trader is the use and understanding of Nasdaq Level II?

Much less important than some would think, and much more important than others think. Many believe that Level II is like the Shangri-La of the market—and that's crazy.

Those that believe it's that strong an indicator become intoxicated by the gyroscopic motion of Level II. Those that use Level II this way become intoxicated money drunks. They think that every tick and every print is telling them something. That is way too microscopic, and those people are going to be harmed by Level II. Conversely, if Level II is used as a confirming indicator or a confirming tool in concert with other tools like charting and technical studies, mathematical indicators, and statistical analysis, then it's an incredibly powerful tool. So, in summary, as stated, not as important as some think, but more important than those that ignore it think. Many technicians ignore it, for example, and this is also a mistake. For example, Level II is a great "precision execution" tool to pick your entry and exit points while making trades to find market liquidity.

Do you believe that day trading is preferable to "swing trading" (three-to-five-day holding period)?

To me day trading and swing trading are the same thing. It's just a difference in your time horizon. Adapting your time horizon to the strategy is what's most important. Personally, I day trade (defined as no overnight positions) more than I swing trade by far, but I will also tell you that my best swing trades are found through day trading. Reading and trading a stock's patterns throughout the day will feed a broader perspective of the stock as well, and when that perspective is seen and confirmed through technical indicators, a swing trade is very desirable.

Two years from now, what major changes do you expect to see in the day-trading arena?

I think it will continually self-cleanse itself in terms of the number of participants. I think you'll see a wider division between the amateur and professional than you see today—and it is already pretty wide. Some people do not want to admit that, because most that engage the market think they are traders, but a true trader is a person with a plan and the discipline to adjust and follow it. I think you'll see day traders congregate more. I believe that traders like to be around traders just like athletes like to be around athletes and actors want to be around other actors. I think that if a person truly has a talent for trading, it is very esoteric and therefore enjoyable to be around other people like you. Therefore, more trading rooms will emerge but with larger barriers to entry, such as a license, higher capital requirements, and of course acceptance from the high-end trader who doesn't want to work with an amateur blaming others for poor results.

What will the day-trading industry look like in five years?

In terms of the technology, you are going to see continual change. But in terms of market psychology, little has changed over the years, and I doubt it will five years from now. Trading is 90 percent to 95 percent psychological, while mechanics (which includes technology) is only 5 to 10 percent, in my opinion. Therefore, relatively speaking, not much will change at all. It's still going to be about people. It's still going to be about supply and demand imbalances based on market reaction. It will still be about recognizing where overreactions and exuberance occur. It will still be about psychology more than technology.

How many of today's day-trading firms will still be in existence in the next three years?

Far less. It is already happening. Just as the market cleanses poor traders out of the market, the market will self-cleanse poor brokerage firms out of the business.

Interview with Steven P. Goldman

Steven P. Goldman's firm is not a day trading firm, but rather a traditional discount broker that has day traders as clients, among other clients. After speaking with Mr. Goldman, I realized that he had unique insights into the day-trading phenomenon. Therefore, I included his comments as part of this interview series.

Mr. Goldman is CEO of Yamner & Co., based in Fairlawn, New Jersey. Mr. Goldman has been with the firm for five years. He was named CEO as of January 2, 2000, and he is the firm's largest shareholder. Steve Goldman is a graduate of the University of Pennsylvania's Wharton School and Cornell University Law School. He has an extensive background in computer sciences, having designed and implemented several computerized trading order management, routing, and execution technologies. He is a series 24, 4, 27, 7, 55, and 63 (trader, registered rep, options and sales principal, and financial principal). Mr. Goldman can be reached at (201) 791-6475 or spgoldman@trademanage.com.

The Interview

What is the focus of your brokerage firm?

We are a traditional discount broker/dealer, exceptionally well-positioned to handle particularly difficult executions—quick executions, large size orders, and active investors. We are not a day-trading shop, but rather our focus is more on institutional and high net worth transactions. Because of the quality of trading technologies required by institutional size, we also attract high net worth retail business. We do not market ourselves as a day-trading shop. We actually discourage day trading.

You discourage day trading—why is that?

I find that day traders without any guidance, in general, do not perceive the risks in their trading. At our firm, we make sure that our clients try to understand the markets the best that they can and reflect on the risks associated with their activities. We speak to clients when we notice that some of the transactions that they may be engaging in are outside the bounds of reasonableness or suitability. The classic example would be some of these "short" stocks—the stocks that are making their way around the short-selling circles. If a person shorts a touted stock at $5 and it goes to $10—he is basically 100 percent out. I've seen a lot of clients get hurt from this type of strategy. Therefore, we try to encourage them to look at other types of investment vehicles and investment strategies more suitable for the type of return that they are looking for—whether it be an aggressive return or something more moderate and in line with traditional expectations.

A lot of people are utilizing the wrong technology to engage in their more active trading. Certain accounts use lower end, traditional, full-service brokers to execute their transactions. These broker/dealer operations are not designed for the more active traders. Many firms do not give their traders access to all the different systems that are out there, and many firms do not get access to the many sources of liquidity on "The Street." Some market makers and liquidity sources will not let certain firms route orders for execution to them. For the end-user, the retail client, this is a serious disadvantage to others on The Street.

An example would be the direct-order entry shops. They usually do not have access to auto-fills or execution technologies linking to the industry's market makers and must then rely on ECN technologies to execute orders. Contrarily, Yamner & Co., Inc. has over twenty-five different sources of liquidity and relationships with market makers that provide auto-fills on large size orders and midpoint pricing on many occasions. This approach may not affect 80 percent of the market, but for the institutional or larger size client or the more active retail client this would be particularly onerous—this could cost you severely if you don't have access to various points of liquidity in the market.

What makes a person a successful trader?

If you're speaking about skill sets, the number one skill set that you must have is discipline. Certain traders may be very good at picking stocks, other traders may be very good at executing orders and understanding technologies, another group of traders may be good at evaluating positions and money management, and others simply have luck. But at the end of the day, what you can bank on, day-in and day-out, is discipline. Where most active traders and active investors fail is not having discipline or the classic trying to do something you shouldn't. There is saying that a lawyer that represents himself has a fool for a client. Most investors are great stock pickers, but really should not be executing their own orders. These are two wholly different skills and require different talents and technologies.

By discipline, I mean whatever your strategy is, whatever your course of action is, you must first define it beforehand—lay down the groundwork and the research, figure out how you are going to invest, test your model, and execute your model. And your model should have protective stops. This is similar to investing in any business. For example, if you were to open a bike shop, you might say that you will run the bike shop in a certain way for seven months. And after that time, you will evaluate how it is doing. You should say to yourself beforehand, "I'm willing to tolerate *x* amount of risk. I will not ruin any family fortunes on any one business opportunity. I'm going to set standards that I'm going to follow. If I don't meet my model, then I'm going to decide that it is over and move on."

I'm a risk adverse person. I like to evaluate a scenario with a risk/reward ratio that favors reward, not risk. Some people get involved with $400 stocks. If their long-term objective was to be in the stocks for three years, that's fine, as long as they can tolerate the stock going down $100. But if you're telling me that they are looking for this $400 stock to go to $410 or $420—a total upside of 20 points and a downsize of 400 points, I'd say in this case, the risk/reward ratio does not favor the reward. This example demonstrates a case of having a tremendous amount of risk for a very little reward.

Also, you have to factor in the liquidity of the stock. At the end of the day, for most traders, the reward of a teenie [sixteenth] or an eighth or a quarter of a point does not justify the risk. If a stock moves $4 or $10 a day and you try to make fifty cents on it, you may get tagged for a $4 loss. So you've have a reward factor of two and a risk factor of ten. This doesn't work. Any day trader must have in his model an evaluation of the risk versus the reward, otherwise the results will be unsatisfactory.

For example, if you are going to trade Intel or Qualcomm and make $2 on it, then don't take a $9 loss. There is old phrase that a guy on the street used to tell me, "Don't eat like a bird and shit like an elephant." Don't go for teenies, eighths, and quarters, and then take a $10 loss. You have to make eighty times an eighth to make up for a $10 loss. If you are going for fifty cents on the upside, then you have to set your limits on the downside—perhaps seventy-five cents or a dollar loss.

If you do not have discipline, just like at the casino table—if you take $200 to gamble and you lose it—then you shouldn't go into your wallet for more money. Don't pull out your credit card, don't try to wish it home, and don't go to a "hot" table to make it back. Because the uglier it gets, the more compulsive it becomes. The farther a stock goes against you, the harder it becomes to sell it, assuming that you are long. It's much easier to take a small fractional loss—as a day trader take a $2 loss, as a position trader a $4 loss, or as a long-term investor a 20 point loss on an $80 stock. As a long-term investor you should try not to buy a stock at $100 and see it go to $20. It's foolish. As a day trader, if you buy a stock a $50 and it goes to $49.50, then you should probably get out. Instead, you may try to wish it back when it keeps falling. This approach is a breakdown in discipline.

The most successful traders that I have seen have rock solid discipline. And many times they may say to themselves, "Damn it, I just sold this stock and now its $2 higher." I can't tell you the number of times that I have seen that occur. I've seen it a million times. The key is that the professionals with discipline are able to be in the market day in and day out and get the return on investment that they want.

Discipline also means that you don't sink every dollar into an investment. You should be allocating *x* percentage of your capital to each trade. You should have criteria when you trade, and you should definitely not run your capital to zero. Give your trade a certain amount of time, and if it does not play out, then you have to say to yourself, "That is it," and you should close the position. It is just like the bike shop example. You're not going to open up different bike shops as each one fails because you have different reasons to blame it on. This approach is hopeful and wishing, and at the end of the day it's not productive. This doesn't mean that if you have one or two bad trades that you should give up. You have to do your research and determine just why you failed on the trade. For example, you should ask yourself, "Did I buy it too early?" or "Did I buy it too late?" and, "What are the criteria and conditions that I used when I bought it?" Don't whitewash the problem. Be honest with yourself. Remember that hindsight is 20/20.

On the other hand, there are many traders that are making a lot of money. So the whole endeavor can be very dynamic. It can be very intense, very challenging, and very stimulating. It's a lot of fun, especially when you are making a lot of money. Trading is such a lure that people are unwilling to give it up. I had a client, a woman physician, who wanted to sell her practice and put the money into the market. I'm not sure if she actually did that. I also had another client who, against all my good advice, sold his restaurant and took the $700,000 proceeds and turned it into $4 million in eight months by buying the hot Internet stocks. I would tell my clients ten times out of ten not to do it. I would never do that with my own money. Most people do not see the downside, they gamble, and they lose. So, therefore, in conclusion, you have to have discipline, you have to approach trading as a business, you have to set your limits, and you have to execute. If it is not in the cards, then you should do something else.

Why do you think people think they can easily day trade and make money?

One of the reasons is that on Wall Street when you speak to money managers you never hear them speak about their losses. People do not say, "I just got killed on a Dell," or,"You should have seen how I got whacked on a Georgia-Pacific." This is not what people do. Good performance is what's accepted. Failure is looked on very negatively, particularly in light of the meteoric rise of the market over the last four years.

Even in the trading community, you'll have traders running around telling you how they made a buck on so and so. What they don't tell you are their losses. To some degree there is a perception of fast money—the casinos let you think you win money. You listen to the lottery ads—"Win a million (scratch-and-sniff and you make $500,000). Remember, 50 cents gets you $250,000 if you win." What they don't show you is at the end of the day the number of people taking their tickets and throwing them away—totally valueless. There is a perception that trading is easy. Trading is just something that comes about. Everybody talks about what they made, but not about what they lost. Others are influenced by it. A person making $30,000 a year may say, "If I only invested my salary in the market last year I could've doubled my money and perhaps even tripled my money. If I keep doing this I would probably make $250,000." This person does not look at the downside at all, not realizing he or she can lose it all.

Interview with Ronald Shear

Ronald Shear is CEO of Carlin Equities Corporation. Long before the Internet, Ron was blazing his own highly successful trading career. During the mid 1970s, after working for Lehman Brothers, Ron became a market maker on the American Stock Exchange. His analytical skills quickly enabled him to become one of the largest market makers on the Amex. His firm, Investors Option Company, eventually managed contracts for nine different U.S. exchanges, including the CBOE, the Pacific Stock Exchange, and the European Options Exchange. In 1984 Ron was awarded the specialist's book for the Major Market Index (XMI), a contract which became so popular that the American Stock Exchange built a separate trading pit to accommodate its volume. Ron still spends a major portion of each day trading.

Company Description

Carlin Equities Corporation was created by professional traders *for* professional traders.

The firm is headquartered in New York City, with offices nationwide. Trades of the firm's customers are cleared through Spear, Leeds & Kellogg, a leading provider of execution and clearing services to the financial community since 1931. Carlin Equities and Spear, Leeds & Kellogg are members of the NASD and SIPC (Securities Investors Protection Corporation).

The Interview

How long has your firm been providing day-trading services?

Carlin Financial Group was founded in 1993 by professional traders for professional traders. The firm's goal is to be the leading provider of trading and execution services to individual professional traders, registered proprietary off-floor traders, and institutions.

How many individuals trade at your firm's office versus remotely?

About two hundred trade in the New York headquarters and another thousand around the country.

Has your firm grown in the past two years?

The firm has grown over the last two years. We have opened many locations and increased our remote client base on the Internet. This was made possible by a major expansion in our communication and network infrastructure. In particular our new marketing department is concentrating on online growth.

Has the Mark Barton incident in Atlanta had any impact on the way you run your business?

Carlin has always maintained a rigorous screening process to evaluate potential traders, well before the tragic event in Atlanta. The firm actually discourages many people from entering the profession if we feel they do not have the temperament, or if someone is immature or does not have sufficient capital (i.e., at least two years of living expenses in the bank).

What responsibility should your firm have, if any, to determine the suitability of a potential client for day trading?

Carlin, as all regulated firms, is required to ascertain information from the client as to the suitability of the individual to day trade, along with disclosing the risks involved. We try to evaluate that person to the best of our ability and make a judgment based on our findings. The decision to day trade is solely up to the individual.

Did you expect that day trading would become as popular as it is today?

I always believed that trading by individuals would become more mainstream as they obtained access to the same tools as professional traders. That has happened gradually over the past few years and I expect that interest to continue to increase.

In selecting a day-trading firm, what should a day trader look for?

The main characteristic is to find a firm at which you are comfortable with the professionalism, depth of information, and expertise of its traders. Essentially, trading is like a community, and you must enjoy the company of those around you.

What characteristics distinguish your firm from the other large firms in the industry?

Carlin goes beyond other traditional retail brokers to bring independent traders the same electronic trading tools and news feeds that the pros use. Carlin caters to sophisticated individual investors and offers a total trading package that includes proprietary research, a state-of-the-art order execution system, market data, and instant news. Importantly, the firm's principals are experienced professional traders who trade at the firm and offer investment strategies to help traders succeed.

If you offer a training program to new customers, how long have you been offering it, what is its length and cost, and how many customers have taken it?

We started a new division of our company called Carlin Mentor Trading for the purpose of training new and prospective clients. We are using advanced Web-casting technology in order to broadcast interactive classes from our headquarters in New York to our office and remote network.

What personal characteristics and attributes does a person need to become a successful day trader?

Given the high intensity work environment, the main requirement is a balanced life. It may sound corny, but you must eat well, sleep well, exercise, and regularly see family and friends.

What personal weaknesses can lead to a trader's downfall?

The more chaotic one's life is, the more unhinged and unprofitable the trader becomes.

Do you expect to see a consolidation among ECNs within the next two years? What impact will this have on the ability of traders to obtain rapid and competitive price execution?

I do believe there will be some consolidation. Carlin's customers can directly route trades to the major exchanges, as well as to market makers and ECNs on Nasdaq, which means trades are faster and can have tremendous value to a customer trying to trade in markets characterized by rapidly changing prices. Costs have come down over recent years, while executions have improved.

Do you believe the regulatory authorities are misguided in their attack on the day trading firms for their aggressive advertising campaigns and their playing down of the dangers of day trading to the general public?

Government has the responsibility to make sure that the public is well informed about the risks and rewards of trading, and we support their efforts.

If you were to list the decision criteria that a person needs to determine if day trading is suitable for him- or herself, then what would they be?

A person has to first seriously decide if he or she wants to make the commitment that is required to be successful. It's not part-time work. It is a profession that requires study, training, and practice. It can be satisfying and rewarding if it is taken seriously and the necessary steps are taken in preparation for each trading day.

If you were to list the steps that a person needs to take to become a successful day trader, what would they be?

Choose the right firm, do your homework, and be patient.

What would your definition of a "professional" day trader be?

Someone who is committed to trading full-time.

Based on your knowledge, what are the odds that a part-time day trader can be successful (make money each year)?

It is highly unlikely that someone who is not fully committed to trading will be a successful active trader.

What advice would you give a twenty-five-year-old and a fifty-year-old who want to day trade full-time for a living?

The advice would be the same. Carefully choose a firm that meets your requirements, don't expect an immediate payback, and use a long-term perspective for short-term trading.

How critical to the success of a day trader is the use and understanding of Nasdaq Level II?

Understanding Level II is of critical importance. That's why we offer a series of online classes on this subject. Traders must be able to distinguish market makers from ECNs, and know how to route orders so as to get the best fill.

Do you believe that day trading is preferable to "swing trading" (three to five day holding period)?

These methods represent different styles of trading. We encourage traders to find a style that is comfortable for them and appropriate to the level of risk that they can assume. Our technology facilitates both styles. We offer powerful technical analysis tools and chart interpretation. We have several systems that facilitate stock selection for this type of trading. Many of these chart patterns resolve over a period of days. It is up to the trader whether he or she wants to trade these stocks intraday or over several days.

Two years from now what major changes do you expect to see in the day-trading arena?

There will be great expansion in trading, particularly by remote users over the Internet. Trading will expand along with bandwidth.

What will the day-trading industry look like in five years?

Wireless trading from hand-held devices will become a factor. In general, online trading will continue to increase.

How many of today's day-trading firms will still be in existence in the next three years?

I think you will see some consolidation in this industry, as evidenced by Schwab's acquisition of Cybercorp. I believe that was just the beginning, because the large institutions realize the future potential of active trading. By the same token, there will be an inevitable shake-out of those firms that don't offer competitive services.

PART FIVE

PRONOUNCEMENTS, PUNDITS, AND PROGNOSTICATIONS

14

REGULATORY FINDINGS ON THE DAY-TRADING INDUSTRY

With so much money at stake, it is no wonder that regulators have zeroed in on the day-trading industry to protect consumers. The explosion of online brokers and online trading has resulted in abuses by some of these firms. At the same time, there has been a parallel growth in the number of day-trading firms and day trading volume. Unfortunately, some regulators and news stories lump online brokers and day-trading firms in the same bucket and assume that they are one-and-the-same. That couldn't be further from the truth, as you probably realized after reading chapter 1.

Nevertheless, between November 1999 and May 2000 there were seven reports issued by various regulators or governmental agencies reviewing the practices of online brokers or day trading. The first three investigations listed here focus on online brokers, while the last four focus specifically on the day-trading industry.

Online investing:

On-Line Trading: Better Investor Protection Information Needed on Broker's Web Sites, United States General Accounting Office (GGD-00–43), May 9, 2000.

Online Brokerage: Keeping Apace of Cyberspace, Report of Commissioner Laura S. Unger to the United States Securities and Exchange Commission, November 1999.

From Wall Street to Web Street: A Report on the Problems and Prom-

ise of the Online Brokerage Industry, Office of New York State
Attorney General Spitzer, November 22, 1999.

Day-trading:

*Special Study: Report of Examinations of Day-Trading Broker-Deal-
ers*, Office of Compliance Inspections and Examinations, U.S.
Securities and Exchange Commission, February 25, 2000.

Day Trading: Everyone Gambles But the House, Staff Memorandum,
Permanent Subcommittee on Investigations, Committee on
Governmental Affairs, United States Senate, February 24, 2000.
(This 197-page report deals solely with the day-trading industry
and was distilled from more than 50,000 pages of data and testi-
mony.)

*SECURITIES OPERATIONS: Day Trading Requires Continued Over-
sight*, United States General Accounting Office (GGD-00–61),
February 2000. (This report reviewed the seven largest day-trading firms, which had 5,300 individuals trading through them.
This represents about 80 percent of all day traders trading at
firms. The GAO also reviewed sixty-seven examinations of day-
trading firms and branches conducted by federal regulators. Go
to www.gao.gov for the complete report.)

Day Trading Project Group Report—Findings and Recommendations,
North American Securities Administrators Association, Inc., August 9, 1999.[1]

Since the focus of this book is on day trading, we will not review
the findings of the regulators regarding online brokers. But if you plan
on using an online broker instead of a direct-access broker (which I
wouldn't recommend), then you should get a copy of the reports and
read through them for more insight into the problems and the potential
remedies. Be aware that most online firms have greatly improved their
operations, customer service, communications systems, and ability to
handle huge transaction traffic since the reports were issued.

The focus of this chapter is the regulatory findings on the practices
and procedures of day-trading firms. Two reports are reviewed with
respect to these findings. The first report reviewed was prepared by the
U.S. Senate and entitled *Day Trading: Everyone Gambles But the House.*

Day Trading: Everyone Gambles But the House

The investigators reviewed the titans of the day-trading industry by formally requesting documents from nineteen firms, resulting in 50,000 pages of material. This was supplemented by interviews with 107 individuals—including the deposing of seven staff members of day-trading firms, current and former day traders, gambling experts, authors, and academicians. Also, regulators from the federal government and individuals from self-regulatory organizations participated. Only three of the nineteen day-trading firms were chosen for a detailed analysis—All-Tech Direct, Inc., Providential Securities, Inc., and Momentum Securities, Inc.

The Senate committee's investigation wanted answers to three critical questions:

1. Is day trading basically just gambling?
2. Are some of the day-trading firms using deceitful and dishonest practices? If they are, then how widespread is the wrongdoing?
3. What is the impact of day trading on individual firms and the securities markets?

Selected Staff Report Conclusions

General Findings

1. Risks not disclosed.

Day trading is a highly speculative activity that can be fairly compared to certain types of gambling. Although there is no definitive study regarding the profitability of day trading, the best evidence suggests that only a tiny fraction of novice day traders are ever profitable and that, even among well capitalized and experienced day traders, a majority will lose money. Moreover, some day trading firms have failed to adequately disclose the risks attendant to day trading in their advertisements and during their interactions with prospective customers. Even when firms have given prospective customers good written risk disclaimers, some firms have undermined that risk disclosure through contradictory verbal statements about the profitability of day trading or the ease with which risk can be avoided. (p. 6)

2. Firms do not follow their policies or train branch staff sufficiently.

    Some firms have failed to heed their own internal policies to obtain the necessary information about the financial data about potential customers to determine their suitability for day trading. These firms allowed individuals with inappropriate investment objectives and financials to open accounts at their firms. Unfortunately, some firms have lowered their minimum requirements (e.g., starting capital) to match those of the less stringent firms, so as not to lose business (e.g., commission revenue) to competing firms.

    Some firms have not hired qualified branch managers, and have also not properly trained or supervised them. Moreover, many firms provide their new day-trading clients with inadequate training programs, which do not properly prepare them to succeed.

3. Firms offer unauthorized funding and allow third-party trading to unregistered traders.

    Many firms provide additional funding for customers who cannot satisfy their margin requirements by having other customers provide short-term loans at excessive interest rates.

    Many firms allow unregistered "retail" day traders to trade the accounts of third parties.

4. Profitable unseasoned day traders are few and far between.

    Only a small number of new day traders will be profitable (even including traders who have sufficient capital and some experience), and the majority will lose. A former manager of one firm's San Diego office indicated in a deposition that 80 to 90 percent of its onsite traders lost money and left the firm within six months. A branch manager of another firm, located in Seattle, indicated that 90 percent of its customers were not making money. At another firm, in their Los Angeles office, the average day trader lost about $50,000 and lasted about a month before calling it quits.

Don Bright of Bright Trading was quoted in the press as saying that less than 10 percent of day traders will make money, if remote day traders are included in the count. He further stated that about 66 percent will leave day trading within one year. In its day training manual, Cornerstone indicated that approximately 70 to 90 percent of new traders will go bust or leave day trading within six to twelve months of their first trade. The staff report states, "While not conclusive, this voluminous anecdotal evidence strongly indicates that, on the whole, day traders lose money and that an extremely high percentage of novice traders fail to achieve profitability. This tentative finding is also generally supported by what little empirical data exist on the success rates of day traders" (p. 33).

5. Day trading is compared to gambling.

According to Ed Looney, executive director of the New Jersey Council on Problem Gambling, "When you look at day traders, you're talking about an activity that attracts people who love action, who love excitement. You're going to see a lot of them who are really in it for the gambling" (p. 30). Mr. Looney further indicates that in 1998 his organization received less than 3 percent of its hotline calls from day traders, but in 1999 they increased to 4 percent—about an average or five to six calls a day. During market corrections, he notes, 40 percent of the calls are from day traders.

"Day trading closely resembles gambling for novice, undercapitalized traders" (p. 27). This conclusion was based on discussions with gambling professionals, regulators, and members of the day-trading industry, as well as documents from the firms, and a review of day trader account profitability. According to the staff report, "Like gambling, which is defined as playing a game of chance for money or other stakes, day trading offers the chance for quick riches. The odds are somewhat longer for the day trader than for the professional blackjack player; however, the day trader pays a commission charge for every trade regardless of whether it is profitable" (p. 27).

6. Day trading is highly unprofitable.

The staff discovered much anecdotal evidence indicating that day trading is "highly unprofitable." In a deposition, a former manager of an All-Tech branch office admitted that 80 percent to 90 percent of the customers lost money and quit in six months. Another manager of a different branch of the firm said that 0 percent of the traders were profitable, while another branch mentioned that 90 percent of its customers lost. An official of the firm indicated that about 33 percent of all day traders become full-time traders.

Don Bright, of Bright Trading, indicated in a press report that less than 10 percent of day traders will be profitable when at-home traders are included in the trader universe. He further indicated that 67 percent leave trading within one year.

According to the report, "On the whole, day traders lose money, and an extremely high percentage of novice traders fail to achieve profitability" (p. 33).

7. Positive impact of day trading.

There are three developments that have made day trading positive for investors. First, day traders have added liquidity to the markets due to increases in volume and the use of ECNs. Second, there has been mammoth growth in low-cost trading execution platforms, which has drastically cut commission costs. Third, the newest technologies developed for day trading have increased transparency (for example, access to information). These three changes have been extremely positive for both traders and investors.

8. Additional findings.

■ Some firms have forged customer documents and engaged in unauthorized trading.
■ Some firms used misleading advertisements and did not properly characterize the risks of day trading.
■ Some firms did not provide potential clients with any risk disclosure prior to opening the trading account.
■ Some firms accepted customers who were clearly unsuitable for trading.
■ Some firms encouraged traders to trade beyond their means and aided them in obtaining short-term loans from other customers to cover their margin calls.
■ Some firms were very poorly managed and supervised.

Report Conclusions

1. Many disturbing practices were found at some day-trading firms, some of which are criminal.
2. Securities regulators should spend more time and money to police this growing industry.
3. The top firms should self-police their own industry.
4. The firms should make sure that potential customers are made aware of the significant risks of day trading.

Day Trading Project Group Report—Findings and Recommendations

The second report to be reviewed was prepared by the North American Securities Administrators Association, Inc., and entitled *Day Trading Project Group Report—Findings and Recommendations*. (The complete report may be obtained from the North American Securities Administrators Association, Inc., 10 G Street, NE, Suite 710, Washington, DC 20002, (202) 737-0900.) The following comments are from this day-trading project group report of August 9, 1999. The report was designed to "serve as a word of caution for those who believe that day trading offers a viable career opportunity, or that frenetic trading is an alternative to prudent, diversified, long-term investing" (p. iii).

Because of technological advances individuals can now handle brokerage transactions electronically. Day traders are considered retail customers of firms whose goal is to profit from intraday incremental changes in stock prices. The firms that offer day trading receive significant revenues from the commissions generated by these traders. The firms have significant overhead as well as other costs that they must cover. Since the customers of these firms have a high dropout rate, the firms must do a continuous marketing effort to replenish lost customers with new customers. This revenue pressure has resulted in certain day-trading firms not living up to the letter of the law according to existing rules and regulations.

The Project Group observed the following problems in the industry:

■ Deceptive marketing, which includes inadequate disclosure of risk.

- Violating suitability requirements.
- Offering questionable loan arrangements, including arranging for the firm's customers to make loans to other customers.
- Abusing discretionary accounts in which a broker trades for the customer.
- Failing to maintain adequate records.
- Failing to properly supervise traders.

The Project Group hired two independent consultants to analyze the trading activity of day traders by sampling random accounts. The findings of one if these consultants indicated that "seventy percent of public traders will not only lose, but will almost certainly lose everything they invest" (p. 1). And only 11.5 percent of the accounts reviewed indicated the ability to produce short-term trading profits. (*Author's note:* The counsel for the Electronic Trader's Association criticized the consultant's findings because the sample size was too small to draw broad conclusions—only twenty-six accounts at one branch office for seventeen trading days were examined.)

The Day-Trading Industry

Day-trading firms offer significantly different services than those of the more traditional brokerage houses. Customers of day-trading firms manage their own accounts using equipment and software provided by the firms, as well as execute their transactions instantaneously using direct access. Other customers of day-trading firms use their own equipment at their home or office to make their trades.

Day traders, in the generic sense, make intraday trades looking for small profits on each transaction and usually close out all their positions by the end of the business day. Since day-trading transactions are made on a very short-term basis, they are particularly speculative.

The old-line brokerage firms, in contrast, provide advisory services, process customer orders, handle discretionary accounts, and provide numerous other services to their clients—typically for a much higher fee than charged by their day-trading competitors. There are some day traders at old-line firms, but they constitute a very small percentage.

Day-trading firms are also different than the typical discount broker. For example, the latter accept orders from customers and do not usually provide stock recommendations. The day-trading firm, on the other hand, promotes day trading as a strategy or method of investing. Many firms also offer their own day-trading courses or seminars, or refer customers to other firms that offer this service. These courses typically provide day-trading strategies. In addition, the firms offer trainers or coaches to help new traders learn the ropes.

The distinction between online brokerage firms and day-trading firms is sometimes confusing. The online firms just provide a service for executing orders over the Internet.

Industry Size and Customer Base

The Project Group determined that there are sixty-two firms that offer day-trading services at 287 branch locations across the country. Most of the firms are registered with the National Association of Securities Dealers (NASD). These firms have customers whom they refer to as traders. Other day-trading firms are registered with the Philadelphia Stock Exchange. These firms' clients register their traders as agents of the firm, not as "retail" customers. Therefore, they avoid registering with the NASD. Typically, at these firms, individuals trade the firm's capital on a highly leveraged basis using the firm's extended margin capabilities. Additionally, these firms require a hefty security deposit to cover losses that may be incurred by their traders. In essence, the traders themselves are exposed to losses.

The Electronic Traders Association (ETA) estimates that there are between 4,000 to 5,000 individuals trading full-time through day-trading firms executing approximately 150,000 to 200,000 trades a day. This represents about 15 percent of the average daily Nasdaq volume.

Day-Trading Industry Problems

The problems uncovered by the Project Group appear to be widespread. First, the group found that firms do not follow basic compliant regulations. They have engaged in practices that are totally unacceptable, especially if they were conducted by traditional brokerage houses. They found that the management of many of the day-trading firms have minimal brokerage experience. Thus, they concluded that many firms are being managed by people with limited knowledge or respect for the legal regulations and standards developed by the securities industry.

Second, they found that all of firms need new customers to replace those that fall by the wayside. Since most of the traders lose money, there is a high turnover, and replacements are needed to keep revenue rolling in. This has led to some firms using questionable tactics to obtain additional capital, including using misleading and deceptive advertising, painting day trading without regard to its suitability for individuals, and encouraging trading by unregistered investment advisers. Some firms have used dubious lending practices so that their customers can meet their margin calls—hoping that they will not leave the firm.

Comparison to Gambling

Day trading is a form of gambling. Therefore, most traders at day-trading firms will lose their money, while the firm itself gains revenue through commission dollars. SEC Chairman Arthur Levitt has indicated that day trading is not just speculation but amounts to gambling. He points out that speculation requires market knowledge and that short-term trading has been the domain of professional traders.

Day trading is similar to determining how a coin flip will turn out. For example, a stock can rise, fall, or remain the same by the close of business. And, of course, the day trader must pay commissions on all trades no matter the turn of events—so the "house" (day trading firm) wins.

Day trading can also be compared to trading in the futures markets. Both types of activity entail using leverage, and both are forms of trading rather than investing. Retail customers have not been very successful in the futures market, as industry leaders have indicated that 80 percent to 90 percent of these customers lose money at their firms.

Kenneth L. Fisher, writing in *Forbes*, August 26, 1985 "Where are They Hiding? Winners at Short-Term Trading," p. 162, indicated that "if you could make good money with short-term approaches, there would be lots of visible folks who had done so. Where are those who have made fortunes as short-term traders?"

Day trading is also comparable to market timing on a microscopic level. Market timers attempt to sell at or near the top and buy at or near the bottom. According to the Vanguard Group, Inc., "The problem is that few investors, if any, can accurately foresee the direction of the stock or bond markets." (www.vanguard.com/educ/module4_8_0. html). Likewise, few traders can accurately predict the short-term direction of individual stocks.

Flaws of Day Trading

Day trading has much more of a speculative bent than long-term trading for two reasons. First, stock price changes on a specific day are usually small. This translates into small profits for a trader. Second, successful traders cut their losses and let the profits run. If day traders close out all positions during the day, then they can cut their losses, but they may also forgo profits. Looking at the real world, most day traders take their profits too quickly and don't cut their losses quickly enough. (*Author's note:* This is what our Day Trader Survey confirmed as the two major weaknesses of traders.)

Over time, commissions coupled with bid-ask spreads will eat up profits rapidly. Since there is rapid turnover of stocks during the day, the profits needed just to break even are high. The average commission charged by online brokerage firms is about $15 ("The Real Virtual Business," *Economist,* May 8, 1999, p. 71).

Paradox of the Existence of the Day-Trading Industry

The very existence of an industry devoted to offering day trading of stocks is paradoxical. For those who wish to speculate, futures and options provide much greater leverage than stocks purchased or sold short on margin, allowing bets to be made on small movements. Futures and options also provide the ability to speculate on the direction of the market, rather than on the price of individual stocks. In short, futures and options may be more effective speculative trading vehicles than stocks.

Perhaps day traders are aware that retail customers usually lose money trading futures and options, so they wish to trade a seemingly safer vehicle. This usually results in the slower loss of capital, but in loss nevertheless. It can also result in day traders compensating for the lack of leverage by trading beyond their means, and trading with funds borrowed from other customers and other sources. (P. 7)

Academic Studies of Trading

Academic studies over the past few years are consistent with the expectation that day traders in general will lose money. Brad M. Barber and

Terrance Odean of the Graduate School of Management, University of California at Davis, have performed a comprehensive study of the performance of individual investors who manage their own money without using the advice of a full-service broker (Brad M. Barber and Terrance Odean, *Trading Is Hazardous to Your Wealth: The Common Stock Investment Performance of Individual Investors*, April 1999). The authors discovered that those investors who trade most actively realize, on average, the lowest net returns. The study's conclusion was that trading was hazardous to your wealth. They found that individuals are overconfident, which leads to too much trading.

The study was specifically designed to exclude intramonth trades, thus excluding short-term trading used by day traders. Therefore, this study did not study the trading patterns and results attained by day traders. However, the authors found that the most active traders in their study had a positive annual rate of return, but they substantially underperformed the market—11.4 percent versus 17.9 percent. Interestingly, the study found an inverse relationship between trading and return, which is consistent with the promise that day traders will lose money.

The project group found that a former branch manager of a day-trading firm testified that of sixty-eight accounts in his office, sixty-seven lost money. Another branch manager of a different firm indicated that someone in his firm's margin department rhetorically asked him, "Why would you even want to be in this business? You know all these people lose money."

Harvey Houtkin, the principal of All-Tech, in the February 12, 1999, issue of *Securities Regulation and Law Report*, stated, "Day trading is a business like any other. It is not wild speculation. And, like other businesses, 95 percent will fail in the first two years" (p. 9).

Day-Trading Firms Fail to Prove Their Claims

Some of the day-trading firms' disseminations to potential clients have used very general and specific claims of their clients' success. The day-trading industry's existence is based on the common belief that day trading is an easy way to make money. However, the day trading industry must prove that its claims—implicit and explicit—are true. According to the Project Group report findings, the industry has not met its obligation to support its claims of day trader success. The project group requested that the ETA provide information from its own organization or its membership with regard to the profitability of day-trading customers. The ETA's counsel responded by letter, dated March 19, 1999, in which he stated: "I am unaware of any ETA report of this nature, although I understand that certain ETA members have informally surveyed part of their operations to provide a rough estimate of such profitability. While such information is probably sound, I doubt if the information prepared to date is all that useful since it is so narrow."

According to an article in the *Los Angeles Times* (Walter Hamilton, " 'Day-Trading' Study Finds Split Results," January 29, 1999, p. C1), a study by Momentum Securites indicated that 58 percent of its clients lost money in the first three months of trading. And after three to five months, of those that remained 65 percent were profitable.

This article also mentions that the study indicates that "there is an extremely high correlation between high profitability [for traders] and high trading volume." Unfortunately, the day-trading industry has not released any analyses supporting this claim. According to the Project Group, the day-trading firms could easily download their records electronically from their computers and from their clearing brokers and have them analyzed. So far, the industry, to our best knowledge, has not analyzed the data nor released its findings, if any.

Misleading and Deceptive Advertising

Advertising by some day-trading firms has been misleading and on occasions deceptive. The major problems include the following:

- Representations that traders are likely to make profits.
- Representations that day trading can be a career opportunity for many individuals.
- Claims of specific success rates.

Examples of deceptive marketing include:

- A firm's brochure that states that "educating others to the unlimited earning potential of day trading."
- A firm's brochure indicating that the firm's principals "help their customers profit from fluctuations in the Nasdaq market."
- A firm's Web site referring to the firm's "giving individuals the ability to maximize their investment potential."
- A firm's Web site and marketing brochure quoting the firm's

principal saying, "You've probably read about the many successes utilizing my trading techniques" and that "some people
claimed I have found the key to financial independence."

■ A firm's Web site asserting that, "We have a success rate of
around 85 percent with customer traders, meaning people who
come here and actually make money doing this over time."

■ A firm's Web site press release stating that its trading and mentoring programs "boast an 85 percent success rate for new traders, unusually high for industry in which some analysts claim
there is a 90 percent failure rate."

■ Newspaper ads claiming "pinpoint accuracy" and "6 to 7 figure
income per year."

■ A firm's Web site indicating that it offered "absolutely the best
trading system in the financial market." Also claimed were "12%
per trading day minus slippage and commissions," and a "profit
to loss ratio [of] better than 12 to 1."

All of the claims indicated have already been eliminated from these
firms' Web sites and written materials due to regulatory actions and
self-policing.

Additional Marketing Problems

Some of the firms' brochures and Web sites encourage individuals to
make day trading a career. One Web site stated:

Electronic Day Trading attracts people dead-ended or un-
happy in their current field of endeavor and people with a
desire to make trading their life's work. Electronic day trading appeals to executives, victims of downsizing or layoffs,
retirees, graduating college students and anyone who recog-
nizes the unlimited earnings potential and quality of life
which an Electronic Day Trader may achieve. Trading allows
people to work a 6½-hour trading day, to take vacations on
demand and to leave for the day on a whim.

Suitability for Trading

The suitability doctrine requires that brokerage firms only recommend
investments that are appropriate for its clients. A failure to comply with

this requirement violates NASD rule 2310 as well as state and federal law. The Project Group believes that the existing rules and policies concerning suitability and risk disclosure create obligations that the day-trading industry should address. The group also believes that the practices of some of the day-trading firms have violated these rules and policies. In summary, the Project Group supports the issuance of rules that specifically specify the industry's obligations in the day-trading arena. On July 29, 1999, the NASD Board of Governors approved new suitability and disclosure rules regarding day trading. These rules will not become effective until they are approved by the SEC after receiving public comment.

The Project Group found that some day-trading firms have not adhered to suitability requirements. Some firms do not even follow their own stated policies concerning minimum account balances. For example, a manager of a day-trading firm misrepresented information on a new account form for a particular customer. The manager listed the individual's income as $25,000 when it was actually $15,000. The net worth of the individual was listed as $50,000 when the actual amount was $10,000 to $15,000. And when the customer was asked about previous investment experience, the manager checked off "yes" when the customer's actual experience was "none."

The brokerage industry is estimated to spend approximately $250 to obtain each new customer, while an "on-site day-trading firm may spend $30,000 on each new customer, counting the outlay on equipment, office space, and training" (Diana B. Henriques, "In Day Trading, Less Thrill and More Chill," *New York Times,* July 18, 1999).

Members of the Project Group have received numerous complaints from day-trading customers indicating that their firms explicitly and implicitly urged them to use a high-volume trading strategy. This is problematic and raises ethical questions, since the firms have high overhead and monthly expenses and encourage their customers to do a lot of trades to keep their revenues up and make a profit. The customers, on the other hand, are paying large commission dollars, in aggregate, which eats into any potential profits that they earn.

Lending Arrangements

Many day-trading firms loan money to their customers. These arrangements are questionable, since they raise significant issues regarding their suitability. Customers who do not have sufficient capital cannot open an account without borrowing funds. The Project Group believes that "day trading is unsuitable for customers who are unable to meet margin calls except by borrowing funds from other customers. Customers with little or no account equity, who would therefore not be able to afford to day trade, are allowed to day trade through the use of the firms' lending arrangements" (p. 17).

Analysis of Customer Day-Trading Accounts

Twenty-six short-term trading accounts were randomly selected from a Massachusetts day-trading firm in 1997–98 in connection with a State of Massachusetts legal proceeding against the firm. The Project Group hired two consultants to review the statements, quantify the trading activity, and to evaluate the trading performance of the accounts. The findings and conclusions of the consultants were as follows:

- Average account was open for four months and had an annual turnover of 278, and a cost/equity ratio of 56 percent. This ratio measures the amount of profit required on the capital employed to pay for transaction costs, alone and breakeven. The ratio in this case is high, indicating that the trader does not have a long life trading.
- Seventy percent of the accounts lost money and were traded in a way that realized a 100 percent risk of ruin, or lost everything they started with.
- Risk of ruin is the probability that a trader will experience a sequence of losing trades that will totally wipe out the funds in the trading account. As a percentage the range of the risk is zero to 100 percent, depending upon the trading strategies employed, the amount of each transaction, the percentage of winners and losers, and the average winning and losing amounts of each trade.
- Only three accounts of the twenty-six evaluated (11.5 percent of the sample) showed an ability to conduct profitable short-term trading.
- The statistically significant day trading (2,754 trades in seventeen accounts) was evaluated. Sixty-five percent of the accounts lost money and traded in a manner that realized a 100 percent risk of ruin.

- There was only one successful day-trading account in the seventeen accounts analyzed. And this account did not have trading returns commensurate with the risks to which the account was exposed.
- The most successful account in the study had limited short-term trading and no day trading.

Ronald L. Johnson, investment consultant, one of consultants on the project, made the following statement in his report entitled *Day Trading: An Analysis of Public Day Trading at a Retail Day Trading Firm*: "Day trading is the ultimate test of market timing in that the trade is opened and closed within the same day."

The purpose of Johnson's analysis was to statistically determine whether public retail customers have been successful day traders. He randomly selected thirty short-term trading accounts at one day-trading firm to analyze. A review of all accounts indicated that the average losing trade was held for 9.53 days, compared to the average winning trade holding period of 4.52 days. The average intraday trade was a losing trade. Traders in these accounts were letting their losses run and cutting short their profits—just the opposite of good money management.

Johnson stated: "If this analysis is representative of public trading, it is abundantly clear that the average public investor should refrain from short-term trading. Only three out of twenty-six accounts (11.5 percent of the sample) evidenced the ability to conduct profitable short-term trading. . . . Day trading is particularly risky. There was only one successful day trading account analyzed."

Counterpoint

The day-trading industry roundly criticized this report because of the small sample size (twenty-six accounts), the use of only seventeen trading days, and the sampling from only one branch of one firm. Moreover, most of the accounts reviewed were not those of day traders. Speaking from a statistical perspective, the findings were clearly not based on an adequate sample of actual day-trading accounts. Therefore, you as the reader should be aware of this major caveat before making any conclusions based on the consultants' findings and recommendations.

SEC Warnings

The Securities and Exchange Commission and its outspoken chairman, Arthur Levitt, have testified before congressional committees, given speeches, and provided the public with their concerns about day trading. One document prepared by the SEC is shown in figure 14-1. This document warns the potential day trader about the risks involved.

If you want to examine the latest findings of the SEC on this subject, then obtain a copy of their latest report: *Special Study: Report of Examinations of Day-Trading Broker-Dealers*, Office of Compliance Inspections and Examinations, U.S. Securities and Exchange Commission, February 25, 2000. This can be obtained on their Web site: www.sec.gov.

The SEC also goes after day-trading firms that it believes are not following the law. An example of an SEC action is shown in the news story at the end of this chapter.

Conclusions

As potential day traders, you should be aware of the pitfalls in dealing with day-trading firms. The regulatory reports provide nonbiased objective findings of regulators' investigations. Be very wary of dealing with any firm that continually is involved in legal matters brought by the regulators. Of course, not all actions by the regulators are considered serious. Therefore, caveat emptor!

For one insider's viewpoint on the day-trading scene, make sure to read chapter 15, written by Saul Nirenberg.

FIGURE 14-1. *Day Trading: Your Dollars at Risk*

Day traders rapidly buy and sell stocks throughout the day in the hope that their stocks will continue climbing or falling in value for the seconds to minutes they own the stock, allowing them to lock in quick profits. Day traders usually buy on borrowed money, hoping that they will reap higher profits through leverage, but running the risk of higher losses too.

As SEC Chairman Levitt recently stated in his testimony before the U.S. Senate, "[Day trading] is neither illegal nor is it unethical. But it is highly risky." Most individual investors do not have the wealth, the time, or the temperament to make money and to sustain the devastating losses that day trading can bring.

Here are some of the facts that every investor should know about day trading:

Be prepared to suffer severe financial losses
Day traders typically suffer severe financial losses in their first months of trading, and many never graduate to profit-making status. Given these outcomes, it's clear: day traders should only risk money they can afford to lose. They should never use money they will need for daily living expenses, retirement, take out a second mortgage, or use their student loan money for day trading.

Day traders do not "invest"
Day traders sit in front of computer screens and look for a stock that is either moving up or down in value. They want to ride the momentum of the stock and get out of the stock before it changes course. They do not know for certain how the stock will move, they are hoping that it will move in one direction, either up or down in value. True day traders do not own any stocks overnight because of the extreme risk that prices will change radically from one day to the next, leading to large losses.

Day trading is an extremely stressful and expensive full-time job
Day traders must watch the market continuously during the day at their computer terminals. It's extremely difficult and demands great concentration to watch dozens of ticker quotes and price fluctuations to spot market trends. Day traders also have high expenses, paying their firms large amounts in commissions, for training, and for computers. Any day trader should know up front how much [he or she needs] to make to cover expenses and break even.

Day traders depend heavily on borrowing money or buying stocks on margin
Borrowing money to trade in stocks is always a risky business. Day trading strategies demand using the leverage of borrowed money to make profits. This is why many day traders lose all their money and may end up in debt as well. Day

(continues)

FIGURE 14-1. *Continued*

traders should understand how margin works, how much time they'll have to meet a margin call, and the potential for getting in over their heads.

Don't believe claims of easy profits
Don't believe advertising claims that promise quick and sure profits from day trading. Before you start trading with a firm, make sure you know how many clients have lost money and how many have made profits. If the firm does not know, or will not tell you, think twice about the risks you take in the face of ignorance.

Watch out for "hot tips" and "expert advice" from newsletters and Web sites catering to day traders
Some Web sites have sought to profit from day traders by offering them hot tips and stock picks for a fee. Once again, don't believe any claims that trumpet the easy profits of day trading. Check out these sources thoroughly and ask them if they have been paid to make their recommendations.

Remember that "educational" seminars, classes, and books about day trading may not be objective
Find out whether a seminar speaker, an instructor teaching a class, or an author of a publication about day trading stands to profit if you start day trading.

Check out day-trading firms with your state securities regulator
Like all broker-dealers, day-trading firms must register with the SEC and the states in which they do business. Confirm registration by calling your state securities regulator and at the same time ask if the firm has a record of problems with regulators or their customers. You can find the telephone number for your state securities regulator in the government section of your phone book or by calling the North American Securities Administrators Association at (202) 737 0900. NASAA also provides this information on its Web site at www.nasaa.org.

Source: http://www.sec.gov/consumer/daytips.htm. Last update: September 16, 1999.

Appendix 1

SEC goes after All-Tech
Day trading firm charged with skirting lending rules
February 23, 2000 Star Ledger

By Sam Ali
Staff Writer

The Securities and Exchange Commission yesterday sued two day-trading firms, alleging they violated margin rules by arranging loans for customers to help them meet margin calls.

Named in the suit: Montvale-based All-Tech Investment Group Inc., a high-profile day-trading company, and seven people connected with the firm for arranging loans when customers didn't have enough cash or equity in their accounts. Also named is Miami-based Investment Street Co., which settled the charges without admitting or denying guilt, the SEC said.

At the heart of the suit is margin lending, which works a lot like a credit card, enabling investors to borrow as much as 50 percent of the total purchase price of a stock.

For day traders, buying on margin is a way of life, enabling them to buy more stock than they could afford on their own and thus trade in high volume. Under strict margin requirements set by the Federal Reserve Board, broker/dealers are prohibited from lending money in excess of this 2-to-1 margin rule.

A margin call happens when a customer in effect maxes out his "credit card" and overextends his buying power or allows the value of the securities in his account to fall too far.

When that happens, customers are required to deposit more money or equities into their accounts. If they can't or don't, the firm can force the sale of the securities in the customer's account in order to bring that account's equity back up to the required level.

In its suit, the SEC alleges that All-Tech extended loans to such customers—violating margin-lending rules that were designed to limit customer borrowing. "When customers indicated they could not meet margin calls, All-Tech, rather than requiring them to meet them or liquidating securities from accounts, extended customers additional lines of credit in the form of loans from persons associated with the firm," said Barry Rashkover, assistant regional director at the SEC's northeast regional office.

Rashkover defined "persons associated with the firm" as employees. Harvey Houtkin, who founded All-Tech 12 years ago and has been butting heads with regulators for years, called the SEC's lawsuit "baseless" and "conspired." He also questioned its timing.

The Senate Governmental Affairs Investigations Subcommittee is scheduled to begin hearings Thursday to examine the day-trading industry and its practices. Houtkin is expected to testify at the hearing this week.

"This is just another case of intimidation right before the Senate hearing," Houtkin said. "It's a sham. It's all orchestrated. They do this every time. We will vigorously fight the charges. We haven't done anything wrong. The SEC has been scrambling for years trying to find anything wrong with anything," he said.

In its complaint, the SEC alleges that the seven All-Tech employees made 103 unsecured loans to customers so that they could meet margin calls totaling more than $3.6 million. Houtkin is not named in the SEC's case against All-Tech.

The SEC alleges that throughout 1998 All-Tech made the loans by withdrawing money from the accounts of: Ralph Zulferino, manager of All-Tech's Edison office; David Waldman, who works in All-Tech's headquarters; and Adam Leeds, who works in All-Tech's San Diego office.

Regulators say these loans are generally made on an overnight basis to traders who would otherwise face a margin call.

Customers typically paid the employee a fee of between $10 and $175 a day for this financial assistance.

An evidentiary hearing will be held before an administrative law judge to determine whether the allegations have any merit and, if so, what sanctions or penalties, if any, would be appropriate, said Rashkover.

The SEC lawsuit comes amid increasing scrutiny of the day-trading industry and of margin-lending rules in particular.

Responding to concerns raised by stock clearing firms and regulators in December, the New York Stock Exchange and the National Association of Securities Dealers approved proposals to set special margin requirements for day traders.

Under the proposed rules, which have not yet been approved by the SEC, customers who engage in "a pattern of day trading" would be required to have at least $25,000 in equity in their margin account at all times.

Currently, any trader who uses borrowed money—who trades on "margin"—needs a minimum of $2,000 in equity. Under the proposed rules, day traders were defined as people who buy and sell the same stock four times in a five-day business week.

Ironically, the proposed new rules may trigger even more margin lending and debt. That's because the new rules would allow day traders to borrow four times the amount of cash or equities they own. Currently, traders can only borrow twice what they have in equity.

A recent study found that margin debt jumped 62 percent last year to $229 billion, according to Ned Davis Research, a Venice, Fla., market-data firm. In 1990, the figure stood at around $35 billion.

15

WHY IN THE WORLD WOULD ANYONE BECOME A DAY TRADER?

Saul Nirenberg

Seventy-five percent of all day traders lose money! That's six out of every seven. Are you going to be that lucky one? And all of this has happened in the biggest bull market in history.

Where am I coming from? I have some relevant experience—twenty-five years as a stockbroker, sales manager of a hundred-man office, a partner in what was the twenty-second largest brokerage house. Moreover, I have an additional ten years as an arbitrator for both the New York Stock Exchange (NYSE) and National Association of Securities Dealers (NASD), a mediator of the NASD, and as a consultant and an expert witness in securities cases (claims by customers against brokerage firms for wrongdoing).

You have already guessed, from the lead-in to this chapter, what I think of day trading, so I won't belabor the point. I am going to relate my observations and those of other professionals and let you decide if day trading is right for you.

Day Traders Are Using the Stock Market as a Gambling Casino

While I do not know what percentage of casino gamblers are losers, I suspect that six out of seven also lose.

Copyright © 2001 Saul Nirenberg. All rights reserved.

However, there are some very big differences between the majority of casino gamblers and day traders. What follows obviously does not apply to everybody; just almost everybody.

- Day traders gamble with substantial amounts of money they have saved over the years.
  Casino gamblers play with much smaller amounts of money they are willing to lose.
- Day traders don't seem to know the odds are stacked against them.
  Casino gamblers know that the odds are stacked against them, but are willing to accept that because they are having fun.
- Day traders are at it every day.
  Casino gamblers only go to casinos occasionally.
- Day traders think they know, or will learn, how to win.
  Casino gamblers know they just have to be lucky.
- Day traders sometimes give up their jobs so they can day trade.
  Casino gamblers go on vacation to gamble.
- Day traders don't realize they are gambling.
  Casino gamblers know they are gambling.
- Day traders often risk much more money than they realize they are risking.
  Casino gamblers know exactly what they are risking.
- Day traders think they are en route to riches.
  Casino gamblers know they are just gambling.

What Day Traders Do Not Seem to Be Aware Of

Any stockbroker working for a reputable firm would be reprimanded if he or she suggested the amount of trading (ten or more trades a day) the average day trader generates. The broker would be told that if his or her client did not trade less, the broker would be fired. The reason? The brokerage firm knows (is 99 percent certain) the customer would lose money, and that the firm would be sued for the losses—and lose. And this has nothing to do with higher or lower commissions.

If a stockbroker for a reputable firm told his or her branch office manager that someone who knew nothing about a company's history, earnings, management, or business, as is true for just about every day trader I have met, wanted to trade in that company's stock, the firm would not approve even opening an account.

Every day trader I have met has been convinced that there is some simple formula (momentum, tape reading, listening to the right person, a certainty that one is meant to get rich) that will bring untold riches. If this were anywhere near the truth, don't you think day trading would have been all the rage years and years ago? Day trading at low commissions has been available to thousands (not millions) of people for years. These were members of the exchange, not too many, and partners in brokerage firms. Between these two groups there were very very few day traders. The odds against them were exactly the same, six out of every seven lost money. They were not willing to accept those odds.

Day trading is a phenomenon of the longest and biggest bull market in history. This has made it possible for a small group to profit from day trading, and the press and the online brokerage houses have publicized these unusual successes. If six out of every seven day traders are losing money in this up-market, what will happen in a down-market? How many day traders got massacred in the April–May 2000 40 percent Nasdaq correction? Probably many more than we'll ever hear about.

Day traders compound their risk by using margin debt, borrowing from the brokerage house, in an outlandish and highly speculative fashion. As you will see, very few, if any, have the slightest idea what can happen to them if their stocks crumble.

Amazing to me is that all day traders seem to think they must be successful. Almost every day trader's account I have seen uses margin. This greatly increases the percentage of profit and the percentage of loss.

If your frame of mind is that you will be a winner, then you will use margin. You will happily borrow money from the brokerage house, speculate on stocks, and win, then repay the broker. It's so easy. You have actually made money with someone else's money. However, it's not quite that simple.

Let's examine the other side of the coin. If you win, the earlier statement is almost correct, except that you had to put up as much of your own money as you borrowed. The rule is that you can borrow an amount equal to what you put into the account. Let's say you put in $10,000, borrow $10,000, invest the $20,000 and sell out for $22,000.

You are ahead $2,000, which is an increase of 10 percent of the money invested, but a 20 percent return on your own money. Notice that your percentage gain has doubled.

But what if you lose? Same example. You put up $10,000 and you borrow $10,000, but this time you sell out for $18,000. You lost 10 percent of the money invested, but 20 percent of your own money. Notice that your percentage loss has also doubled. If you have had any problem understanding this example, you are not ready to buy stocks on margin.

But day traders are going far beyond just borrowing an amount equal to their own money. Here's what happens: Under Regulation T, the Board of Governors of the Federal Reserve System controls how much money a brokerage house can lend you. Any time you purchase a listed security or an "OTC margin stock" you must put up 50 percent of the purchase price. This can come from either funds you send in or what is called the free balance in your account. This calculation is made at the end of each trading day by your firm. However, if you buy and sell a stock the same day, you do not have to put up any money according to Regulation T.

The second point is that, at the end of any day, with some exceptions, your equity, the amount of money that would be left in the account if everything were sold at the closing prices of that day, has to be a minimum of 25 percent. (If your stocks were worth $40,000 and your debit was $30,000, then your equity would be $10,000, which is 25 percent.) If your equity falls below 25 percent, you will get a margin call, demanding you put up more money or sell stock to bring your equity up to a minimum of 30 percent. Every brokerage house has the right to set the minimum equity requirements, at 30 percent, 35 percent, or 40 percent. They can do this *whenever they think it is in their best interests to do so,* for your entire account or just for particular stocks. And the Federal Reserve has the right to increase *or decrease* equity requirements at any time. *Whenever this is done, all customers are immediately affected and must put up any additional monies these changes require.*

Because of this loophole, day traders can buy huge amounts of stock, far in excess of their own equity, eight, ten, twelve, or even twenty times as much, as long as the stock is sold that very same day. As you will see in the example that follows, with only $20,000 of your own money you can buy $200,000 worth of stock! You just cannot hold it overnight.

For example, assume your account has an equity value of $22,000 *and a portfolio value of $80,000.* Let's say you bought 1,000 shares of America OnLine (AOL) at 130 ($130 per share), then another 500 at 140. That adds up to $200,000—almost eight times your equity. Your average cost was 133 ($130 per share). AOL suddenly drops six points before you sell it for a loss of $9,000. That's more than 40 percent of the account's equity. This loss causes a margin call of $11,000. Let's assume you did not have the cash immediately available to cover the call. In order to meet the margin call of $11,000, stock worth $36,000 was sold by the brokerage house. (This is a real case in which a customer was suing because he said the brokerage firm did not give him enough time to send in the $11,000. The customer lost.) *If you do not completely and easily understand this example, you should not be using margin debt.*

In my experience, most day traders do not understand how much stock must be sold as a result of a margin call. If your account goes below 25 percent equity, and you do not have the cash to put in the account, a margin call is only satisfied by bringing your equity up to at least 30 percent. If the stocks in your account are worth $50,000 and your equity is $5,000 (short by $7,500), the brokerage house will issue a margin call for $10,000. (They will want you to increase your equity from $5,000 to $15,000, which is 30 percent of $50,000.) If you do not have that $10,000, they will sell $33,000 of your stocks!

In my experience, and unfortunately in the experience of some day traders, not only can the brokerage house increase the percentage equity they require, but they can demand that a margin call be met within as short a period as a few hours. Generally, margin calls may be met in two to three days, but not always.

The question that needs an answer is: Are you ready for the kinds of drastic situations described here? Are you trading in ways that make you vulnerable beyond your worst expectations?

While we know that six out of every seven day traders lose money, let's assume you are one of those that has made money. How well have you really done? Compare your results with the Dow Jones Industrials and the Nasdaq for the last five years, shown in table 15-1. Enter your results. How have you done?

Proponents of day trading, including every brokerage house that

TABLE 15-1. *Annual Percentage Increase*

	Dow Jones Annual Percent Increase	Nasdaq Annual Percent Increase	Your Results
1995	33.5	39.9	_____
1996	26.0	22.7	_____
1997	22.6	21.6	_____
1998	16.1	39.6	_____
1999	25.2	85.6	_____

has gotten into the act, proclaim that there is a new millennium (which seems to have jumped the gun and started in 1997 or 1998), a new economic paradigm.

As far as I can tell, this new paradigm holds that it is no longer true that what goes up must come down. This would imply that greed will no longer spur people to purchase stocks based only on their desire to become rich, that fear will no longer make people sell good stocks just because they are afraid of what will happen, that knowledge and experience are no longer important, that recessions, much less depressions, are a thing of the past.

Does this make sense to you? Have you noticed that plain untarnished greed no longer lures people, that fear of the future is not a factor, that knowledge and experience don't count?

A few examples from the current market (June 2000) seem appropriate:

- iVillage came out at 24, went to 95 the first day, and is now 7.
- Value America came out at 23, went to 70 the first day, and is now 1½.
- DrKoop came out at 9, went to 13 the first day, climbed to 45 within a month, and is now 2.
- iTurf came out at 22, went to 60 the first day, and is now 3½.
- PriceLine came out at 16, went to 81 the first day, went down to 50, climbed to 100, and is now 45.

Did greed enter into any of this? Fear? Do you really think there will never be another recession? Is there really a whole new paradigm? Is that your experience?

Now let's take a look at your strategy as a day trader. Write down what guides you during a trading day. What are the important things you have learned as your progress has continued? What are some of the foundations of your trading strategy?

These are questions that most of us have to answer regarding our own jobs or professions. Salesmen know what works for them. Carpenters know what tools they need and how the materials they use will react under different circumstances. The same is true for diamond cutters. Plumbers learn about pipes, fittings, pumps, corrosion, and more. Gardeners know as much as possible about soil and light conditions, and the best way to trim trees and shrubs. I wouldn't hire any of these service providers if they could not tell me how they go about their business. Would you?

Think about your day trading. What have you learned? What makes you a good day trader? Here are some of the things professional financial people take into consideration when they go about their business. Compare what they want to know to what a day trader thinks about. Who do you think has the edge?

First, they want to know as much as possible about the overall market environment. The idea is to have a sense where the entire market, or a section of the market, is heading. This would include how much money is coming into the U.S. stock or bond markets from abroad; whether the Fed is expanding or decreasing the money supply; whether the overall economy is expanding or contracting; and whether the various consumer confidence surveys are positive or negative. When the market is down, what groups of stocks have historically done well before the market averages start going up? When the market is up, what have been the historical signs that the market is too high? What stocks usually get hurt when interest rates go up or get helped when interest rates go down?

Second, who and what are the companies they are buying. Day traders, of course, don't think any of the following fundamentals are important. Who do you think has the right idea?

- Facts and figures of the companies; past, current, and estimated future earnings, dividends, and price earnings ratios. What research analysts are saying, what the company management is saying, whether previous management statements have been on target, and more.

- Quality of management. Is there a sound and complete management team or is it a one-man show.
- The present and potential competition.

How do you think you can do compared to people who are armed with that kind of information? Peter Lynch, probably one of the most successful money managers (he managed the Magellan Fund for twenty-three years and consistently outperformed the Dow Jones average on an annualized basis), said he never bought the stock of a company that he could not understand.

Let's talk about the role of your emotions when trading stocks. Of course, if you think that greed and fear are no longer relevant, just skip this section. Do you ever get carried away, throw caution to the wind? Do you ever get so scared that you want to run away?

Both scenarios, when managing money as a day trader, can mean disaster or, at best, lost opportunities. You will be called on to make immediate decisions at moments of the greatest stress. You have to overcome these kind of emotions to be successful. How many of us are that tough?

An interesting and generally very successful way of managing large amounts of money is to hire someone to manage it for you. This is done by the largest, most sophisticated financial people. If you had these huge amounts of money, would you hire you?

And how about those commercials by Ameritrade, E*Trade, and others. They do make you smile for at least thirty seconds. But think about what they are saying to the people viewing the commercial.

Ameritrade has a commercial they think is very successful. I say that because it has been running for months. A young kooky office worker named Stuart tries to make a copy of his face on a copy machine, then convinces his boss to open an account at Ameritrade. Do you think that has ever happened? Would you take advice from someone who puts his face in a copy machine?

An E*Trade commercial shows a group meditating. The group suddenly veers into everyone going gaga over the low E*Trade commissions. Are low commissions really a reason to become a day trader? Another commercial shows a Russian rapturous about the wonders of low commissions! Not one of these commercials has anything to say about any qualifications you should have before investing, much less day trading.

Arbitration

If customers have complaints against their stockbrokers, they can seek to get their money back through arbitration. In an arbitration there are usually three arbitrators who listen to the customer and the broker, and decide if the customer should get back some, or all, or none of his or her money from the brokerage house.

If the stockbroker was responsible for the ten, twenty, or thirty trades a day that a day trader generated, the brokerage house would lose the case 90 percent of the time. Actually, no brokerage house like Merrill Lynch, PaineWebber, Morgan Stanley Dean Witter, or Prudential Securities would permit that kind of trading (it is called "churning") in a brokerage account. They know they would get sued and lose.

The SEC and the New York Stock Exchange say a brokerage house must know all the essential facts about their customers. This is Rule 405 of the New York Stock Exchange. Recommending speculative stocks or speculative trading strategies to unsophisticated customeres with limited money and limited knowledge is often a violation of Rule 405. Most day traders have limited money and limited knowledge, and are financially unsophisticated. But they cannot successfully sue a brokerage house when they lose money.

Just recently, Commissioner Laura Unger of the SEC issued a report (115 pages)* making it clear that online brokerage firms don't have any responsibility for anything that happens as a result of unsuitable purchases. They are at this time only responsible for proper executions of orders they receive. Her report removes the obligation of a brokerage house to make sure that their day-trading customers are not gambling with all their money and are not buying stocks that are too speculative for their ability and means.

If your idea of fun is day trading, and you can afford to lose all the money in your account, plus additional funds that might be demanded as a result of a margin call, then by all means, have a good time. But if you are day trading to earn your keep, be very very careful.

---

*See page 331.

16

PUTTING IT ALL TOGETHER

You've probably realized by now that day trading can be dangerous to your wealth if you are not fully prepared mentally, financially, and educationally. Nevertheless, the number of day traders continues to grow because of the ease of entry and the excitement of playing the market.

But day trading is not a video game without consequences. It must be taken seriously or you will lose it all. Small businesses fail at a high rate because most entrepreneurs do not have a practical business plan, adequate capital, and the expertise to survive. Day trading is a small business that requires all of these three factors and more. The probability of success for a beginning day trader is quite low.

To be a survivor as a day trader, you need a trading plan in order to make clear and intelligent decisions. First, determine the buy and sell prices on specific stocks. These decisions should be based on back- and forward testing of data. Additionally, have sufficient capital to maximize your chances of staying power, which is needed to survive the market volatility. Become educated about the markets, trading principles, trading software, order execution, margin, and numerous other factors so that your chances of success are higher.

Nevertheless, a career as a day trader can provide you with a comfortable living and, in some cases, make you wealthy. As you've learned from the traders and CEOs interviewed in chapters 12 and 13, there are certain individual traits and approaches that can be used to increase the odds of being a successful trader. You're now aware of the importance of the psychology of trading, the importance of minimizing your risk, and the tax consequences. A thorough trading education is a prerequisite to building a solid foundation.

In summary, day trading can be a lucrative career choice if you:

■ Treat it as a full-time business, whether trading remotely or at a day-trading firm.

■ Have a stable personality.

■ Possess key trader attributes—discipline, patience, independence, decisiveness.

■ Have sufficient capital that you can afford to lose to open your trading account.

■ Have a passion for trading that is based on real interest in the subject, rather than just trading for the monetary rewards.

■ Obtain an in-depth trading education, one that provides critical knowledge about the markets, trading, psychology, money management, and technical analysis.

■ Use a state-of-the-art trading software package including real-time quotes, charts, and so on.

■ Use a direct-access broker for executing your trades.

■ Use a specific approach, methodology, or system to select stocks for purchase that has been thoroughly tested.

■ Pay attention to technical indicators, chart patterns, and the overall market condition.

■ Have tight rules for taking loses but letting profits run.

■ Use money management principles to limit your positions and risk level with individual securities (e.g., not placing more than 5 percent of your capital in any one position).

■ Realize that success (making a profit) will not come instantly but may take six months to two years.

■ Realize that losses are part of the trading scene.

■ Take a rest if the market turns against you.

■ Don't jump from system to system searching for the "holy grail"—it doesn't exist.

■ Don't listen to so-called experts on a TV business show, and don't go to chatrooms for tips. Select your own trading vehicles (e.g., stocks and indexes), do your own research and check the charts (e.g., technical analysis, patterns, and other tools) that you have tested to find the entry and exits points for your trades.

Future Scan

Predicting the future is fraught with uncertainly. For example, I remember reading an article in the *Wall Street Journal* about five years ago on forecasts by approximately fifty top economists concerning interest rates and other indicators for the forthcoming year. Not one economist predicted the correct direction of interest rates in the year ahead. Trying to predict where day trading will be next year or in five years is very difficult because of all the variables. Insight into the future of day trading was provided by most of the CEOs interviewed in chapter 13, "Interviews with Firm CEOs." Reread that chapter to gain their interesting perspectives.

Where is day trading headed in the future? Certainly it is not going away. Day trading will continue to experience tremendous growth in the number of players and in the volume of transactions because of the perceived rewards. Day-trading firms will continue to open new branch offices, but the overwhelming majority of the new traders will likely trade remotely (at home). Assuming there are 20,000 full-time traders today (including professional traders trading their firm's money), I expect that the number of full-time day traders to mushroom to a million by 2005. My estimate includes day traders in other parts of the world—where the profession will explode. The overseas traders will trade their own equity markets, if they are liquid, or focus on the markets of the more developed countries and trade globally. Day trading will be an accepted and sought-after career by 2005.

The technology and systems used to day trade will continue to become more automated, faster, easier to use, and less expensive. The choice of investment vehicles (e.g., stocks, futures, indexes, options) will continue to expand, not just domestically but internationally. Look for a twenty-four-hour global market that is never closed. Wireless trading will arrive and change the face of the industry. Imagine being able to trade from anywhere, anytime, with real-time data and connections at high speeds. Wireless high-speed trading on portable PCs is certainly a few years away, but it is eagerly awaited by the connected generation.

Expect to see a handful of day-trading firms capture 95 percent or more of the business, with the smaller firms being absorbed or out of business. ECNs will undergo consolidation, with a few remaining. The cost of trades will level out at a price between $5 to $15, but some firms will act as matchmakers to match buyers with sellers—and they may charge no commission at all.

By 2005, the world of day trading will undergo radical change with respect to the ease of trading, the speed of execution, the markets available to trade, and the portability of trading. But new day traders will still need to be prepared for the profession. Otherwise, they will fall by the wayside.

One Possible Scenario—Expert Trading System Software

By 2005, I expect to see one or more expert trading systems become available. This software will be able to execute all trades automatically based on an expert trader's preprogrammed trading rules or your own rules. Expert systems have been available for years. For example, in the medical field, one expert system is used to diagnose diseases. In the banking field, a West Coast bank uses an expert system to trade foreign exchange contracts, and in the mutual fund industry, one large fund family uses an expert system to select stocks to buy.

Before using an expert trading system, determine the methodology used by the trader (if revealed) to see if it fits your style of trading. Otherwise, you may be better off developing and testing (back- and forward testing) your own rules.

How will an expert system work? Here's a possible scenario. Each night after the market closes your expert trading system would:

- Scan last night's stock universe (e.g., entire Nasdaq market) for those stocks that have certain attributes (e.g., making new all-time highs on volume of at least 50 percent higher than the average for the past four weeks).
- Graph the stock for periods of one year, three years, and five years, six months, three months, one month, and intraday, using specific technical indicators (e.g., ten and twenty period moving averages, trendlines, and MACD) that generate buy signals.
- Evaluate which of the stocks has the highest probability of success based on prior history of previous breakouts and other factors that you've programmed into the software.

■ Issue a buy order for a certain number of shares at a certain price based upon the total capital in your account and your money management parameters. A confirmation will be received, stored, and forwarded to you via your trading software, e-mail, and cell phone depending upon your preference.

■ Automatically issue a sell order based upon your preprogrammed sell criteria (e.g., trend line broken or stock drops below a resistance level or previous intraday low). You will be notified of this transaction immediately after the sell order has been executed.

In this constrained trading environment, you won't miss a stock breakout. You will be notified of all buys and sells. This system will not guarantee that you'll be a profitable trader, but if your rules are based on sound principles, you have set tight stops, and your risk levels are controlled, your chance of success will be higher than that of the novice trader lacking a thorough understanding of what he or she is getting involved in.

Expert systems, in general, have been slow to develop over the last decade, but in the future these systems will be applied to day trading. Their success remains to be seen. So, before you decide to buy the system software, do your homework.

The future looks bright for day traders and the day-trading industry. As more and more people strive for the American dream, the number of day traders will reach unprecedented levels. If you've decided that day trading is for you, good luck. If not, then you've made a wise decision.

CONTRIBUTING
AUTHOR BIOGRAPHIES

Richard V. Rueb is currently executive director of **www.DayTraders USA.com**. He is also an active direct-access short term trader with three years of experience. During 1999, he was affiliated with the Online Trading Academy as a one-week Boot Camp instructor. Richard was the executive director of the Information Systems Security Association (ISSA) from 1987 to 1992, where he grew the membership fivefold.

www.DayTradersUSA.com provides active traders the essential *networking* needed to survive in a most challenging profession. It has a well-developed education and training program offered to short-term traders around the world through which they may focus their learning. Mr. Rueb can be reached at Daytradersusa@home.net.

Gibbons Burke is a trader, writer, and software developer living in Silicon Valley, California. He operates TraderCraft.com, a Web site devoted to providing the tools and information you need to master the craft of trading. He is also editor of the MarketHistory.com site by Logical Information Machines. Gibbons has twenty-three years of experience in the financial markets at companies such as CompuTrac/Telerate, Futures Magazine, Logical Information Machines, Dow Jones Markets, and Quote.com. He has published hundreds of columns and articles in *Futures Magazine* and spoken at industry conferences on topics such as the Internet, technical analysis and system development, and money management principles. Mr. Gibbons can be reached at gibbonsb@io. com.

John Piper has been a full-time trader of futures and options since the 1980s, first as a private trader and now managing client monies. As well as trading, he takes on a select number of traders each year and trains them to become successful also. He is the author of the acclaimed book *The Way to Trade* and publishes a twice monthly newsletter, together with daily hotline reports (available by e-mail). He can be contacted at JOHN@ttttt.freeserve.co.uk or telephone 011-44-208-789-0169, fax 011-44-208-399-7735.

Oscar Goldman is a master scientist of the human mind. He has not only academic understanding (doctorate in psychology, master of Neuro Linguistic Programming, and developer of the Neuro Explosive Trading Technology, or NETT), but also practical real world experience, having lost and made millions of dollars as an entrepreneur.

Goldman has been successfully trading and coaching traders around the country with phenomenal results for the past eight years. He is an international speaker on the psychological aspects and modeling of the world's top traders. He is also the president of Trader Tech University which is the *only* true university-type education in the commodities and equities arena in the world. You can contact Mr. Goldman at (310) 281 1676 or at oscar@tradertechuniversity.com.

Ryan Jones started trading stock options when he was sixteen years old. By the time Ryan was twenty-one, he had experience with trading stocks, stock options, mutual funds, futures, future options, with spreads, and with nearly every major strategy type. At the age of twenty-two, Ryan began to focus on money management strategies and techniques and has since become one of the most sought after speakers and authorities on the subject. Ryan has also developed more than five hundred trading strategies and systems and entered the year-long 1999 Robins Worldcup Trading Championship with less than one month remaining. At the end of that event, he was ranked third with a 43 percent return. Ryan is affiliated with Trader Tech University, a firm dedicated to providing the most extensive education products and services in the industry. He can be reached at the firm's Colorado Springs office at (800) 978-6379 or (719) 527-0477, or by e-mailing him at aspenrj@aol.com.

Ted Tesser is president of Waterside Financial Services, Inc., with offices in Delray Beach, Florida. He has a master's degree in accounting from New York University, with a specialty in investment related taxation. Tesser started Waterside Financial Services in 1986 as a company that specializes in tax reduction strategies for traders.

His popular seminar series entitled "Cut Your Taxes in Half!" has been attended by many prominent and successful investors who wish to gain insight into the areas of retirement planning, tax planning, and developing a plan for passing wealth down to their heirs and establishing a family legacy. Tesser's work has been reviewed by such prominent publications as the *Wall Street Journal, Technical Analysis of Stocks and Commodities,* and *Futures* magazine. He is currently a contributing editor to *Active Trader* magazine.

Waterside Financial Services specializes in counseling traders on tax reduction strategies, retirement, and estate and financial planning issues. To contact Ted Tesser or one of his tax professionals, call (800) 566-9829 or (561) 865-0071, or contact him at TedTesser@TaxTrader.com. The firm's website is www.TaxTrader.com.

Saul Nirenberg is president of Saul Nirenberg & Co. since its inception in 1990. He has been in the securities industry for more than thirty years. Associated with him are a group of experts from various areas of the industry. Mr. Nirenberg started his financial career in 1966 with a major brokerage firm, L. F. Rothschild & Co. Starting as an account executive, he became both the sales manager of a hundred-man branch office in New York City and a partner of the firm in 1983. He joined Oppenheimer & Co., Inc., in 1988 as a senior vice president, leaving there to start Saul Nirenberg & Co. in 1990.

During his years at Rothschild and Oppenheimer, he was involved as a broker, sales manager, and partner in every aspect of the investment world. The primary business of Saul Nirenberg & Co. has been as consultants and expert witnesses in securities arbitration cases. The firm's specialists have been consultants and expert witnesses in more than four hundred securities cases since 1990. He can be reached at (212) 852-1555 or e-mail at saulnir@aol.com. His websites are www.portfolio strategies.com and www_broker_complaint.com.

INDEX